DEREGULATION AND DIVERSIFICATION OF UTILITIES

Topics in Regulatory Economics and Policy Series

Michael A. Crew, Editor
Graduate School of Management
Rutgers University
Newark, New Jersey

Previously Published Books:

Rowley, C., Tollison, R., and Tullock, G.:
  Political Economy of Rent-Seeking

Frantz, R.: *X-Efficiency*

DEREGULATION AND DIVERSIFICATION OF UTILITIES

edited by
Michael A. Crew
Graduate School of Management
Rutgers University
Newark, New Jersey

Kluwer Academic Publishers
Boston/Dordrecht/London

Distributors for North America:
Kluwer Academic Publishers
101 Philip Drive
Assinippi Park
Norwell, Massachusetts 02061 USA

Distributors for the UK and Ireland:
Kluwer Academic Publishers
Falcon House, Queen Square
Lancaster LA1 1RN, UNITED KINGDOM

Distributors for all other countries:
Kluwer Academic Publishers Group
Distribution Centre
Post Office Box 322
3300 AH Dordrecht, THE NETHERLANDS

Library of Congress Cataloging-in-Publication Data

Deregulation and diversification of utilities / edited by Michael A.
Crew.
    p.   cm. — (Topics in regulatory economics and policy series)
  The result of two seminars held Oct. 30, 1987, and May 6, 1988, at
Rutgers University.
  Includes index.
  ISBN   0-89838-299-8
  1. Public utilities—Unites States—Deregulation. I. Crew,
Michael A. II. Series.
HD2766.D47 1989
363.6'0973—dc19   88-29752
                                                CIP

Printed in the United States of America

Contents

AUTHORS AND DISCUSSANTS

Shimon Awerbuch, Assistant Professor of Finance, University of Lowell

Lawrence P. Cole, Pricing Analysis and Plans Manager, GTE Service Company

Michael A. Crew, Professor of Economics and Director of the Center for Research in Regulated Industries, Graduate School of Management, Rutgers University

Catherine C. Eckel, Assistant Professor of Economics, Virginia Polytechnic Institute

Theresa A. Flaim, Senior Economist, Economic Research Department, Niagara Mohawk Power Corporation

Michael Frierman, Assistant Professor of Economics, Graduate School of Management, Rutgers University

Robert A. Gerber, President, Hackensack Water Company

Michael L. Goetz, Associate Professor of Economics, Temple University

Susan S. Hamlen, Associate Professor of Operations Analysis, State University of New York at Buffalo

William A. Hamlen, Jr., Associate Professor of Economics, State University of New York at Buffalo

Krishna G. Hegde, Assistant Professor of Finance, Graduate School of Management, Rutgers University

John A. Helmuth II, Assistant Professor of Economics, Rochester Institute of Technology

Scott R. Herriott, Assistant Professor of Strategy, University of Iowa

Leonard S. Hyman, Vice President, Merrill Lynch

Jeffrey Lahm, Staff Manager, New Jersey Bell Telephone

William W. Lanen, Assistant Professor of Accounting, The Wharton School, University of Pennsylvania

James Leva, President, Jersey Central Power and Light

Eileen A. Moran, Assistant Treasurer, Public Service Electric and Gas Company

Chieu Nguyen, Senior Engineer, GPU Service Corporation

H. Edwin Overcast, Director–Rates and Economics, Northeast Utilities Service

Almarin Phillips, Hower Professor of Public Policy, Economics and Law, University of Pennsylvania

Anthony P. Pusateri, District Manager, New Jersey Bell Telephone

Mark Reeder, Chief of Economic Research, New York State Department of Public Service

Rob Rockefeller, Staff Director–Regulatory Policy and Analysis, NYNEX Service Company

Charles K. Rowley, Dean of the Graduate School, George Mason University

Donald L. Schlenger, Vice President–Business Development, Hackensack Water Company

Joseph C. Schuh, Director of Economics, Orange & Rockland Utilities

Saikat Sen, Manager–Marketing Plan Implementation, AT&T Communications

Roger Sherman, Professor of Economics, University of Virginia at Charlottesville

Richard E. Simnett, District Manager–Public Policy Issues Analysis, Bell Communications Research

Sheldon Switzer, Senior Rate Analyst, Baltimore Gas and Electric

Theo Vermaelen, Associate Professor of Finance, INSEAD

P.V. Viswanath, Assistant Professor of Finance, Graduate School of Management, Rutgers University

Ingo Vogelsang, Professor of Economics, Boston University

Heidimarie West, Research Analyst, Merrill Lynch

PREFACE AND ACKNOWLEDGMENTS

This book is a result of two seminars held at Rutgers–The State University of New Jersey on October 30, 1987, and May 6, 1988, entitled "Deregulation and Diversification of Utilities." Ten previous seminars in the same series resulted in *Problems in Public Utility Economics and Regulation* (Lexington Books, 1979), *Issues in Public Utility Pricing and Regulation* (Lexington Books, 1980), *Regulatory Reform and Public Utilities* (Lexington Books, 1982), *Analyzing the Impact of Regulatory Change* (Lexington Books, 1985), and *Regulating Utilities in an Era of Deregulation* (Macmillan Press, 1987).

Like the previous seminars, these seminars received financial support from leading utilities. The views expressed, of course, are those of the authors and do not necessarily reflect the views of the sponsoring companies. I thank AT&T, Atlantic Electric Company, Elizabethtown Gas Company, Elizabethtown Water Company, Garden State Water Company, GTE Service Company, Hackensack Water Company, Jersey Central Power & Light Company, New Jersey Bell Telephone Company, New Jersey Natural Gas Company, New Jersey–American Water Company, New York Telephone Company, Niagara Mohawk Power Corporation, Northeast Utilities Service Company, NYNEX Service Company, Public Service Electric and Gas Company, Rockland Electric Company, Shorelands Water Company, South Jersey Gas Company, and United Telephone Company of New Jersey. The support went far beyond financial assistance. Company managers freely gave their time and advice and, on several occasions, provided information about their industries. I especially thank George Baulig, Peter Ciccone, Bill Cobb, Lawrence Cole, Don Conyers, Frank Critelli, Frank Delany, A. Noel Doherty, Kevin Fennell, Theresa Flaim, Robert Iacullo, Edward Jones, Patricia Keefe, Alfred Koeppe, Brian Lane, James Lees, Clifford Mastrangelo, Russell Mayer, Edwin Overcast, Henry Patterson III, Glenn Phillips, Don Schlenger, Joseph Schuh, Paul Schumann, Christopher Turner, Michael Walsh, George Wickard, and Bill Wiginton.

Many thanks are owed to the distinguished speakers and discussants, listed on pages vii and viii, for their cooperation in making the seminars and this book possible. They all worked very hard in achieving deadlines, without which the speedy publication of this book would have been impossible. I would especially like to thank Linda Brennan, Adminstrative Assistant in the Center for Research in Regulated Industries. Not only did she provide able editorial and research assistance but she also mastered *PagePerfect*, the pc-based typesetting program used to provide the camera-ready copy for this book.. The usual disclaimers are applicable. None of the people named here is responsible for any errors. The views expressed are the views of the authors and not of the sponsoring companies.

MICHAEL A. CREW

DEREGULATION AND DIVERSIFICATION OF UTILITIES

1

COMPETITION, DIVERSIFICATION, AND DISINTEGRATION IN REGULATED INDUSTRIES
Michael A. Crew

In telecommunication, electricity, gas, and even water, there has been significant entry by competitors and an increased trend toward diversification on the part of existing regulated utilities. Even before the breakup of the Bell System on January 1, 1984, there had been entry into the long distance business which had formerly been the exclusive province of AT&T. Since 1984, the seven Regional Holding Companies (RBOCs) have proceeded to diversify into other (usually closely related) businesses. In addition they have attempted to remove, relax, and change the regulation of their traditional businesses.

The same kinds of trends have been evident, if to a lesser degree, in gas, water, and electricity. In the case of electricity, a further change has begun to emerge; the traditional vertical integration of generation, transmission, and distribution has come under attack. The entry into traditional utility markets has been further encouraged in electricity by the Public Utility Regulatory Policies Act of 1978 (PURPA), which encouraged generation by independent producers and allowed traditional utilities to enter the independent generation business. Indeed, many utilities set up independent cogeneration subsidiaries, and others even went so far as to disintegrate vertically, producing power through independent and unregulated subsidiar-

1

ies. The entry of non-utility generators and the spinning off by utilities of their traditional generation business may be perceived as an attempt to avoid some of the effects of regulation.

The question of whether such changes will result in a more efficient governance structure has been subject to considerable debate. Even in telecommunications, which seems on the surface to offer a potential for competitive governance structures, there are problems. For example, Phillips (1982) raised fundamental questions on the feasibility of competition in telecommunications. Similarly, writing shortly after the AT&T divestiture, Phillips (1985) examined the need for and feasibility of some form of reintegration in telecommunications. Electricity, from a technological point of view, apparently presents more problems for competitive governance structures than telecommunications. Herriott in Chapter 9 and Jurewitz (1988) note the difficulties associated with the loss of integration and coordination efficiencies as restructuring proceeds. The problems of formalizing the cooperation requirements in electricity generation and transmission are formidable, whether they are performed through market exchange or long-term contracts.

The contributors to this book continue the debate as to whether the effects of deregulation and diversification on utilities will lead to greater efficiency. Implications for the structure of utility industries, as well as the nature of regulation, are examined. Questions on the progress and extension of deregulation and the potential for reregulation are raised. Some of the challenges posed to regulation by diversification and deregulation are considered. New forms of regulation are examined.

Chapter 2 by Crew and Rowley employs a public choice analysis to examine the forces affecting the evolution of regulatory institutions and the possible illusory nature of deregulation. Vogelsang in chapter 3 provides an analysis of a new form of regulation, price caps. While he is concerned with the application of his analysis to telecommunications, price caps may have potential application to other industries. Chapter 4 by Roger Sherman and chapter 10 by Leonard Hyman and Heidimarie West are concerned with the implications for financial structure, cost of capital, and regulation of actual diversification by electric utilities. Chapter 5 by Shimon Awerbuch and chapter 6 by William and Susan Hamlen are concerned with the interaction of economics and accounting. Awerbuch is especially concerned with the differences in accounting treatment of regulated and competitive firms. The Hamlens are concerned with the problem of joint cost allocation, which may be particularly important when some markets are regulated and others are not. Crew and Crocker (1988) examine the effects of allowing a regulated firm to enter unregulated markets where there exist economies of scope. Translating their results into practical policy is by no means simple, as they note. Chapter 7 by Almarin Phillips examines the question of efficient governance structures in telecommunications and provides some interesting international comparisons with the United States. Richard Simnett in chapter 8 provides an analysis of the competitiveness of the long distance telecommunications market based upon the contestability analysis of Baumol, Panzar, and Willig (1982). Chapter 9 by Scott Herriott is concerned with the important problem of achieving cooperation in generation and transmission between electric utilities where competitive entry is allowed. Chapter 11 by Catherine Eckel and Theo Vermaelen is concerned with how the risks of nuclear power were perceived by the financial markets as a result of Chernobyl. While this topic is not directly related to the diversification by electric utilities, it does throw light on another reason why electric utilities may wish to diversify. They may wish to avoid some of the risks associated with nuclear power, which may be compounded by governmental and regulatory actions.

There are many aspects of deregulation and diversification that are not addressed in this book. Several directions for research and policy are apparent. The bulk of electricity, gas, water, and telecommunications is still very much subject to rate-of-return regulation. While new forms of regulation, like price caps, are under consideration, it remains to be seen how significant they will become. Traditional regulation is strong in utilities and is likely to remain so. Indeed, in some industries, such as telecommunications, new regulation may be implemented as technologies change. While deregulation and diversification have not yet had a major effect on utilities, they have certainly started to play a role for companies and regulators. It is too early to say what their effects will be on the future structure of utilities. Some utilities are becoming more market-oriented. Regulatory commissions are becoming increasingly concerned about this trend and are seeking ways to avoid cross-subsidization by the regulated business of the competitive ventures. Designing appropriate incentive systems is critical for future developments. This book provides some ideas on how to proceed.

References

Baumol, William J., John C. Panzar, and Robert D. Willig. 1982. *Contestable Markets and the Theory of Industry Structure*. New York: Harcourt Brace Javanovich.
Crew, Michael A., and Keith J. Crocker. 1988. "Diversification and Regulated Monopoly." Rutgers University, Graduate School of Management, Working Paper, #87-001.
Jurewitz, John L. 1988. "Deregulation of Electricity: A View from Utility Manage-

ment." *Contemporary Policy Issues* 6 (No. 3, July): 25-41.

Phillips, Almarin. 1982. "The Impossibility of Competition in Telecommunications." In *Regulatory Reform and Public Utilities*, edited by Michael A. Crew. Lexington, MA: Lexington Books.

Phillips, Almarin. 1985. "The Re-integration of Telecommunications: An Interim View." In *Analyzing the Impact of Regulatory Change*, edited by Michael A. Crew. Lexington MA: Lexington Books.

2

FEASIBILITY OF DEREGULATION:
A PUBLIC CHOICE ANALYSIS
Michael A. Crew
Charles K. Rowley

Deregulation is evident not just in the United States economy but also in much of Western Europe, notably the United Kingdom where there is an effective move toward *privatization*.[1] Following the abolition of the Civil Aeronautics Board on January 1, 1985, the deregulation of the airline industry in the United States is frequently cited as the most important example of successful deregulation. The divestiture by AT&T of its operating companies and the deregulation of several telecommunications services is perhaps the most significant example of the trend toward deregulation in the area of public utilities or natural monopoly. Similar developments are observed in the electricity and gas industries. Even water utilities with, arguably, the strongest case for being classed as a natural monopoly, are diversifying into other businesses.[2] The holding company structure, with its obvious potential for allowing diversification, is becoming increasingly popular. One important difference between these industries and the airlines is that, while the trend is firmly toward deregulation and diversification, regulatory commissions still exist and still exercise regulatory oversight over these industries. Another important difference is that they still have some of the characteristics of natural monopolies, perhaps even of a sustainable nature. Contrast the above with, for example, taxicab services, which are bereft of natural monopoly characteristics and yet show little or no sign of deregulation.[3]

This chapter attempts to explain such paradoxes. How is it that there are instances of successful deregulation of apparent natural monopolies and yet observed durability of regulation in industries that might otherwise be competitive? The approach taken in this chapter will be to examine the political economy of regulation. Modern political economy, we shall argue, drawing upon public choice and the new institution economics, is the most effective and insightful framework for analyzing the forces at work and drawing implications for the issue of the organization of industry. The second section examines some of the main economic theories of regulation. In the third section we show how public choice theory can be employed to offer unique insights into the deregulation issue. Finally in the last section, we derive implications for the relevant organization of industry. Paradoxically, our approach provides a powerful intellectual case for deregulation while at the same time casting serious doubts on its feasibility.

Critique and Review of the Major Economic Theories of Regulation

There are several theories purporting to explain the nature and significance of regulation. All of them are flawed.

The Public Interest Theory

Public interest theories of regulation are based upon the notion that regulation is intended to be "in the public interest," for "the good of all," for the "commonweal," and the like.[4] The concept is purposefully vague. Public interest clearly means different things to different people. For example, monopoly regulation is often advocated in the public interest as a means of eliminating monopoly rents. Rent is a return to a resource owner over its opportunity costs. In the case of monopoly, any profits earned are rents, or payments in excess of what is needed to keep the resources employed in that use. A public interest regulator might regard such rents reflective of unearned enrichment and view their elimination as important on equity or income distribution grounds. Others might stress efficiency criteria. Yet others might say that they are aiming to replicate the competitive market. Rate-of-return regulation, in attempting to provide utilities with a "fair" rate of return on capital, computes the allowed rate of return based upon the notion of the rate of return earned by investments of equivalent risk.[5] The problem, however, with this approach is that application of the methodology allows considerable scope for discretion, and all sorts of self-seeking are seen to masquerade behind the veil of public interest rhetoric.[6]

Capture Theory

At its simplest, capture theory views regulation as a device deployed by firms to establish or to enhance monopoly power. Companies subvert the power of government, through regulators, to provide barriers to entry, a cartel office, or monopolist price discrimination not readily available except by manipulating a regulatory process. The expenditures on forming, maintaining, and manipulating the regulatory process are treated as cost-effective business investment outlays.

Economic Theories of Regulation

Economic theories of regulation, while drawing in part from capture theory, are much more sophisticated analytically and more satisfying to neoclassical economists. They arise primarily from the Chicago School, especially the work of Stigler (1971), Peltzman (1976), and Becker (1983). True to Chicago, they attack capture theory for its lack of theoretical sophistication, for its absence of a tight prior equilibrium, and for its failure to yield predictions that are robust enough for testing.

The seminal article by Stigler (1971) initiated the study of the economics of regulation. This new thrust was consolidated by Peltzman (1976), who developed a formal market model in which regulations were viewed as commodities brokered via political markets in response to bids and counter-bids by those who stood to gain or to lose from specific regulation outcomes. The subsequent contribution by Becker (1983, 1985) added insights and institutional flesh to the Stigler/Peltzman embryo, confirming regulation as an integral component of mainstream market economics, while recognizing that efficiency-reducing transfers will occur through political markets.[7]

An important implication of such contributions, even in the case of Becker as we shall show, is that regulation for the most part confirms resource efficiency within market process; that political markets, in the absence of political entry barriers, are as effective as competitive commodity markets in achieving economic efficiency.

Becker (1976) first questioned implications of Peltzman's (1974) theory that appeared to depend on the assumption that voters are fooled systematically concerning the effects of regulation policies. Utilizing the methodology of the rational expectations school, and squeezing out all notions of systematic voter illusion, he assumed that voters correctly perceive, at least in equilibrium, the gains and losses from all policy alternatives. On this basis, he suggested that "industries are regulated . . . because industrial regulation may be a *relatively* efficient rather than inefficient way of transferring benefits to specified groups" (p. 247). More than this, Becker suggested that the particular regulations that survive the keen competition for votes do so precisely because they are relatively efficient ways to distribute resources:

the methods used to accomplish any given end tend to be the most efficient available, in the public as well as the market sector. . . . this approach leaves little room for economists to suggest improved methods in the public sector . . . (1976, 248).

In 1983, however, Becker shifted the emphasis away from the vote motive as the fulcrum of the political market for regulation. Together with politicians and political parties, voters were viewed as agents whose purpose is "mainly to transmit the pressure of active groups" (p. 372). Interest groups were seen to compete within the context of rules that translate expenditures on political pressure into political influence and access to political resources. This view was consolidated in his 1985 paper.

In Becker's view, competition among interest groups largely serves efficiency objectives. Active groups produce pressure to raise their political influence. All influences are jointly determined by such competing pressures. Competition for influence is a zero-sum game. Since interest groups always confront a free-rider problem, potential benefits from pressure exert an important role. Pressures that limit deadweight losses (and thus maximize appropriable benefits) are likely to prove more successful than pressures that fail to do so. Therefore, political market competition favors efficient (defined as relatively low deadweight cost) policies over less efficient alternatives:

> Policies that raise efficiency are likely to win out in the competition for influence because they produce gains rather than deadweight costs, so that groups benefited have the intrinsic advantage compared to groups harmed. Consequently, this analysis unifies the view that governments correct market failures with the view that they favor the politically powerful by showing that both are produced by competition among pressure groups for political favors (p. 396).

Yet, Becker does not endorse the essentially policy-impotent perspective of Stigler that "what is, is efficient."[8]

Stigler (1976) had earlier attacked the concept of X-inefficiency by asking the important question: What is output? His answer was that output could be defined only in utility space:

> When more of one goal is achieved at the cost of less of another goal, the increase in output due to (say) increased effort is not an increase in "efficiency"; it is a *change* in output (p. 213).

And X-inefficiency proponents endured the Chicago lash:

> This tunnel vision of output seems entirely unrewarding: it imposes one person's goal upon other persons who have never accepted that goal (p. 214).

In Stigler's view, waste arises only as error in an economy inhabited by maximizing individuals. He is totally unprepared to "take the mighty methodological leap into the unknown that a nonmaximizing theory requires" (1976, 216).[9] In the absence of a theory of error, waste is not a useful concept within Stigler's analytic framework. Such a view, coupled to Becker's interpretation of interest group politics, paints a rosy picture for politico-economic regulation in sharp contrast, as we shall demonstrate, to the contributions of public choice theory.

Contractual Theories of Regulation

The notion of regulation as a governance contract stems primarily from the work of Goldberg (1976) and Williamson (1976, 1985). Although not as forcibly stated as the Chicago School, its bottom line is essentially the same. It supports the view that regulation is relatively efficient, given the transactions cost of alternative governance structures and the failure of classical contracting to provide for efficient outcomes in environments characterized by asset specificity, long-term relationships, and opportunities for strategic behavior.

The contractual theory of regulation views regulation as a governance structure, relevant in particular for markets characterized by natural monopoly.[10] A governance structure describes the framework, or set of transactions, in which contracts are initiated, monitored, negotiated, enforced, adapted, and terminated. Thus there may be a number of governance structures for natural monopoly. The New Institutional Economics would analyze such governance structures by means of a comparative institutional assessment. Such analyses tend to be supportive of some form—not necessarily the current form—of regulation.[11] This is true particularly of Williamson (1976) and Goldberg (1976).

The arguments of the New Institutional Economics are attractive in certain respects and provide insights on the "hold-up" problem. Because of the transactions specific investments required by such utilities, they are subject to opportunistic behavior with respect to quasi rents. For example, plant in the ground is sunk both literally and economically. It has little or no value except for the current use. In such cases there is always a risk *ex post* that customers will expropriate quasi rents. Goldberg and Williamson both argue that regulation provides a comparatively efficient governance structure to deal with this problem. The regulatory commission is seen as an independent arbitrator which guarantees non-expropriation of quasi rents by providing an exclusive franchise in its service territory, thus giving the company the incentive *ex ante* to make transactions specific investments and to provide service, while protecting the consumer from monopolistic exploitation.

Williamson compares regulation with franchise bidding, an alternative governance structure proposed by Demsetz (1968). Williamson's argument emphasizes the high transactions cost of franchise bidding relative to regulation. In particular he is concerned with the problem of periodic re-bidding.

If, after a few years, the franchise is put up for renewal and the current incumbent loses it, the problem of compensating the incumbent for its sunk assets is a non-trivial one. Such a revaluation process, Williamson argues, generates uncertainty and is transactions-cost rich. As a result, it is likely to provide inadequate guarantees for transactions-specific investments. Furthermore, complex auctions will be required if natural monopolies are to price at marginal cost, in the absence of a lump-sum general subsidy.

In analyzing regulation as a governance structure, the New Institutional Economics (especially Williamson) stresses the importance of considerations of fairness as well as efficiency in the contract governance process.[12] Correctly, he argues these concepts are positively valued. The question is whether the additional benefits provided by the regulatory process are worth the incremental transactions costs, i.e., is "fairness" efficiently delivered through a contract governance regulatory market.

Posner's Nihilistic Theory of Regulation

Posner's writings on regulation, while impressive in terms both of volume and of insight, also represent a powerful attack on regulation. In this respect, they contrast sharply with the Chicago view, embraced elsewhere by Posner (1986), that "what is is efficient." His basic notion is that regulation is a reservoir, an institution rich in transaction costs, that perhaps benefits only certain actors, such as lawyers. In view of Posner's own formidable writings arguing that the common law is efficient, his attack on regulation is particularly interesting, reminiscent of Hayek's (1973) views, putting him at odds in this area with the Chicago School.

Posner (1969) provided a blistering attack on natural monopoly regulation at a time when the enthusiasm for regulation was approaching its zenith. His criticisms owed much to his ". . . personal experience, as a government lawyer involved in regulatory matters" (1969, 549). His conclusion is that ". . . even in markets where efficiency dictates monopoly we might do better to allow natural economic forces to determine business conduct and performance subject only to the constraints of antitrust policy." He argued that monopoly regulation was ineffective. It failed to prevent monopoly profits and instead redistributed them in the form of cross-subsidies, at a high price in terms of X-ineffiency and other transaction costs. In addition, there existed dynamic inefficiencies from protecting the regulated monopolist from entry.[13] Further, monopoly profits were unlikely to result in large welfare losses, particularly in the context of second best "world of monopolies" where the gains from moving one sector to efficient pricing are likely to be small.

In Posner (1975) he attempted to quantify the effects of allowing unregulated monopoly, compared to regulation. By extending his analysis to include the effects of the transactions costs of the regulatory process, he was led to conclude that ". . . the costs of monopoly are quite probably much greater in the regulated sector than in the unregulated despite the greater size of the latter sector" (1975, 821). Posner employed the rent-seeking insight of Tullock in a way almost unheard of in mainstream Chicago economics, with the recent exception of Becker (1985).

The Public Choice Theory of Regulation

Public choice theory[14] offers a unique insight into the political economy of regulation, combining Olson's (1965) theory of interest groups with Tullock's (1967) theory of rent-seeking behavior. In contrast to Becker, Olson's logic of collective action emphasizes that competition among interest groups introduces significant bias into political markets.[15] Underpinning this bias is the differential impact of the free-rider problem on the formation and effective mobilization of various kinds of interest groups. Unlike Becker's theory, in which free-riding was viewed as vulnerable to the magnitude of the benefits available, Olson emphasized the importance of privatizing such benefits to individual group members and of excluding non-performers from the benefits that are won.

In such a perspective, if the common good of a potential interest group has pronounced publicness characteristics, the free-rider problem will hinder group formation and weaken group pressures. Typically this is a serious problem for large groups of individuals in the absence of membership coercion. Large pressure groups, to be effective, must be organized for other purposes which provide selective benefits to the membership. They must be able to pressure the common interest essentially as a by–product of the selective benefits. This by–product theory explains the existence and success of organizations representing agriculture, labor, and the professions. Consumer groups typically fail the selective benefits pre–requisite.

Smaller organizations may engage successfully in collective action, without recourse either to coercion or to selective benefits, by utilizing their "special interest" advantages. Although the existence of such a special interest, usually in the form of a significant expected benefit to individual members with any limited publicness features, overcomes the free-rider problem, outcome bias is still predictable. Specifically, there is a systematic tendency within such groups for the "exploitation" of the large member by the small, with the larger demander of public policies bearing a disproportionate share of the burden of collective action. The special interests theory explains the existence and success of organizations that represent business interests.

Olson's theory suggests that interest groups introduce significant bias into political markets that otherwise might respond to the median voters' preferences. It further suggests, even on the assumption of zero transactions costs, that competitive interest groups in political markets will divert resources from efficient allocation, given the underlying willingness-to-pay criterion. As such it contrasts sharply with the naive view of Becker that competition between pressure groups tends to correct market failure and to minimize social welfare losses in the process of wealth redistribution.

Olson's view of interest groups, realistic though it was, incorrectly emphasized the costless transfer nature of political markets. In 1967, Tullock corrected this false vision with his seminal paper on rent-seeking and destroyed the notion that interest group lobbying is a costless, even a wealth-enhancing exercise. Interest groups, following Tullock, are viewed as rent-seekers, expending resources in institutional settings where attempts at wealth transfers generate social waste, rather than social surplus, usually (though not exclusively) through the invasion of political markets.

Rent is a return to a resource owner in excess of opportunity cost. It plays an ambivalent role in resource allocation, since its existence is not necessary to insure the commitment of resources to a plan. However, all utility-maximizing individuals seek rents. In competitive markets there exists the potential for a transitory gain from entrepreneurship or innovation to the entrepreneur and an ensuing efficiency gain to society as a result of initiated

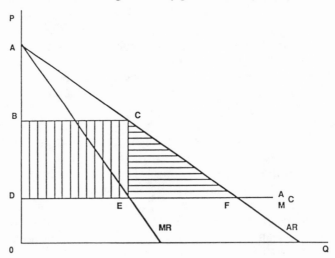

Figure 2-1. Illustrating Efficiency Losses from Regulated Monopoly

change. However, seeking rents in the case of monopolization, whether through regulation or via the machinery of government, imposes efficiency losses for society, as figure 2.1 outlines.

Using the Tullock insight, the welfare losses from (regulated) monopoly are not the traditional, horizontally shaded triangle, CEF, but, in addition, include the vertically shaded rectangle, BDEC. The rectangle, BDEC, in traditional theory, would represent monopoly rents to the monopolist—4ea simple transfer having no welfare economic consequences. However, Tullock argued that these potential rents would be the target of rent seekers who would be prepared to invest resources in their pursuit. In the limit, such expenditures would be sufficient to exhaust the entire rent available, in which case the welfare loss would be the shaded trapezoid, BCFD, rather than just the triangle, CEF. Indeed, Posner's (1975) high estimate of the welfare losses from regulated monopoly was based on the assumption that the deadweight loss was equal to the trapezoid. Moreover, the rectangular part is likely to be much larger than the triangular part.[16]

So far Tullock's rent-seeking theory seems to lead in the same direction as that of Posner's theory of regulation. Both show that the efficiency losses from regulated monopoly are much greater than traditionally argued. Both highlight an institutional example of political market failure. Tullock, however, offers additional insights into the problem, while at the same time providing less of a basis for a solution.

Presumably the implication of Posner's argument is that if society would simply rid itself of regulation, then the problem would disappear, and efficiency losses would be reduced. As such, it bears an inescapable "nirvana" flavor of the new welfare economics. The implications of the Tullock theory are very different and of far greater explanatory and predictive power. Tullock's theory, when linked to public choice theory, shows that it is far from easy to eliminate regulation once it has been politically brokered.

In the public choice approach,[17] politicians are modelled as providing a brokering function in the political market for wealth transfers. Voters and special interest groups capable of effective economic organization "demand" such transfers. Other voters, and more general groups, incapable of such effective economic organization, "supply" such transfers, albeit at a political price. The politicians effect market equilibrium, balancing benefits against costs at the margin, thus maximizing their own utility functions, weighted variously in terms of expected wealth, expected votes, and ideology.

The concepts of demand and supply in this stylized model require a special interpretation. Demand consists of willingness to pay, in money transfers and/or in votes, by voters and interest groups for policies carrying an expected positive net present value. Such returns, which represent rent and not profit, since overall wealth is diminished by such behavior, induce rent-seeking behavior as defined by Tullock (1967). The rent-seekers who represent demand are not merely the direct beneficiaries but are also such secondary recipients as those departments of government, members of regulatory agencies, government-dependent private contractors, consultants and expert witnesses, whose budgets and/or expected net wealth can be enhanced by the transfer mechanism.

Supply consists of the unwillingness or inability of those from whom wealth transfers are sought, at the margin, to protect themselves by countervailing offers of money transfers or of votes to the brokering mechanism. Supply in this sense is equivalent to rent-protection, which is equally as destructive of wealth as is rent-seeking. For this reason, the relative absence of regulation does not necessarily indicate an absence of rent dissipation in a transfer-oriented society.

Where political market discretion exists, rent-seeking interest groups predictably will emerge with the principal objective of transferring rights (more narrowly wealth) to their respective memberships. Such interest groups are a major source of rent dissipation both in the democracies and autocracies. The emergence of countervailing rent protection further serves to dissipate potential wealth in such an environment.

Regulation thus has several advantages when compared with the traditional tax and subsidy instruments available to the brokers of political influence. Its principal advantage is its non-transparency relative to these other instruments. While voters may eventually rebel at a transparent transfer in the form of a tax or a subsidy, the potential of cross subsidies to escape the voters' attention is a great advantage both to politicians and to interest groups. As such, it extends the effective margins of the rent-seeking society.

Accordingly, it is predictable that cross-subsidy will be one of the hallmarks of regulation; and there is much evidence to support this. Empirical research by Trapani et al. (1987) and Nelson, Roberts, and Troup (1987) support the view that electricity prices depart significantly from Ramsey optimal prices, with residential customers subsidized by commercial and industrial customers. Long-distance telephone service traditionally has subsidized local services, at least prior to partial deregulation in the United States. Dense routes have tended to subsidize sparse routes. Such cross-subsidies were also apparent in the U.S. airline industry, prior to deregulation. They still exist on international routes.

In telecommunications, following the divestiture by AT&T of its operating companies, the cross-subsidy from long distance to local has been reduced, as can be illustrated by the changes in the access charges charged to long distance companies by the local operating companies. Before divestiture, approximately 15 cents per minute of use was charged to long distance to cover the so called "non-traffic-sensitive" costs of the network.[18] This charge is currently 4.33 cents. As noted by Crandall (1988), this decline in access charges has been reflected in a decrease in the rates for toll calls and an increase in rates for local service—both in real terms, by around 8 percent per annum and by about 5 percent per annum, respectively. In electricity the effect of entry by cogenerators and small power producers has made electric utilities more concerned about their rates for large users, and negotiated rates for large industrial customers are becoming increasingly apparent.

Another area where the opacity of regulation may assist political brokers is through the use of bureaus. Bureaus are public sector organizations in which employees/owners cannot appropriate directly any rents as personal income, and in which a significant part of recurring revenues derive from other than the sale of output at a per unit price. However, they are conduits through which influence can be directed by the influence brokers through their agents, the bureaucrats. There may be costs of using bureaus, especially the loss of some control through agency. However, there are compensatory benefits conferred by such bureaucracies in terms of patronage and reduced accountability. Moreover, bureaus provide additional ways of obfuscation. Take, for example, the conservation programs that are currently being undertaken by electric utilities and regulated by state public utility commissions. Such programs provide subsidies for customers who undertake measures intended to save energy. The subsidies may be paid directly to the customer or to an energy service company.[19] The subsidies are financed by an increase in the cost of service allowed by the regulatory commissions. Thus the subsidy provided to conservation is derived from all the customers of the utility. It is a classic example of the few receiving benefits from the many along Olson (1965) lines. It provides yet another example of the success of regulation at providing subsidies that would not be forthcoming except through obfuscation.

In addition to the commissioners, many appointments are political, with the obvious potential to reward loyalty, to pay "political debts," and so on. With a more transparent instrument this would be more costly politically. Another advantage of regulation is the ability of politicians to identify with the successes of regulation and yet to avoid being marred by its failures. The former is possible just by claiming responsibility for any successes, the latter by blaming the bureaucrats and by seeking additional influence by initiating a "reform program."

Implications

Stigler, Peltzman, and Becker are correct in emphasizing that the political market in regulation is evaluated most appropriately from the perspective of a tight prior equilibrium. Indeed, this is one of the major contributions of the Chicago School. Even in a rent-seeking environment where regulatory equilibrium reflects significant wealth losses to society and in which wealth redistribution occurs on some non-transparent margins, the political equilibrium may be invulnerable to outside attack. Illusion plays an important role in this solution. Thus, the glue that holds together the balance of rent-seeking and rent protection outlays may prove to be of an uncommonly adhesive nature, despite the absence of full information.

Because of the benefits regulation confers on political influence brokers, they are unlikely to wish to give it up. In addition rent-seekers and rent-protectors, even those that are making only normal returns may oppose the ending of regulation. The problem can be illustrated by reference to the "transitional gains trap" of Tullock (1975). Rent-seekers, such as lawyers and economists servicing regulated industries, may only be making a normal return on their investment. They may have sunk some transaction-specific investment that, in the absence of regulation, would be worthless. For a lawyer who has expertise in the law of public utility regulation, the ending of utility regulation would make acquired skills nearly valueless. Economists, in the expert witness business, would recognize a similar problem. In the case of the lawyer, he might have to take a lower paying job in another branch of law. For an academic economist on the faculty of a university, it might be almost as painful, being now obliged to do research at a significantly lower income. The mechanism is the same as Tullock's taxi cab medallions. The existing owners make only a normal profit from the regulated monopoly in taxis. Therefore, if regulation were abolished they would lose their investment.

By employing public choice theory, it is possible to provide powerful arguments and insights into why it may be extremely difficult to follow Posner's essentially right-headed desire to abolish natural monopoly regulation. Public choice, by synthesizing influence-brokering, rent-seeking, and the transitional gains trap, implies that the quest for efficiency by abolition may be a chimera. What then can be done? Is the situation reflective of an absence of effective choice, in which case the Chicago School perspective essentially is correct? We suggest a few possibilities for reform and imply that institutional choices always exist, with the definite implication that what is is not necessarily efficient.

First, we stress the value of research and education. We must never underestimate the power of ideas. The intellectual endeavors of Marx, Keynes, and more recently of Friedman and Buchanan and Tullock, have had a profound influence on the institutions and management of economic systems. The role of the political economist as entrepreneurial provider of hypotheses concerning institutional reform (Buchanan 1959) is not to be underestimated.

Secondly, rent-seeking and rent-protection may become so unprofitable and impose such large wealth losses that they disintegrate without outside influence. However, when this occurs the economic system typically is already severely damaged, as is evidenced by current attempts at institutional reform in the USSR. It would be far better for such damage to be avoided. Indeed, the power of ideas may be the only means of avoiding serious damage once rent-seeking has become pervasive. One example of this impact is recent experience in the United Kingdom. There is reason to believe that rent-seeking and rent-protection had become excessive and that the economy had been severely damaged by 1979 when the Conservative Government of Thatcher was elected into office. By employing a few basic principles of free market economics, the government radically improved the performance of the U.K. economy during the 1980s. Britain's economic success has been much more dramatic than that of the United States especially when the considerably lower underlying potential of its economy is taken into account. Whether progress can be maintained without the resurgence of rent-seeking remains to be seen. Differences in the political system may also play a significant role. The extent to which the British political system leaves less of the power of influence brokerage in the hands of individual politicians may play a role in moderating rent-seeking abuses. The extent to which logrolling and vote-trading in political markets is lessened by the British Parliamentary system may also attenuate the extent of regulatory equilibrium.

Ultimately, the problem that faces the outside researcher is the existence of a tight prior equilibrium in which government itself is an endogenous element. In such a situation, outside shocks alone will shift the outcome unless inside preferences and technologies shift sharply in favor of deregulating reform. The informed public choice analyst can pinpoint the problems. He cannot expect to shift entrenched self-interest embedded, even as it often is, in a negative sum game. It would be tragic indeed if economics must await, as Olson (1984) suggests they must, defeats in major wars or internal socio-economic disintegration as the only effective vehicles against rent-seeking. If so, public choice may yet merit the label that often is levelled against it—the most dismal branch of the dismal science.

Notes

1. The United Kingdom, as a result of the policies of Labour governments since the Second World War, had placed several industries in addition to traditional natural monopolies under public ownership. The government of Mrs. Margaret Thatcher, with its election in 1979, embarked on a policy of making the economy more subject to market forces rather than government command and control mechanisms. Prior to its re-election for a third term in June 1987, it had returned 51 percent of the telephone service, British Telecom, to private hands. During its third term, it plans to restructure the publicly owned electricity supply industry and to return it to some form of private ownership.

2. Privatization of U.K. water authorities was an election commitment of the Thatcher Government.

3. Teal and Berlund (1987) examine the extent of deregulation and distinguish four consequential benefits and some disadvantages to producers and consumers.

4. For a recent re-appraisal of the "morality tales" that underpin this notion, see Reich (1987).

5. For a comprehensive discussion of the methods employed by financial economists in attempting to compute the allowed rate of return see Kolbe et al. (1984).

6. Even Reich (1987), a self-designated liberal, recognizes this. "The problem comes when a changing environment outpaces the political culture. When we become so enchanted with our fables that we wall them off from the pressures for adaptation, the stories may begin to mask reality rather than illuminate it. Instead of cultural tools for coming to terms with the challenges we face, they become means of forestalling them."

7. Becker (1985, 335): "Aggregate efficiency should be defined not only net of dead weight costs and benefits of taxes and subsidies, but also net of expenditures on the production of political pressure . . . since these expenditures are only rent-seeking inputs into the determination of policies."

8. See Becker (1985, 335): "Restrictions on campaign contributions, regulation of and monitoring of lobbying organizations, limitations on total taxes and public expenditures, and other laws may be evidence of cooperative efforts to reduce 'wasteful' expenditures on cross-hauling and political pressure."

9. On this issue, see Reder (1982), especially at page 11: "In essence the Chicago View . . . is rooted in the hypothesis that decision makers so allocate the resources under their control that there is no alternative allocation such that any one decision maker could have his expected utility increased without a reduction occurring in the expected utility of at least one other decision maker."

10. See Crew and Rowley (1988).

11. Crew and Kleindorfer (1986) give an example of such a comparative institutional assessment. See Williamson (1985, 193): "Transaction cost economics maintains that it is impossible to concentrate all of the relevant bargaining action at the ex ante contracting stage. Instead, bargaining is pervasive—in which case the institutions of private ordering and the study of contracting in its entirety take as critical economic significance."

12. See Williamson (1985, 177): "Contract doctrines that permit excuse from strict performance were originally explained by reference to fairness. . . . More recently, however, impossibility and related doctrines have been interpreted with reference to efficient risk bearing."

13. See Posner (1969, 548): "The most pernicious feature of regulation would appear to be precisely its impact on change—its tendency to retard the growth of competition that would erode the power of regulated monopolists."

14. See Crew and Rowley (1986, 1987, 1988).

15. See Becker (1985, 344): "Indeed, no policy that lowered social output would survive if all groups were equally large and skillful at producing political influence, for the opposition would always exert more influence than proponents. The condemnation of special interest groups is more justified when there is unequal access to political influence."

16. Becker (1988) has emphasized the non-empirical nature of such statements. "Do you know of anybody who has shown with real data and not with speculations (the rectangles involved are only upper bounds) that rent seeking expenditures are a more important 'distortion' than deadweight costs?" His stricture is well-taken.

17. See Rowley, Shughart, and Tollison (1987) for an empirical test of the model here briefly outlined.

18. In addition the long distance companies pay the local companies for the "traffic-sensitive" costs. These average about 5 cents per minute of use. This 5 cents is the total charged at both the originating and the terminating end of the call.

19. Interestingly, direct subsidies for energy conservation used to be given in the form of Energy Tax Credits to households. These were abolished with the Tax Reform Act of 1986. Such subsidies were obvious and did not satisfy the politicians' requirement for obfuscation.

References

Becker, Gary S. 1983. "A Theory of Competition Among Pressure Groups for Political Influence." *Quarterly Journal of Economics* 96 (3): 371-400.

Becker, Gary S. 1985. "Public Policies, Pressure Groups, and Dead Weight Costs." *Journal of Public Economics* 28:325-347.

Becker, Gary S. 1988. "Letter to Charles K. Rowley." March 31.

Crandall, Robert W. 1988. "Surprises from Telephone Deregulation and the AT&T Divestiture." *American Economic Review* 78 (no. 2, May): 323-327.

Crew, Michael A. (ed.) 1987. *Regulating Utilities in an Era of Deregulation.* New York: St. Martin's Press.

Crew, Michael A., and Paul R. Kleindorfer. 1986. *The Economics of Public Utility Regulation.* Cambridge, MA: MIT Press.

Crew, Michael A., and Charles K. Rowley. 1988. "Toward a Public Choice Theory of Regulation." *Public Choice* 57 (March): 49-67.

Demsetz, Harold. 1968. "Why Regulate Utilities?" *American Economic Review* 11 (April): 55-66.

Hayek, F.A. 1973. *Law, Legislation and Liberty,* Vol. 1. London: Routledge and Kegan Paul.

Kolbe, A. Lawrence, James A. Read, and George R. Hall. 1984. *The Cost of Capital.* Cambridge, MA: MIT Press.

McCormick, R.E., W.F. Shughart III, and R.D. Tollison. 1988. "The Disinterest in Deregulation: Reply." *American Economic Review* 78 (no. 1, March): 284-285.

Olson, M. 1965. *The Logic of Collective Action.* Cambridge, MA: Harvard University Press.

Peltzman, Sam. 1976. "Toward a More General Theory of Regulation." *Journal of Law and Economics* 19 (August): 211-240.

Posner, Richard A. 1969. "Natural Monopoly and Its Regulation." *Stanford Law*

Review 21 (February): 548-643.

Posner, Richard A. 1975. "The Social Costs of Monopoly Regulation." *Journal of Political Economy* 83 (August): 807-827.

Reder, M.W. 1982. "Chicago Economics: Permanence and Change." *Journal of Economic Literature* 20 (no. 1, March): 1-38.

Reich, R. 1987. *Tales of a New America: The Anxious Liberal's Guide to the Future.* New York: Random House.

Rowley, C.K., W.F. Shughart III, and R.D. Tollison. 1987. "Interest Groups and Deficits," pp. 263-280. In *Deficits*, edited by J.R. Buchanan, C.K. Rowley, and R.D. Tollison. Oxford: Basil Blackwell.

Stigler, George J. 1971. "The Economic Theory of Regulation." *Bell Journal of Economics* 2 (no. 1, Spring): 3-21.

Stigler, George J. 1976. "X-istence of X-inefficiency." *American Economic Review* 66 (no. 1, March): 3-21.

Teal, Roger F., and Mary Berglund. 1987. "The Impact of Taxicab Deregulation in the U.S.A." *Journal of Transport Economics and Policy* 21 (January): 37-56.

Tullock, Gordon. 1967. "The Welfare Costs of Tariffs, Monopolies, and Theft." *Western Economic Journal* 5 (June): 224-232.

Tullock, Gordon. 1975. "The Transition Gains." *Bell Journal of Economics* 6 (Autumn): 61-68.

Williamson, Oliver E. 1976. "Franchise Bidding for Natural Monopoly—In General and with Respect to CATV." *Bell Journal of Economics* (Spring): 73-104.

Williamson, Oliver E. 1985. "Assessing Contract." *Journal of Law, Economics and Organization* 1 (no. 1, Spring): 177-208.

3
PRICE CAP REGULATION OF TELECOMMUNICATIONS SERVICES: A LONG-RUN APPROACH
Ingo Vogelsang

Introduction

With its recent *Notice of Proposed Rulemaking* the United States Federal Communications Commission (FCC 1987) has opened a discussion about the possible use of price caps to replace rate-of-return regulation for telecommunications services. The basic idea of these price caps is closely related to the RPI–X formula suggested by Littlechild (1983) for British Telecom and implemented there, along with British Telecom's privatization, in 1984. This formula says that over a period of at least five years British Telecom is constrained in adjusting the prices for a basket of its basic services by the condition that the weighted average of these prices increase by no more than the Retail Price Index less "X" percent. In the prices of its other (nonbasic) services, British Telecom is only constrained by the market and by general laws on competition.

Littlechild and the FCC argue carefully about the virtues of such a pricing scheme. In short, it should provide incentives for the regulated firm to produce efficiently, and it should protect customers from monopoly exploitation. Also, the administrative burden of price regulation on regulators and firms is likely to be reduced substantially.

The previous analysis of price caps has at least two shortcomings. First, it concentrates almost solely on the issues of (1) cost efficiency by the regulated firm and (2) equity for certain consumer groups. The issue of allocative price efficiency (that is, correctly dividing up services to the consumers who value them most) has not been raised. This analysis does precisely that and shows, at the same time, what the implications are for issues (1) and (2). Second, the current literature has examined price caps under a very limited time horizon. This would be acceptable if the regulatory agency could and wanted to commit itself to total deregulation within this time span. Otherwise, one has to ask, what will happen when the time is up for a general review of the price caps? Specific suggestions for answering this question are given below.

In this chapter, I present the argument that the RPI–X or price cap scheme has to be seen from a long-term perspective that includes adjustments of the formula over time. The question of allocative efficiency of the resulting mechanism can and should be addressed, in addition to productive efficiency and fairness. This discussion is substantially facilitated by the fact that the RPI–X formula can be interpreted as a modification of the regulatory adjustment process suggested by Vogelsang and Finsinger (1979), hereinafter called V-F.

The second section briefly describes the V-F mechanism and discusses its virtues and problems. The third section deals with modifying the mechanism to make it equivalent to a long-run version of the RPI–X formula. This modification is done in several steps, each of which highlights a particular problem that so far had not been solved for the V-F mechanism. These problems include adjustments to changes in cost and demand conditions and incentives for cost reduction and productivity increases. The main V-F findings continue to hold: Consumer surplus will increase over time, and in the long run the structure of price caps will resemble Ramsey prices. By using price caps, all this can be achieved at substantially lower administrative costs to the regulator than by using rate-of-return regulation. The final section gives a short conclusion.

The V-F Mechanism[1]

Consider a regulated multi-product enterprise in an intertemporal setting. The firm's objective is to myopically maximize profits $\pi_t = p_t q_t(p_t) - C(q_t)$ for each consecutive time period t, t∈N, N={1,...,∞}. p_t and q_t are price and output vectors for the m products that the firm produces. The firm faces a stationary cost function $C(q_t)$ and a stationary demand function $q(p_t)$. There are no intertemporal cost and demand effects. The management of the firm is assumed to know both these functions. The regulator is assumed to know neither of them. However, he or she can observe current posted prices and the last period's output quantities and total cost. The regulator is interested in social surplus $S=\pi(p)+V(p)$, where $V(p)$ is consumer surplus without income effects. The regulator would like the firm at least to break even, $\pi(p)\geq0$. The heart of the V-F mechanism is a constraint Rt that defines the set of allowed prices for the firm in each consecutive period t. This constraint is defined as

$$R_t \equiv q_{t-1}\,p_t - C(q_{t-1}) \leq 0. \qquad (3.1)$$

Constraint (3.1) says that in period t the firm may only charge prices that would produce no (excess) profit if applied to the last period's outputs and cost. The regulator requires the firm to fulfill all demand at current prices. Figure 3-1 provides a two-product example of the constraint. It is drawn in price space. The fact that p_{t-1} is inside the zero-profit contour, $\pi(p)=0$, indicates that the firm has been making a positive profit in t-1. Now the shaded area on and below R_t defines the allowed prices in period t. As the figure is drawn, the firm can make a profit in period t. Maximizing profits, it will end up at a point like p_t. Then a new constraint R_{t+1} will be imposed, which will leave the firm less room for profit maximization. The process continues in this manner and will eventually converge at a point on the

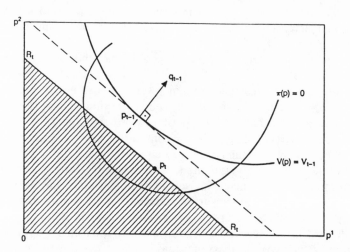

Figure 3-1. The Regulatory Constraint R_t

zero-profit contour. The key result is that, for this final price vector, consumer surplus attains the highest level possible without the firm incurring losses. Prices with this property are called "Ramsey" prices. Because of the gradient property $\partial V/\partial p = -q$ (Roy's identity without income effects), the demand vector q_{t-1} is perpendicular to the social indifference curve V_{t-1} through p_{t-1}. Therefore, by construction, the constraint R_t is parallel to the social indifference curve through p_{t-1}. The constraint always moves in the direction of the steepest increase in consumer welfare.

A simple interpretation of the constraint R_t is that it forces the firm to reduce its prices in each period on average by the last period's profit margin. Here the average is defined by a Laspeyres chain index; that is, prices are weighted by last period's quantities. As can be seen from figure 3-1, individual prices may well be increased as long as other prices are sufficiently decreased.

Four assumptions on the cost and demand function are needed for the V-F process to converge to Ramsey prices.

Assumption 1: The cost function has to exhibit decreasing ray average cost. That means that, if all outputs of the firm are increased proportionally, then total cost has to go up less than proportionally.

Decreasing ray average cost is closely related, although not identical, to natural monopoly. This assumption is needed to assure nonnegative profits for the firm. The reason is simple. Although the firm may increase individual prices, the pricing constraint requires the firm to reduce its prices on average by the amount of the last period's profit margin. Hence, on average it will have to increase outputs. If that increase in output leads to a less than proportional increase in cost, then the firm can still make a profit. Otherwise it may face a loss.

Assumption 2: The demand function has to be such that consumer surplus is convex in prices.

This property requires that consumer surplus does not decrease if, at current prices, consumers can still buy the last period's quantities without paying more in total than before. In other words, we apply the axioms of revealed preference to the aggregate of consumers. This assumption assures convergence. Every time the firm makes a profit the constraint is tightened, and every time the constraint is tightened consumer surplus increases. Hence, we get a monotonically increasing sequence in consumer surplus which is bounded by the maximum consumer surplus compatible with nonnegative profits. It will normally converge to this maximum, which, under the assumption of decreasing ray average cost, coincides with the Ramsey optimum.

In my view, the two crucial assumptions just discussed are not very restrictive. They are unlikely to be violated by regulated telecommunications carriers. However, the following two assumptions are restrictive.

Assumption 3: Cost and demand functions faced by the firm are required to be stationary over time.

This stationarity assumption is unlikely to hold in reality, creating a problem for any lagged mechanism. The mechanism therefore has to be adjusted to changes in the firm's environment.

Assumption 4: The firm maximizes profit myopically for every period t.

Sappington (1980) has shown that strategic behavior violating this assumption could undermine the welfare implications of the V-F mechanism even though it eventually converges. The basic argument behind his derivation is that the regulated firm may inflate its costs in early periods in order to postpone more stringent regulation. While V-F regulation always benefits consumers, it has no built-in mechanism that will always induce cost efficiency.

Modifications of the V-F Mechanism

A Differentiated Lag Period

The V-F mechanism has two major weaknesses, due to Assumptions 3 and 4 (the requirements of a stationary environment and of myopic profit maximization). I will now address those weaknesses.

Let us start with the problems caused by Assumption 4. Sappington's main finding was that under V-F the regulated firm may strategically waste resources. This may happen in particular at the beginning of the process, as the firm attempts to postpone a tightening of the regulatory constraint. Sappington suggested that this would become less likely the more the firm discounted the future: Wasteful expenditures have to be borne by the firm now, while the relaxation of the profit constraint occurs with a lag of one period. The firm's discount rate per period obviously depends on the length of the time period involved. A discount rate of 10 percent for a period of one year becomes 61 percent for a period of five years. Thus, by increasing the regulatory lag period, one can solve the problem of potential waste (and lack of incentives for productivity gains). However, this would also reduce the number of iterations of the regulatory process in a given time span. This could slow down the convergence speed, which would increase the weight of Assumption 3.

To mitigate these problems, I suggest differentiating between two types of adjustments. Long-term adjustments by means of a profit-based reexamination should occur only at multi-year intervals. The relevant interval, or period, is designated by subscript t. Such a general reexamination ought to be done after a prespecified period of five to ten years. The only way an earlier reexamination could be triggered would be if an emergency situation arose for the carrier (e.g., Chapter 11 filing). As a result of the reexamination, the average caps would be adjusted once and for all reflecting the actual profitability of the carrier. In this chapter we assume that the length of t is external to the regulatory process.[2]

Short-term adjustments in any subperiod of t (designated by subscript μ) occur at short intervals which we call *subperiods*. *Subperiods* can span a year or can be irregular. In the latter case, the carrier should take the initiative for price changes. The carrier would have to file changes with a demonstration that they comply with the caps. The filing would automatically result in new tariffs after one month, unless the FCC or an interested party shows that the new tariffs violate the caps. Again, in the following we assume that the length of *subperiod* μ is set externally.

The regulatory constraint now becomes

$$R^1_{t,\mu} \equiv \frac{1}{T}\,\delta_{t,\mu} \sum_{\theta=1}^{T} \pi_{t-1,\theta}\beta^\theta - (p_{t,\mu-1} - p_{t,\mu})q_{t,\mu-1} \le 0. \qquad (3.2)$$

Here T is the number of *subperiods* in each *period* t, and $\delta_{t,\mu}$ is the Kronecker symbol with $\delta_{t,\mu}=1$ for $\mu=1$ and $\delta_{t,\mu}=0$ otherwise. Subscripts t,μ represent a lexicographical ordering. Dropping subscript μ means that we look at the entire *period* t. Also, we define $t,0 \equiv t-1,T$. β is the discount factor applied by the firm and is assumed to be known to the regulator. Constraint (3.2) means that in *subperiod* μ of *period* t the firm may set prices which, if applied to *subperiod* μ-1's outputs, would reduce gross revenues by the average (excess) profit of *period* t-1 discounted to the beginning of period t-1. Whereas the *structure* of prices will be adjusted in every *subperiod*, the *level* of prices is only adjusted once at the beginning of each *period*.

If we had only one *period* t the term

$$\sum_{\theta=1}^{T} \pi_{t-1,\theta}\beta^\theta$$

could be interpreted as a lump-sum amount by which the firm's price level would have to be reduced at the beginning of period t. In all *subperiods* μ of t a Laspeyres chain index of prices would have to be held constant. If t is a *period* of infinite length, if cost and demand functions of the firm do not change over time, and if the firm maximizes the discounted stream of future profits, then this one-*period*, infinitely-many-*subperiods* process will converge to Ramsey prices at the profit level defined by the constraint in the steady state.[3] The firm will also minimize costs in every *subperiod* after the first.

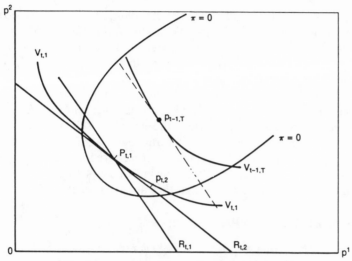

Figure 3-2. The Regulatory Constraint $R^1_{t,r}$

Figure 3-2 shows how the firm moves toward more efficient pricing. In the first *subperiod* $\mu=1$ of *period t,* the firm faces constraint $R^1_{t,1}$ which has been constructed just like constraint $R_{t,1}$ in figure 3-1. As can be seen, the social indifference curve $V_{t,1}$ reached at the point chosen by the firm will usually cut constraint $R^1_{t,1}$. The new constraint $R^1_{t,2}$ for *subperiod* $\mu=2$ now has the property that it goes through $p_{t,1}$ and is tangent to $V_{t,1}$. Under myopic profit maximization, we could now use a revealed preference approach to the firm to determine that for *subperiod* $\mu=2$ the firm would choose a point southeast of $p_{t,1}$ on the new constraint, though for strategic reasons it may choose not to do so. However, in either case, consumers' surplus weakly increases in every *subperiod* until the process converges at some profit level higher than the initial profit level $\pi_{t,1}$. This ultimate profit level may be deemed too high from a social point of view. That is one of the reasons why the RPI–X formula has to be adjusted from time to time.

We do precisely that by *assuming that there are many (nevertheless long) periods t.* The major change introduced by this assumption is that π_{t-1} becomes a variable that is influenced by the firm's behavior.

π_{t-1} depends on both revenues and costs during t-1. Provided that *periods* t-1 and t are long enough, the firm will have little or no incentive to incur excessive costs or charge excessive prices just to manipulate the constraint in *period t.*[4] On the contrary, the longer the *period,* and thus the lag, the greater the incentive to engage in innovative and cost-reducing activities.

Again, this is the reason why the RPI–X formula for British Telecom will only be reviewed after five years. With an infinite number of *periods t*, a finite number T of *subperiods* μ, and under similar assumptions as before, it can again be shown that prices converge to Ramsey prices.[5] This time, however, they would involve zero excess profits.

Constraint (3.2) stipulates that the firm has to adjust the price *level* for its products at the start of every *period* but not for every *subperiod*. From one subperiod to the next only the base of the chain index changes, not the level. This is neither in line with the RPI–X formula nor a sufficient adaptation to a changing environment. To decide on a procedure for adaptation, we have to discuss which potential changes we want to adapt to. We then suggest several indices with the property that they are easily observable.

Adjustments for Input Price Changes

Without any adjustment, price caps will eventually lead to some crisis situation, either one of financial distress or one of unduly high profits, for the regulated firm. Assuming that one wants to avoid such a crisis, the main question remains to what extent adjustments should be automatic and to what extent they should require a formal rate review. Since an automatic mechanism cannot be perfect, price caps will have to be formally revised from time to time. However, automatic adjustments can help stretch the time span between formal reviews. The more an automatic adjustment reflects the actual cost changes of the carrier, the longer this time span can be. However, at the same time, cost-accounting problems grow, and the incentive to cut costs weakens. To strike a balance, actual cost changes should be used for large items that cannot be influenced by the carrier, such as carrier access charges and taxes. These changes should be given their respective weight in total costs, and the remaining cost changes should be factored in by using industry-wide or nation-wide indices.

Changes in the firm's environment can occur with respect to costs and demands. Costs are the sum of products of input prices and input quantities. Costs may therefore change as a result of price changes for inputs or changes in input requirements.[6]

Let us first concentrate on the question of input price changes. These could become relevant during a *period* or a *subperiod*.

To solve this problem for the *period*, I suggest allowing cost increases computed for the previous *period's* input quantities to fully pass through. This would not change constraint (3.2), but would mean that, for instance, $\pi_{t-1} < 0$ would result in a higher allowed price level in *period t*. Because the regulatory lag (on average) is quite long, the firm would have an incentive to hold input prices down. However, in the interim, the firm would not be shielded against input price increases outside its control. To allow for this *pass-through* of input price increases during *subperiods*, the regulatory constraint has to be changed. Assuming that there are n inputs with quantities denoted by the quantity vector v_t and prices denoted by the price vector w_t, the constraint would be

$$R_{t,\mu}^2 \equiv \frac{1}{T} \; \delta_{t,\mu} \sum_{\theta=1}^{T} \; \pi_{t-1,\theta} \beta^\theta - (p_{t,\mu-1} - p_{t,\mu}) q_{t,\mu-1} + (w_{t,\mu-1} - w_{t,\mu}) v_{t,\mu-1} \leq 0. \quad (3.3)$$

The last term on the left hand side is a generalization of the notion of fuel adjustment clauses used in regulated energy utilities. It has the advantage over these clauses that no bias is introduced because all inputs, in principle, are treated symmetrically. It also contains $R_{t,1}^1$ as the special case where v is constant over time. Compared with constraint (3.2), the additional information requirement for constraint (3.3) is quite substantial. However, regulators normally have access to the firm's accounting data, which should reveal input prices and quantities.[7] Aside from the large amount of data to be handled, the problem of intertemporal cost effects also remains. While inputs of labor and raw materials are usually consumed within one period, capital inputs by definition span several periods. Thus, measuring the correct amount of capital inputs may pose a problem.

The obvious disadvantage of a full input price adjustment is that it substantially lessens incentives for the firm to keep input prices down. That is why the FCC wants to restrict the use of adjustment clauses to just those inputs whose prices the firm cannot influence. If the contribution of these inputs to total costs is high and if they are few, then including them in such an adjustment clause may make both administrative and economic sense. The administrative burden for the firm and the regulator would be small, and the flexibility gained would be substantial. If the contribution of these inputs to total costs is small, then additional *adjustment indices* are needed. These could relate to individual inputs, such as a wage index for construction workers, or to a large composite of inputs, such as a producer price index. In these cases, again, the administrative burden would be low. At the same time, however, there would be the danger that the firm's individual input prices on average would deviate substantially from the index. The more this is likely to be the case, the shorter the *period t* to be chosen.

A realistic adjustment to changing input prices requires a combination of *pass-through* and indexing in such a way that all or almost all inputs are covered. The resulting price constraint reads

$$R^3_{t,\mu} \equiv \frac{1}{T} \, \delta_{t,\mu} \sum_{\theta=0}^{T} \pi_{t-1,\theta}\beta^{\theta} - (p_{t,\mu-1} - p_{t,\mu})q_{t,\mu-1} + (w^*_{t,\mu-1} - w^*_{t,\mu})v_{t,\mu-1} \leq 0. \quad (3.4)$$

Here $w^*_{t,\mu} = (w^1_{t,\mu}, \ldots, w^k_{t,\mu}, w^{k+1}_{t,\mu} PI^{k+1}_{t,\mu}, \ldots, w^n_{t,\mu}PI^n_{t,\mu})$ and $PI^j_{t,\mu}$ is the price index for input j in *subperiod* μ-1. w^j_{t-1} is the price of input j in the last *subperiod* of *period t*. The indices PI could be aggregated for a number of inputs and would be weighted accordingly. Assuming that one of the firm's aggregated inputs is capital, we can see that our constraint can also be formulated as a rate-of-return constraint. This can be done by substituting the allowed rate of return, s_t, for the cost of capital r_{t-1}. Since r is hard to observe we generally will have s_t unequal to r_{t-1}. This would make regulation asymmetric with respect to input prices. That is why s_t should only be adjusted once for every *period t*.

Instead of adjusting an initial profit constraint for input price changes, the RPI–X formula used for British Telecom adjusts the allowed price level by the change in consumer price index (RPI in the United Kingdom or CPI in the United States). This procedure holds two basic advantages. First, the RPI is extremely simple to apply, and its movements are widely understood by the public. Second, it is fair to consumers in the sense that it neutralizes real price changes. At the same time RPI movements are likely to be somewhat in line with movements of input price indices. So, the RPI adjustment also provides some flexibility to the supplying firm. In many regulated industries, however, input price changes have been substantially different from changes in the RPI. Examples include electric utilities and transportation industries which are heavily dependent on energy inputs. Similarly, telecommunication costs could be highly sensitive to changes in interest rates, which may move in quite different ways than does the RPI. Somewhat closer to the carrier's input price movements would be the Gross Domestic Product (GDP) deflator and the Producer Price Index (PPI), but again these would not take care of peculiarities of a particular regulated industry. Assuming that one chooses the RPI to allow for price adjustment, this could, as in the case of British Telecom, completely replace any input price adjustment. The relevant constraint in this case would be

$$R^4_{t,\mu} \equiv \frac{1}{T} \delta_{t,\mu} \sum_{\theta=1}^{T} \pi_{t-1,\theta}\beta^{\theta} - (RPI_{t,\mu-1} p_{t,\mu-1} - p_{t,\mu})q_{t,\mu-1} \leq 0 \quad (3.5)$$

where $RPI_{t,\mu-1}$ is the consumer price index for *subperiod* μ-1 based on the last *subperiod* of *period t-1*. We cannot use the current consumer price index, because that is only available after the current *subperiod* is over. Thus, the process is always going to contain some lag that cannot be completely adjusted for.

What can we do if the index used deviates significantly from the actual movement of weighted input prices? One correction is built into the mechanism already. It is the adjustment at the end of each *period* for excess (otherwise insufficient) profit over that *period*. This, however, does not undo the index problems of the past. It only shifts the base for the index. Furthermore, if the index has a built-in bias, the same index problem can surface again and again. To wit, if the RPI systematically understates the average increase in input prices, the firm will see its profits eroded during the course of each *period*. We therefore have to *correct the index itself after each period*. Among the possible ways to do this I suggest one of the following three methods:

First, one may perform a counterfactual experiment by simulating the past with other indices. Then the index (or combination of indices) that best reflects the actual input price movement of the firm is selected.

Second, one can regress the firm's actual weighted input price development during the last *period* against the index used during that *period*. If this regression yields strong results, the resulting parameters can be used to adjust the index formula.

The third method combines the first two: Use regression analysis both to identify the best index (or combination of indices) and to project into the future the difference between this index and the actual input price movement experienced by the firm.

These methods are technically straightforward, but they may arouse public discussion, particularly because they are unfamilar tools for policy-making.

Adjustments for Productivity Improvements

We now come to the "X" in the RPI–X formula. Aside from input price changes, the firm's costs are influenced by technical changes in the input quantity requirements. Generally, we only expect technical progress to occur. That is, over time we expect to see a reduction in input quantities for a given quantity of outputs. We nevertheless sometimes observe that certain outputs seem to require more inputs now than in the past; there can be three reasons for this. First, the quality of inputs, such as the purity of an ore or the education or motivation of a worker, may have deteriorated. Second, the quality of the output, such as the brakes, acceleration, or durability of a car, may have improved. Third, unmeasured inputs or outputs (externalities) may vary over time. None of these factors can be excluded *a priori* for the telecommunications sector. However, current indications are that technical progress, in the form of productivity increases and new outputs, is most likely to continue in this industry. Then the questions arise: How should we adjust our constraint for productivity increases, and how should we adjust for new products?

It has to be noted that, under the constraints (3.2) through (3.5), the firm is allowed to keep all productivity increases until the beginning of the next *period*. This lag can generate some excess profit, the expectation of which should boost the incentive to engage in productivity-enhancing activities. After the lag, consumers should benefit from the firm's productivity increases. Rather than relying on this lagged adjustment, the RPI–X formula forces the firm *ex ante* to agree to give away productivity increases to the consumers in the form of price reductions in real terms amounting to X percent per *subperiod*. This procedure has some drawbacks but also has a number of advantages. The main drawback is that the firm carries all the risks of productivity increases. If it cannot reduce its real costs by (approximately) X percent, then it may incur losses. It may also have difficulty, engaging in types of R&D that will only pay off in terms of cost reductions much later. The firm will therefore want to negotiate conservatively in setting X. Also, the initial price and profit level of the firm will have to be higher than if no X factor is included. On the other hand, as part of the initial adjustment formula, the carriers, wishing to implement the rate-setting reform, are likely to commit themselves to higher productivity increases than they can safely predict.

I see four major advantages in the X percent adjustment of the ceiling for every *subperiod*. The first is that consumers immediately enjoy increasing benefits for some time (that is, until t+1). Second, carriers will be reluctant to use their allowed tariff increases in times of high productivity growth and high profits.[8] So consumers lose little if X is set too low. Third, high rates of productivity growth over a longer time period will result in lower caps and higher productivity adjustment at the time of a general reexamination of the price caps. Fourth, with some good judgment regarding X, *period t* can be made quite long, mainly because the rate of return achieved by the firm will be within some reasonable range.

There is reason to believe that a predetermined X percent will be too generous initially and may be too tight later. Under the RPI–X approach, at least four potential forces can increase the profitability of the firm. The first is general productivity increases attributed to innovations. The time pattern of such increases is hard to predict. On one hand, the pool of potential innovations decreases over time. On the other, the RPI–X scheme may initially help open up the pool. The second potential force is improvements under current technology that have not been realized because of regulatory distortions or lack of cost-minimizing incentives. A key intention behind the RPI–X is to initiate a one-time improvement here. The third force comes from economies of scale that can be realized through growth of demand and lower prices. The RPI–X scheme would, in particular, have the effect of moving the firm down the demand curve. Economies of scale are increasingly exhausted at larger output quantities, so their effect diminishes over time. The fourth force comes from changes in the price structure. To the extent that cross-subsidization is reduced (or, more subtly, consumer welfare is increased), the firm can make additional profits which reduce the current tightness of the constraint. Again, these gains are more easily achieved at the beginning of the adjustment process than later. On the other hand, to avoid overshooting, the firm may want to explore demand reactions of consumers in small steps.

There are various possibilities for including projected or negotiated productivity increases in the regulatory constraint. The simplest way within our framework is to insert RPI–X instead of RPI in constraint (3.5):

$$R^5_{t,\mu} \equiv \frac{1}{T} \delta_{t,\mu} \sum_{\theta=1}^{T} \pi_{t-1,\theta} \beta^\theta - [(RPI_{t,\mu-1} - X)p_{t,\mu-1} - p_{t,\mu}]q_{t,\mu-1} \leq 0. (3.6)$$

This essentially makes us arrive at the Littlechild approach. Rewriting constraint (3.6) yields:

$$\frac{p_{t,\mu} \, q_{t,\mu-1}}{p_{t,\mu-1} \, q_{t,\mu-1}} \leq RPI_{t,\mu-1} - X - \frac{\delta_{t,\mu} \sum_{\theta=1}^{T} \pi_{t-1,\theta} \beta^\theta}{T \, p_{t,\mu-1} \, q_{t,\mu-1}}. \qquad (3.6')$$

Compared to (3.6') the RPI–X constraint used by Littlechild would read

$$\frac{p_{t,\mu} \, q_{t,\mu-1}}{p_{t,\mu-1} \, q_{t,\mu-1}} \leq RPI_{t,\mu-1} - X. \qquad (3.7)$$

The difference between constraints (3.6') and (3.7) is that, as a result of our long-term approach, we introduce an adjustment factor as the third term on the righthand side of constraint (3.6'). This adjusts for excess profits (otherwise for insufficient profits) from *period t-1* at the beginning of each *period t*. Such an adjustment is not necessarily required at the time the process is introduced, because under the previous cost-of-service regulation the firm may have earned only a normal rate of return. Also note that, on the lefthand side, constraints (3.6') and (3.7) use a Laspeyres *chain* index with changing weights for every *subperiod* μ. The reason is that the chain index reflects the changed consumption patterns over time. At the same time, it shares with the simple Laspeyres index the characteristic property that it underestimates (overestimates) welfare improvements (deterioration). This is an advantage over the Paasche index, which has the additional drawback that it can only be measured after the period is over.[9]

As discussed above, the factor "X" could contain various cost and demand effects such as economies of scale, technical change, increase in demand, and reductions in cross-subsidies.[10] The most important of these influences could be captured in the expected relative change in total factor productivity (TFP): X = dTFP/TFP. If we use a Laspeyres index to measure total factor productivity this can be expressed conveniently as

$$X = \frac{p_{t-1}\,(q_t - q_{t-1})}{p_{t-1}\,q_{t-1}} - \frac{w_{t-1}(v_t - v_{t-1})}{w_{t-1}v_{t-1}}, \ or \qquad (3.8)$$

$$X = \frac{p_{t-1}\,q_t}{p_{t-1}\,q_{t-1}} - \frac{w_{t-1}\,v_t}{w_{t-1}\,v_{t-1}}.$$

The basis for an adjustment factor reflecting productivity increases should be the carrier's past performance of total factor productivity over an extended period of five to ten years. Assuming that this past performance can be separated for AT&T and the Local Exchange Carriers (LECs), different future standards should also be set for the different carriers. Initially, productivity measures should not be separated into regulated and unregulated services, but rather an overall value should be used. Exogenous changes in demand cannot be separated accurately from productivity increases, so they should also be combined, given the carrier's responsibility of forecasting demand and installing the correct capacity and correct type of equipment.

To estimate the X factor *ex post*, the regulator would need to know the same data required to calculate the input price adjustment in the form of constraint (3.3) above. This leaves us with several possibilities to set the X in constraint (3.6'). First, we could take from constraint (3.8) the average relative change in TFP from the last *period* and set this as the standard for the current *period*. Second, we could regress actual relative changes in TFP against time in order to establish a trend that is then extrapolated to the future. Third, productivity increases applied to the price cap formula could be negotiated *ex ante*. Fourth, one could establish a sharing rule for the actual relative change in TFP from each last *subperiod* $t,\mu\text{-}1$ to establish $X_{t,\mu}$.

Such a sharing rule has been used successfully by French public enterprises (Marchand, Pestieau, and Tulkens 1984). Because there is a lag, one may also assume that the full relative change in TFP is passed on to the consumers. To preserve incentives, the lag should then be length t rather than length μ. In this case substituting (3.8) into constraint (3.6') and using a Laspeyres input price chain index instead of the RPI gives us

$$
\frac{p_{t,\mu}\, q_{t,\mu-1}}{p_{t,\mu-1}\, q_{t,\mu-1}} \leq \frac{w_{t,\mu}\, v_{t,\mu-1}}{w_{t,\mu-1}\, v_{t,\mu-1}} - \frac{p_{t-2}\, q_{t-1}}{T p_{t-2}\, q_{t-2}} + \frac{w_{t-2}\, v_{t-1}}{T w_{t-2}\, v_{t-2}} - \frac{\delta_{t,\mu} \sum\limits_{\theta=1}^{T} \pi_{t-1,\theta}\, \beta^{\theta}}{T\, p_{t,\mu-1}\, q_{t,\mu-1}}. \qquad (3.9)
$$

Output Price Index	Input Price Index	Output Quantity Index	Input Quantity Index	Profit Adjustment

This inequality can be readily interpreted. The term on the very right gives the average price adjustment done every T years to account for excessive or insufficient profits over this time span.

Leaving out this term, the remainder of constraint (3.9) consists only of price and quantity indices for inputs and outputs. It can be interpreted in two ways: Either the sum of an index of output prices and an index of output quantities (lagged) has to be kept smaller than the sum of an index of input prices and an index of input quantities (lagged); or the difference between the index of output prices and the index of input prices has to be smaller than the lagged difference between the index of input quantities and the index of output quantities.

Using constraint (3.9) would determine the long-run price caps quasi automatically. This would be administratively easy. However, it might leave the regulated firms with some risks arising from lags.[11] In an uncertain environment, the probability distribution of profits is truncated from above by the price caps. If this leads to losses, the regulated firm can only make up for them through a relaxation of the price caps at a later time. In some way the firm may have to be compensated *ex ante* for this truncation.

New Services

New services potentially have four properties that weigh against capping their rates initially. First, conceptually, genuinely new products are related to productivity increases. Both may require innovative activity represented by R&D. This means that they may have to be rewarded by the opportunity to make supernormal profits on them for some limited time. Second, their introduction is risky and may require low introductory prices which would induce customers to try them out. Third, almost by definition they usually do not represent vital services for customers. Fourth, without any change in the formulas, our approach would give new products no quantity weight in the *subperiod* of their introduction: They were not produced in the *subperiod* before. They could therefore initially be priced at the firm's discretion. In the next *subperiod* their pricing would be constrained, however. Even if R&D may be treated as a current expense, a *subperiod* of unconstrained pricing may be too short in general to give enough incentives to the firm for product innovations. Hence, genuinely new products should go uncapped for at least one *period*.

A danger inherent in this policy toward new products is that the regulated firm might simply repackage old products and present them as new, at the same time abandoning the old service that was capped before. This would not be allowed under the current approach because the firm would still have to serve the demand for the old service at the capped price. To rid itself of an old service, the regulated firm would have to set its price so high that no one would buy it any more. This, however, would usually be prevented by the quantity weight previously attached to the old service. This does not imply an inability of the regulated firm to fool its customers about the nature and quality of its services. Quality control and quality information by the regulators remain essential.

The Scope of Price Caps

We have so far assumed a multi-product monopoly firm facing a regulatory price constraint on all its outputs. The price cap approach has, however, also been suggested for only a subset of the firm's outputs and for firms operating in a more competitive environment. These suggestions may be complementary to each other. A firm facing competition in some services but being a monopolist in others may need price caps only in its monopolistic services. I have argued elsewhere (Vogelsang 1984) that an adjustment process like the one described by constraint (3.6) can also be fruitfully applied to single services. This can still lead to an allocatively efficient outcome, provided that the other (noncapped) services are supplied competitively. In case the regulated firm has market power for the other services, price caps for regulated services may lead to cross-subsidizing the capped services in the long run. The reason is that, in the absence of cost separation among the services, a long-run adjustment of price caps will occur under an overall rate-of-return constraint for the firm. Assuming that the firm can generate above-normal returns for its other services, it may (with a lag) be forced to charge noncompensatory rates for the capped services. Politically, this kind of cross-subsidization may be quite acceptable. If not, in the absence of fierce competition for the other services, some cost allocation will have to be made to separate costs of the capped services. This means that the administrative regulatory burden is likely to be greater if not all services are price capped under the same constraint.

Now, what happens if some of the services under the constraint are offered in competition to other firms while some services are not? The scope of price caps has to be determined by considerations of competition and equity. Competition can force the firm to choose more efficient prices at any point in time. Under normal circumstances, the constraint should give the regulated firm enough flexibility to handle both competition and price caps. Three problems could arise, though.

First, the constraint may not be sufficiently adjusted to the risks of a competitive industry. In part this is a problem of measuring the cost of capital including risk. In part it is the problem of ups and downs in a competitive environment. The constraint may truncate profits on the upside but not on the downside.

Second, in the short and medium term, competition will mean lower prices for competitive services, but this may mean higher prices for the monopolized services. This may be unfortunate for the captive customers. There is no long-run alternative short of entry barriers or subsidies, though. Third, although predation is unlikely to occur under a price cap approach, it cannot be fully ruled out. Using average rates for capped services overall, the regulated carrier might lower its rates in competitive areas below the efficient level and charge fully profit-maximizing rates in monopoly areas with the average complying with the caps. After successfully driving out its competitors it would reduce the previous monopoly rates and increase the previous predatory rates, again leaving the average within the capped range. The carrier would not gain an overall price advantage from this. However, there might be an advantage in terms of larger sales because the carrier would not have to share the market with others. The theoretical possibility exists that these additional sales represent enough of a motive for predation. By not including in the overall average the rates of services deemed to be supplied under competition, such an incentive for predation by means of cross-subsidization might be reduced. There still remains the problem that the carrier may raise uncapped (or even capped) rates after driving out competitors. However, the initial profit sacrifice will put the firm in a situation of low overall earnings that neither management nor shareholders will like. To be fully on the safe side, predatory acts by regulated carriers may have to be watched just like predatory acts by other firms.

Conclusions

By combining the price cap approach with the V-F mechanism, we have shown that improvements toward allocative efficiency of pricing can be combined with incentives for cost minimization. The basic idea has been to fix the price level of services of a regulated carrier with reference to a basket of changing quantity weights over time. The allowed price level would be adjusted by a formula that is related to the development of prices outside the firm's control and to a factor of productivity increases. The main functions of this formula are to increase the regulatory lag while providing immediate benefits to consumers. Within the limits of the firm's price level defined by this formula, the carrier would be allowed to change the price structure. Maximizing the discounted stream of profits, such a carrier would want to move the price structure toward that of Ramsey prices. This holds because Ramsey prices resemble the structure of unconstrained profit-maximizing prices. At the same time, since the firm's price level is constrained through a Laspeyres price index, consumers are induced to improve their choices as well. By differentiating short subperiods, during which the price cap formula would apply, from long periods, at the end of which general revisions would occur, we were able to show that price cap regulation can be seen as an open ended process. While the flexibility introduced in this chapter for the pricing of individual services may allow the regulated firm to meet competition, there is no built-in device against predatory pricing. This will have to be dealt with via the antitrust laws. Similarly, the incentives provided for cost reduction may interfere with those for setting optimal quality. Thus, under the approach of this chapter, the regulator will have to bother less about prices and more about the quality of service.

Notes

This paper was funded under a grant from the John and Mary R. Markle Foundation to the RAND Corporation. Further thanks are owed to Leland Johnson and Bridger Mitchell for many insightful suggestions.
 1. The following description is based on Vogelsang (forthcoming).
 2. The advantage of flexible intervals is that they add a random element to the process which may be desirable. See Bawa and Sibley (1980) and Logan, Masson, and Reynolds (1986).
 3. A sketch of the proof is given in the Appendix.
 4. If we did not discount within this constraint, there would remain incentives for strategic behavior toward the end of period t. For example, a cost-reducing innovation may be profitably

postponed to the beginning of period $t+1$. The averaging of profits in period t, however, would mitigate this problem.

5. A sketch of the proof is given in the Appendix.

6. Clearly, changes in the price of inputs trigger changes in input requirements for a cost-minimizing firm.

7. As formula (3.8) below shows, these data may have to be collected and used anyhow to measure productivity increases of the firm.

8. The carrier should be able to carry forward such unused allowable adjustements to later years; otherwise, the carrier would fully utilize the adjustements earlier with no advantage for customers.

9. Independently the problem of these weights is also discussed by Bradley and Price (1987) and Brennan (1987).

10. Changes in demand are treated in Brennan (1987).

11. If capped prices on average are expected to follow a downward trend over time, the carrier should be required to apply the adjustment factors and recalculate average price caps once a year. More likely is that average caps can be expected to go up in nominal terms. Thus, the carrier has a self-interest in making the allowed price increases that it needs.

Appendix: Outline of Proofs

In this appendix we state two propositions more formally and outline their proofs.

Assumptions 1, 2, and 3 are stated in the main part of the chapter.

Assumption 4A: The regulated monopoly firm knows its cost and demand functions and maximizes the discounted stream of profits over an infinite horizon and subject to the regulatory constraint defined by constraint (3.2). At the beginning of the process, profit is positive.

Proposition 1: Under assumptions 1, 2, 3, and 4A the regulatory adjustment process defined by constraint (3.2) will converge for $t=1$ and $T=\infty$ to Ramsey prices at the profit level achieved in the steady state.

Sketch of proof: The proof is very similar to the one given more formally in Vogelsang (1987). It goes as follows:

Step 1: The discrete-time Euler equations are derived for the firm's constrained maximization problem. It is shown that in the steady state, if it exists, they imply the structure of Ramsey prices.

The firm maximizes

$$L = \pi_{1,1} + \lambda_{1,1} [\pi_0 - (p_0 - p_{1,1})q_0] +$$

$$\sum_{\mu=2}^{\infty} [\pi_{1,\mu} + \lambda_{1,\mu}(p_{1,\mu} - p_{1,\mu-1})q_{1,\mu-1}]\beta^{\mu-1}. \qquad (3.10)$$

The first-order conditions for this problem are

$$\frac{\partial L}{\partial p_{1,\mu}} = [p_{1,\mu} + \frac{\partial C}{\partial q_{1,\mu}}] \frac{\partial q_{1,\mu}}{\partial p_{1,\mu}} + q_{1,\mu}(1 - \lambda_{1,\mu+1}\beta) + q_{1,\mu-1}\lambda_{1,\mu}$$

$$+ \lambda_{1,\mu+1}\beta(p_{1,\mu+1} - p_{1,\mu}) \frac{\partial q_{1,\mu}}{\partial p_{1,\mu}} = 0, \text{ for all } \mu = 1, \ldots, \infty. \quad (3.11)$$

In the steady state, if it exists, all the relevant variables are stationary. Then we can drop time subscripts and (3.11) becomes

$$\frac{\partial L}{\partial p} = [p + \frac{\partial C}{\partial q}] \frac{\partial q}{\partial p} + q(1 + \lambda - \lambda\beta) = 0 \quad (3.12)$$

This implies

$$[p + \frac{\partial C}{\partial q}] \frac{\partial q}{\partial p} = -q(1 + \lambda - \lambda\beta) \quad (3.13)$$

Noting that $\partial q/\partial p$ is an n x n matrix, while p, $\partial C/\partial q$, and q are n x 1 vectors, we see that (3.13) describes the Ramsey price structure.

Step 2: By not changing prices at all the firm can always make a profit if it made a profit at the beginning of the process.

Step 3: Due to the convexity of consumer surplus, consumers are better off after each period in which the firm made no loss: They can still buy what they bought last period without paying more. The firm can gain nothing strategically by making a loss in any period because that does not affect the level of allowed prices for the future. This implies a monotonically increasing sequence of consumer surplus levels. This sequence is bounded by the Ramsey optimum. Hence, it must converge. Step 1 then establishes the result.

Proposition 2: Under Assumptions 1, 2, 3, and 4A the regulatory adjustment process defined by constraint (3.2) will converge for t = 1,...,∞ and finite T to Ramsey prices with no excess profits (π=0) in the steady state.

Sketch of proof: The proof is quite similar to that of Proposition 1.

Step 1: The discrete-time Euler equations to the firm's maximization problem are shown to imply the structure of Ramsey prices in a steady state. The firm maximizes

$$L = \sum_{t=1}^{\infty} \sum_{\mu=1}^{T} [\pi_{t,\mu} + \lambda_{t,\mu} (\frac{1}{T} \delta_{t,\mu} \sum_{\theta=1}^{T} \pi_{t-1,\theta}\beta^{\theta}$$

$$- (p_{t,\mu-1} - p_{t,\mu})q_{t,\mu-1}\}]\beta^{tT+\mu}. \quad (3.14)$$

The first order conditions for this problem are

$$\frac{\partial L}{\partial p_{t,\mu}} = \frac{\partial \pi_{t,\mu}}{\partial p_{t,\mu}} [1 + \frac{\beta^{T+1}}{T}] + \lambda_{t,\mu} q_{t,\mu-1}$$

$$+ \beta \lambda_{t,\mu+1} [(p_{t,\mu+1} - p_{t,\mu}) \frac{\partial q_{t,\mu}}{\partial p_{t,\mu}} - q_{t,\mu}] = 0 \qquad (3.15)$$

for all $t=1,...,\infty$ and $\mu=1,...,T$.

If the steady state exists (3.15) becomes

$$\frac{\partial L}{\partial p} = (p - \frac{\partial C}{\partial q}) \frac{\partial q}{\partial p} [1 + \frac{\beta^{T+1}}{T}] + q(\lambda - \beta \lambda + 1 + \frac{\beta^{T+1}}{T}) = 0. \quad (3.16)$$

This implies

$$(p - \frac{\partial C}{\partial q}) \frac{\partial q}{\partial p} = -q[1 + \frac{\lambda(1 - \beta)T}{T + \beta^{T+1}}]. \qquad (3.17)$$

A steady state in this case can only exist if profits vanish, because otherwise the constraint could not be stationary. Hence (3.17) would imply Ramsey pricing.

Step 2: Assuming that the firm made a profit over the previous *period*, it will have to reduce its prices for the current *period* in such a way that it would just break even if it sold the old quantities. Actually it will have to sell more on average because of the (on average) lower prices. Because of decreasing ray average cost this will be profitable to do.

Step 3: This step is almost the same as Step 3 for the previous sketch of proof. The difference is that now the firm can gain a relaxation of the profit constraint in the next *period* by making a cumulative loss in the current *period*. We cannot totally dismiss this possibility if the firm discounts the future very little. However, the firm would only do this if such a strategy enabled it to make larger profits in the future than it foregoes now. Hence, finite subsequences of profit levels always exist that add up to positive sums. These finite subsequences themselves form an infinite sequence of positive profit levels associated with a monotonically increasing level of consumer surplus. Since positive profit levels are associated with a tighter constraint in the next *period*, the constraint tightens more and more over time. Hence profits will eventually go to zero. Again consumer surplus converges to the Ramsey optimum.

References

Bawa, V.S., and D.S. Sibley. 1980. "Dynamic Behavior of a Firm Subject to Stochastic Regulatory Review." *International Economic Review* 21:627-642.

Bradley, I., and C. Price. 1987. "The Economic Regulation of Private Industries by Price Constraints." Department of Economics, University of Leicester, England (September).

Brennan, T.J. 1987. "Capping 'Average' Prices of Regulated Monopoly Firms." Graduate School of Arts and Sciences, George Washington University, Washington, D.C. (October).

Federal Communications Commission. 1987. *Notice of Proposed Rulemaking*. FCC Docket No. 87-313 (August).

Littlechild, S.C. 1983. *Regulation of British Telecommunications' Profitability*. Report to The Secretary of State, Department of Industry, London (February).

Logan, J.W., R.T. Masson, and R.J. Reynolds. 1986. "Efficient Regulation with Little Information: Reality in the Limit?" Mimeo, Cornell University (March 24).

Marchand, M., P. Pestieau, and H. Tulkens. 1984. "The Performance of Public Enterprises: Normative, Positive, and Empirical Issues." In *The Performance of Public Enterprises–Concepts and Measurement*, edited by M. Marchand, P. Pestieau, and H. Tulkens, pp. 3-42. Amsterdam: North-Holland.

OFTEL. 1986. *Review of British Telecom's Tariff Changes*. A report issued by the Director General of Telecommunications (November).

Sappington, D. 1980. "Strategic Firm Behavior Under a Dynamic Regulatory Adjustment Process." *Bell Journal of Economics* 11:360-372.

Vogelsang, I. 1984. "Incentive Mechanisms Mimicking German Electric Utility Regulation." *Proceedings of the 11th E.A.R.I.E. Conference*, Volume 1. Fontainebleau (August 29-31): 87-109.

Vogelsang, I. (forthcoming). "Regulation of Public Utilities and Nationalised Industries." In *Public Sector Economics–A Reader*, edited by P.G. Hare. Oxford: Basil Blackwell.

Vogelsang, I., and J. Finsinger. 1979. "A Regulatory Adjustment Process for Optimal Pricing by Multiproduct Monopoly Firms." *Bell Journal of Economics* 10:157-171.

4

EFFICIENCY ASPECTS OF DIVERSIFICATION BY PUBLIC UTILITIES

Roger Sherman

Introduction

Diversification by public utilities is growing. The trend has brought efforts on one hand to remove barriers that stand in the way of diversification, such as the Public Utility Holding Company Act of 1935, and on the other hand efforts to limit diversification further. In both the House and the Senate, for example, proposals have been introduced to modify the Public Utility Holding Company Act, specifically with regard to public utility diversification.[1] The holding company played an important role in developing the electricity industry early in this century, but its complexities were abused, and limits on its use were imposed through the 1935 Act. If diversification by public utilities can improve efficiency, then such restrictions on it need to be evaluated.

The Public Utility Holding Company Act of 1935 forced divestitures that greatly simplified the organizational structure of public utilities, making independent operating companies the major form of electric utilities, for example, and greatly reducing the number of holding companies.[2] Under the Act, a public utility holding company could persist if it and its subsidiaries operated only in the state where it was organized or in contiguous states, with each subsidiary being predominantly intrastate.[3] Such cases would be expected to fall more effectively under state regulation, so the federal Act did not have to be controlling. The Securities and Exchange Commission (SEC) was given substantial discretion in allowing such exemptions, however, for in granting them it had only to interpret the public interest, or the interest of investors or consumers, which it could do in a variety of ways. Many telephone companies were exempted. Exemptions are not seen today as having been allowed on a consistent basis, or as true exemptions without restraint, by either the public utilities or the SEC.[4]

Before the Public Utility Holding Company Act was passed, there had been widespread concern over public utility holding company practices, which brought Congressional and Federal Trade Commission studies showing that complicated interrelationships had been abused. Holding companies exacted high fees for paltry services to their subsidiaries; they arranged deals among the companies that they held, in order to raise asset values fictitiously; they used intercompany borrowing for speculative purposes; and they included interest payments in construction projects, which raised asset values while they claimed the interest as earnings elsewhere. Outright violations of laws occurred in sales of securities, paying of dividends from capital surplus, or evasion of federal income taxes. The abuses resulted in excessive borrowing which made the risk of insolvency high and also resulted in manipulated security values. It was through the great complexity of the holding company structure, made even less comprehensible by occasional reorganization, that these abuses had been able to navigate without detection. The Public Utility Holding Company Act of 1935 was passed to clear away the tangles and allow more effective regulation.

Thus the Act of 1935 came in response to a serious problem in controlling regulated monopolies, and it did lead to important organizational changes. By limiting the acceptable forms of organization that can be used, the Act prevented regulatory efforts from being subverted. The times now are very different from 50 years ago, however, and new issues need to be considered. In particular, greater economies of scope may exist in regulated industries today, and restrictions that limit diversification into other goods or services can be inefficient because they prevent realization of such economies (Baumol and Willig 1985; Mac Avoy and Robinson 1985). To the extent this is true, there is a trade-off between gaining efficiencies from freer product-line decisions by public utilities, which can realize the economies of scope, and the possible loss of regulatory effectiveness that also may accompany diversification.

An important issue that is usually raised by any diversification possibility is its effect on risk-bearing. Debt holders of formerly separate firms have claim to a broader earnings pool after the merger, for example, while shareholders have increased exposure to risks of failure. Before considering diversification directly, I therefore examine the rate-of-return regulated public utility itself, to emphasize the way in which its risks are created and borne. Apart from these risk patterns, the pros and cons of diversification can vary from case to case, and generalizations are difficult.

Portrait of a Public Utility

Allow me to present a stylized description of a public utility. I do this because I want to portray the institution in a way that emphasizes its special characteristics, instead of implicitly regarding it as a regular private firm except for minor differences that are caused by regulation. Regulation affects risk-bearing in fundamental ways that need to be considered if the effects of diversification are to be understood. You may think my portrait is off the mark, but it can still be useful for the issues it raises, and I ask you to consider it in that way.

Public utilities are privately owned legal monopolies producing the vast majority of electricity, telecommunications, and gas in the United States. Some new discovery could, of course, bring any monopoly position to an end. But most public utilities operate technologies that have developed over many years and are apt to continue to play an important role in the economy, so their monopoly positions can be regarded as secure. The market values of these monopoly positions depend, however, on regulators' decisions. Indeed, for well over half a century, starting from the time privately owned enterprises were granted monopoly franchises as public utilities and made subject to regulatory oversight, regulators have struggled with the question: What profit should the utility be allowed?

Drawing guidance from previous court decisions, state regulatory commissions now establish a rate base for a public utility, which is an accepted valuation of the utility's assets, and then allow a rate of return on that rate base to establish a profit level for the utility. The allowed profit level is then combined with the utility's costs to determine its revenue requirement, and a set of prices is determined that is expected to generate that revenue. The resulting revenue is expected to cover costs and yield the allowed level of profit. The rate base and rate of return determinations are extremely important because the assets are enormous; an electric utility's assets can easily be worth two or three times as much as the utility's annual sales. This means, for example, that allowing a 10 percent return on the assets of an electric utility can require that 20 or 30 percent of the value of its sales be devoted to that purpose.

Whether to use original cost or replacement cost to value assets and calculate allowed profit is an old, and major, issue for the institutions of public utility regulation in the United States. These institutions grew largely from court decisions establishing the power of states to regulate certain private enterprises in the last quarter of the nineteenth century and the first quarter of the twentieth. Because the price level was falling in the late 1800s and rising in the early 1900s, it was very difficult for parties to agree on original asset value or replacement cost as a generally applicable basis for calculating profit allowances. This asset base and profit allowance question was a perennial issue in the early days of regulation, and today's practices and procedures are a reflection of the way that it was solved.

The Hope Natural Gas Company decision, which still provides the main guidelines for determining allowed profit, took a compromise position in urging that historical cost be used for the debt portion of capital structure, while a current cost is used for equity.[5] The Hope mixture of historical return (for debt) and current returns (for equity) does not apply in unregulated competitive markets, however, where current returns for both debt and equity influence an entrant's decision. Nor is the Hope mixture consistent with theories of firm valuation (e.g., Modigliani and Miller 1958). Only tax effects or a threat of bankruptcy allow the current mixture of debt and equity to affect the firm's value according to accepted valuation theory, whereas the Hope mixture allows capital structure to have a direct effect on the allowed return.[6] Thus, as the conflict in how to determine utility profit was solved, regulators probably cannot match the market valuation process, even if they wish to, as long as they abide by the Hope guidelines. And there is evidence that regulators do not mimic financial markets successfully; public utility equity values behave more as fixed coupon bonds than as true equities, especially in periods of rapid inflation (Archer 1973; Keran 1976).

In contemporary practice, quasi-judicial rate hearings are held to determine what rates ought reasonably to be charged for a public utility's services, and the rates thus determined are imposed until another hearing is called to consider new rates. In the intervals between rate hearings, utilities bear risks for which there is no true equivalent in unregulated competitive markets. When demand varies from expectation, or if an input cost changes, in an unregulated market all firms would ordinarily be affected and market price would change. But since the public utility's rates are held fixed, gains or losses can result, and that possibility constitutes a new form of risk. Automatic adjustment clauses can moderate this risk for price changes in some major inputs, but only imperfectly, and they bring unwanted consequences for efficiency (Baron and DeBondt 1979; Scott 1980).

An efficiency advantage is also gained from these intervals between rate hearings, because the inability to change price gives the utility the incentive to control costs in order to make profit. But the fact that price is unchanged does not solve other problems of regulation. In proposing rate structures at hearings, for instance, the public utility will be influenced by relative demand elasticities, due to its monopoly position, and also by the marginal capital requirements of different services (Sherman and Visscher 1982; Wellisz 1963; Westfield 1965). The interval of unchanging prices does nothing to moderate these capital biases and monopolistic demand elasticity considerations since they are built into the utility's changing rate structure. As a rate hearing approaches, the utility will naturally want to justify costs as high, while claiming also that operations are efficient, in order to win high rates for services in the ensuing interval.

Where the regulators decide to set rates that will apply in the next interval, we may assume they will allow only a small fraction of the profit that would be available to the monopoly if prices were not regulated. Indeed, the regulator decides what fraction of the potential monopoly value will actually be realized. These decisions of regulators are so important to the financial fortunes of public utilities that investment advisory firms seem to devote as much attention to evaluating the "regulatory climates" they create as to evaluating the utilities themselves. Ratings of regulatory commissions have been prepared and published by many investment advisory firms. They tend to be correlated with public utility bond ratings and stock values (Dublin and Navarro 1982), and also with whether commissioners are appointed or elected, the latter being less favorably rated on average (Navarro 1980). Whether commissioners are appointed or elected does not seem to determine allowed returns (Hagerman and Ratchford 1978). Although not significant at normal levels, regulatory climate assessments have been found positively correlated with market-to-book value ratios (Delano and Howard 1973). Expert witnesses apparently influence the outcomes of rate hearings also (Joskow 1972).

In deciding how much of the monopoly power to use, regulators have great discretion, for they can squeeze out a barely competitive result or allow virtually a monopolistic one. This great range of possibilities makes the financial risks of a regulated firm quite different from those of unregulated firms. In ordinary unregulated private firms, the holders of debt are given assurances about their interest earnings and their rights in the event of bankruptcy only because they have priority over the equity ownership; bondholders have first claim to earnings or to assets in the event of failure. In the regulated public utility more than the equity position is available to satisfy debt obligations; there is, in reserve, a great monopoly power that can be called upon, perhaps to protect bondholders or even shareholders. Since regulators are unable to mimic perfectly the competitive market process from instance to instance—or from rate hearing to rate hearing—the extent to which they draw on monopoly power may vary. As a result, we have a very different institution than that of the ordinary private corporation operating in competitive markets. The valuation of the firm in capital markets may depart from the Modigliani-Miller theory because of the reserve monopoly power, which can absorb residual effects that ordinarily would fall to equity (Sherman 1977; Taggart 1981).

This brings us back to the idea of determining a utility's profit from the amount of assets it devotes to public service, rather than from some genuine test of how effectively those assets actually served the public over their useful lives. In the absence of free entry and exit, it is difficult to create a regulatory equivalent of the competitive market test for investment success. State regulatory commissions essentially have imposed two requirements: (1) that assets be "used and useful" in order to receive a return; and (2) that the investment decisions pass a prudency test, requiring that, with information reasonably available at the time of the decision, it was a prudent action. When power plant construction projects have been cancelled, some state commissions have not allowed any amortization of their costs. And some state commissions also have reduced in some way the rate base eligible to receive a return, when they conclude—usually by the used-and-useful standard—that the utility has built excessive, or unneeded, capacity. In these latter decisions especially, state commissions have attempted to produce results somewhat like a competitive market, where excessive capacity in relation to demand will not earn a normal return.

The question of how to deal with cancelled plants and excess capacity has become a major regulatory issue in the 1980s (Pierce 1984). For instance, in 1988 the largest electric utility in New Hampshire, Public Service of New Hampshire, was denied a return on its investment in the Seabrook nuclear power plant and forced to seek bankruptcy protection. The New Hampshire Supreme Court had advised that allowing a return would have violated a 1979 state law prohibiting returns on investments not in commercial operation, since the Seabrook plant had not yet qualified for a Nuclear Regulatory Commission license to operate. Of course the nuclear accident at Three Mile Island in Pennsylvania in March 1979 penalized investors, too. In these cases, genuine problems arose in the provision of service, and, in unregulated competitive markets, investors certainly would have borne financial responsibility for them.

In 1984 the Montana Power Company's 30 percent share in a coal-fired generating unit, called Colstrip Unit No. 3, was removed from the firm's rate base by the Montana Public Service Commission.[7] Its per-KWH cost was higher than that of other sources in the area. So, in view of current competitive conditions prevailing at the time of the judgment, the capacity was seen as unnecessary, or not used and useful. Rather than consider how the decision might have looked when initially undertaken, as a test of prudence, this decision used eventual market conditions to evaluate investment success.

In the mid-seventies, seven New York State electric utilities proposed a consortium to construct generation facilities, to be called Empire State Power Resources, Inc. (ESPRI). Nominally, they would share risk and make possible the use of more debt financing, but the proposal also would have had other important effects. Cost responsibilities, and consequences for rates, were to be binding whether capacity was actually used or not, so that capacity could not be disallowed from the rate base. The New York Public Service Commission did not approve the proposal,[8] in part because it was seen to contain incentives that would not serve efficiency.

It is very difficult to construct artificially a competitive market test of public utility investments. Where departures from market outcomes are large and transparently obvious, its use is possible, but even then the basis for decision requires justification. Making more subtle distinctions is very difficult, in part because there often is no market to allow comparison. To the extent that a market test is not achieved and returns on assets are simply allowed, the competitive market process will be turned on its head. Rather than prices and costs determining returns, allowed returns and costs will then determine prices. Since much discretion rests with regulators, we may consider how perfectly, or even how consistently, they will function. To the degree that they vary, there can be more uncertainty, or risk, introduced by the regulatory process itself.

Thus, the regulated public utility submits to long intervals during which its prices are held fixed. When it proposes rates for such an interval the utility may use more capital because of rate-of-return profit allowances, perhaps by not using peak-load pricing, for example. The utility can also be expected to follow monopoly urgings that regulation does not suppress, such as using demand elasticities as important influences on prices. The interval between rate hearings, in which prices are unchanged, does induce some cost control incentive, but it also creates new risks for the utility to bear, and it does not moderate pricing distortions. Since no competitive market is available to test performance, investment mistakes, or costs above the most efficient level, may go undetected. If such faults go unnoticed, which is to be expected in all but extreme cases, greater monopoly power will be drawn upon to pay adequate returns to investors. Whether the regulator will correctly evaluate these matters is difficult to predict, so uncertainty about that decision is another new source of risk, a risk that is unique to the regulated public utility.

Advantages of Diversification for a Public Utility

The utility that we have described could have a sudden change in its fortunes due to some external factor, such as a demand shift or a marked change in an input price. With its prices regulated, it might have to endure a delay of months—perhaps more than a year—before output prices could respond to the change. In that interval, a diversified enterprise could either draw resources from other activities, if necessary, or expand and improve those other activities, if that was warranted. The enterprise could respond more effectively, in other words, to events that affect earnings between rate hearings. In addition to short-run risk caused by regulatory lag, the public utility faces a longer run risk that regulatory decisions might be misguided. The utility presently has no way to escape the harmful consequences of such a decision, for it can be every bit as much a captive of its regulatory agency, as utility customers are of the utility that serves them. Does the utility's desire to have some operations outside its regulated orbit undermine regulation, in which case it should be avoided, or does having scope to operate in unregulated fields protect the utility from misguided regulation with which it should not have to contend?

It might be said that the utility can act through capital markets rather than by diversification. But the costs of transacting in capital markets each time are bound to be higher. First, information must be gained about alternative activities, information that would already be part of the diversified organization. Second, without diversification, a very substantial investment portfolio would be necessary for it to be an effective source of funds when earnings are reduced and another source of funds is needed. Although, in the event of good fortune, the investment of extra earnings in stocks or bonds might be possible without diversification, such investment would require careful explanation in each case, and the payment of higher dividends might be urged instead. Of course, if dividends are paid to shareholders rather than shifted within the firm, an extra tax loss will be felt. We know also that when favorable capital gain taxation was important, diversification could advantageously provide it, since internal investment for capital gain was more apt to be possible within a conglomerate (Sherman 1972). But the more important point is that reinvestment within the firm can avoid the tax payment that accompanies dividends, and for that reason alone it can be desirable. Since growth and investment opportunities in some fields where public utility organization is very important—such as electricity and gas—have diminished in recent years, the utilities have a tax reason for seeking investment outlets beyond their traditional regulated industries.

Recall that the regulatory commission has a difficult task. Suppose that it makes a serious mistake and allows a rate of return on assets that is well below the capital cost of a single-service utility. The utility can survive for a time, but eventually it will have difficulty attracting capital to expand its service or even to replace existing facilities. The more talented management may have departed by then. A severe problem could face the utility's owners and the regulatory commission, which by this time may even have different members. A diversified utility might be able to respond more quickly to such a regulatory mistake by applying available funds in more promising, perhaps unregulated, areas. As a consequence of this recourse to alternative opportunities, the mistaken regulatory action would have to be confronted more directly and more immediately. If the alternative opportunities of the utility cannot subvert sound regulation, then their existence might actually improve overall performance by eliciting more competent and responsible behavior from regulatory agencies.

If the regulatory commission errs in the other direction and allows a return that is too generous, the undiversified utility has limited scope in which to apply the resulting earnings. It might make inefficient application of excessive resources to its industry or develop organizational slack, with attendant waste. A diversified firm might apply the handsome earnings more effectively instead in other, perhaps unregulated, markets. This action could offer tax savings, compared with paying the earnings out as dividends, and could offer greater benefit to shareholders, given the regulatory commission action. As a result, it might reduce the cost of capital, leading to lower revenue requirements and lower rates for consumers. The overgenerous return is not desirable, but, if it occurs, efficiency may be greater with diversification than without it.

Returns do not have to be excessive for diversification to be useful to a utility. In the electricity industry, for example, internal investment opportunities are limited for many utilities, because current capacity is large relative to demand. Internal investment offers a tax advantage for shareholders who want to maintain rather than sell their investments. This advantage could be achieved through diversification, which would provide internal investment opportunities in other industries.

One motive for geographic diversification is the desire to change regulatory jurisdiction. This possibility arises because of the distinction that has developed between retail sales of electricity to final customers, which are regulated by state commissions, and sales at wholesale from one producer to another, which have come to be regulated by the Federal Energy Regulatory Commission (FERC). For example, the New York State ESPRI proposal would have had ESPRI sell electricity to member utilities at wholesale, so that rates would have been regulated by FERC rather than by the New York State Public Service Commission. The same result can be accomplished by organization as a holding company with generation, transmission, and distribution subsidiaries, so that more transactions qualify as wholesale transactions at FERC-approved rates. Since FERC is seen as a more lenient regulator than most states, especially when it comes to allowing investments in the rate base, it is natural that some utilities might organize such that more of their sales occur at the wholesale level, where they will be regulated by FERC (Pfeffer and Lindsay 1984; Pierce 1984).

Of course, there are other genuine benefits of diversification for the utility, most notably when economies of scope can be realized by producing another, perhaps unregulated, good or service beyond the regulated one. Technological developments in computing and telecommunications may offer such economies, for example, since computers now play an important role in operating the telephone network, and data communications has become so important in computing operations (Baumol and Willig 1985). In addition, there is a security value in diversifying into fuel sources, to avoid being closed down by fuel scarcities in the future.

Although it can be claimed as an advantage of diversification generally, the training ground it fosters might be especially valuable to a regulated firm. The utility that is diversified into some unregulated fields may find the experience with competitive market forces to be an especially valuable testing ground for its management and other personnel. Competitive markets discipline decision makers harshly, and their lessons might be valuable for regulated firms, yet they are ordinarily unavailable to them. From their experience in unregulated subsidiaries, the managers of utility operations might develop a greater understanding of the demands for efficiency and greater skill in making effective decisions.

Diversification and Financial Performance

In view of these incentives to diversify, one would expect that the regulated public utility might do so, to enlarge its range of possible responses to regulatory treatments and to bring tax advantages to shareholders. If we could control for regional and other revenue-relative-to-cost factors, to focus on regulatory climate, we might wonder how climate would interact with diversification to influence firm performance. For example, with P representing performance, X representing control variables, RC representing regulatory climate (3 if very favorable, 2 if favorable, and 1 if unfavorable), and D a dummy variable for diversification (1 if diversified and 0 otherwise), consider estimating with cross-section data the equation

$$P = \alpha_0 + \alpha_1 X + \alpha_2 RC + \alpha_3 D + \alpha_4 RC \cdot D + e,$$

where e is a homoskedastic error. We would ordinarily expect $\alpha_2 > 0$ and, if diversification improves performance, we should find $\alpha_3 > 0$. If regulatory climate and diversification also interact favorably together, then $\alpha_4 > 0$.

Ideal data for estimating the equation above are not available. In 1980 the Edison Electric Institute (EEI) surveyed a group of 125 electric utilities in order to find whether they operated any nonutility business (Edison Electric Institute 1981). They found that fuel exploration, real estate, and energy conservation[9] were the major areas of activity for these utilities, but only a little more than half of the respondents (79) indicated that they were involved in some other activity beyond electricity. The Cabot Consulting Group narrowed the EEI groups of diversified and nondiversified companies by considering as diversified only those that also reported nonutility revenue in their income statements for the period between 1976 and 1980 and as nondiversified only those with no such revenue in the same period (Cabot Consulting Group 1982). The resulting samples of nondiversified electric utilities and diversified ones are listed in table 4-1 and table 4-2, respectivley.

Measures of market-to-book value ratios and revenue per kilowatt hour (KWH) from the Cabot study are shown for the sample in the tables along with a measure of regulatory climate.[10]   At least 20 Wall Street firms have rated the state regulatory agencies, based not only on how generous are their rate-of-return allowances but on how quickly they complete rate cases, how they handle construction work in progress and other accounting matters, or whether they allow future test years or fuel adjustment clauses. A composite of major ratings was prepared as a regulatory climate indicator for the year 1978 by Navarro (1980) and is included in the tables.[11] The market-to-book-value ratio was higher for diversified companies, but the difference was not significant at the 0.05 level (it would almost be significant at the 0.10 level). There was virtually no difference in electricity revenue per KWH for diversified versus nondiversified utilities. If anything, the average regulatory

Table 4-1. Nondiversified Electric Utilities

	Market-to-Book Ratio	Revenue (cents) per Kilowatt Hour	1978 Regulatory Climate*
Central Hudson Gas & Elec.	0.66	6.15	2
Central Illinois Light	0.62	5.12	2
Central Illinois Pub. Serv.	0.77	4.66	2
Cincinnati Gas and Elec.	0.76	4.13	2
Hawaiian Electric	0.70	7.01	3
Illinois Power	0.82	3.92	2
Interstate Power	0.63	4.48	1
Iowa-Illinois Gas & Elec.	0.74	4.23	1
Kansas Gas and Elec.	0.72	3.75	2
New York State Elec. & Gas.	0.68	4.71	2
Northern Indiana Pub. Serv.	0.66	4.93	3
Oklahoma Gas & Elec.	0.77	3.36	2
Portland General	0.67	3.53	2
Potomac Elec. Power	0.73	5.17	2
Pub. Serv. Co. of Indiana	0.83	3.42	3
Pub. Serv. Co. of New Hampshire	0.68	5.64	2
Savannah Electric	0.41	5.41	1
Southern Indiana Gas & Elec.	0.75	3.48	3
Tucson Electric	0.87	4.96	3
United Illuminating	0.62	7.72	1
Virginia Elec. & Power	0.56	5.22	2
Average	0.70	4.76	2.06
Standard Deviation	0.096	1.16	

Note: Because observations could not be obtained for them on a comparable basis, these firms in the Cabot sample of nondiversified utilities are omitted: Allegheny Power, Eastern Utilities, Kentuck Utilities, Louisville Gas and Electric Company, and Texas Utilities.
Key: 3 = Very Favorable; 2 = Favorable; 1 = Unfavorable.

climate ratings suggest that diversified utilities tend to face less favorable regulatory commissions.

Taking the market-to-book-value ratio as a performance measure (P) and allowing revenue per KWH to serve as a control variable (X) despite its obvious shortcomings, we can estimate the equation above with regulatory climate (RC) and the diversification dummy variable (D). Ordinary least

Table 4-2. Diversified Electric Utilities

	Market/ Book Ratio	Revenue cents/kWh	1978 Regulatory Climate*
Baltimore Gas and Elec.	0.64	4.98	2
Boston Edison	0.59	7.06	1
Commonwealth Edison	0.67	5.89	2
Consolidated Edison	0.54	10.43	2
Detroit Edison	0.55	5.19	2
Duke Power	0.79	3.22	3
Gulf States Utilities	0.75	3.20	1
Houston Industries	0.81	3.88	3
Indianapolis Power & Light	0.77	3.55	3
Iowa Elec. Light & Power	0.64	5.20	1
Iowa Public Service	0.78	5.33	1
Kansas City Power & Light	0.64	5.12	1
Montana Dakota Utilities	1.06	4.05	1
Montana Power Company	1.11	2.49	1
Northern States Power (MN)	0.76	3.61	2
Northern States Power (WI)	0.76	3.61	3
Ohio Edison	0.76	4.81	2
Pacific Gas & Electric	0.68	5.01	1
Pacific Power & Light	1.00	2.51	2
Pennsylvania Power & Light	0.63	3.91	2
Philadelphia Electric	0.67	6.40	2
Public Serv. Co. of Colorado	0.87	4.22	2
Public Serv. Co. of New Mexico	0.85	5.03	3
San Diego Gas & Electric	0.73	7.67	1
Sierra Pacific Power	0.79	5.57	2
South Carolina Elec. & Gas	0.77	3.99	2
Southern California Edison	0.77	6.11	1
Union Electric	0.69	4.02	1
Washington Water Power	0.70	1.75	2
Wisconsin Elec. Power	0.71	4.29	3
Wisconsin Power & Light	0.82	4.01	3
Average	0.75	4.75	1.87
Standard Deviation	0.13	1.71	

Note: Northern States Power is included twice because its assets can be divided between the two states in which it operates. This division only affects the Regulatory Climate measure, because other variables cannot be divided between states.
Key: 3 = Very Favorable; 2 = Favorable; 1 = Unfavorable.

squares estimates with no interaction term (RC • D) are

$$P = 0.860 - 0.039\,X + 0.013\,RC + 0.052\,D, \quad n = 52$$
$$(11.440)\ (-3.847)\ (0.603)\quad (1.749)\qquad R^2 = 0.30$$

where t-statistics are indicated in parentheses below the coefficients. Regulatory climate has a positive coefficient, but it is not significant. Diversification affects performance positively at the .05 level of significance with a one-tailed test. When we allow for interaction between diversification and regulatory climate we obtain

$$P = 0.752 - 0.040\,X + 0.067\,RC + 0.217\,D - 0.083\,RC \bullet D, \ n = 52$$
$$(8.266)\ (-4.043)\ (1.951)\qquad (2.450)\quad (-1.966)\qquad R^2 = 0.35$$

where t-statistics are again in parentheses. Now diversification has a larger positive effect on performance. Among undiversified firms, a more favorable regulatory climate improves performance significantly. But climate essentially has no effect among diversified firms, since the coefficients for RC and $RC \bullet D$ virtually offset each other. The average market-value-to-book-value ratio is about the same for undiversified firms in very favorable climates as for diversified firms in all climates. But it is lower for undiversified firms operating in less favorable regulatory climates.

These results must be tentative in part because the data are limited. The amount of diversification is modest, and revenue per KWH cannot account adequately for all the regional and other influences we should like to control for. In addition, there is some evidence of heteroskedasticity when the predicted value of the dependent variable is used for sorting extreme observations in order to apply the Goldfeld-Quandt test. Coefficients retain the same signs when observations yielding the highest and lowest one-third of the predicted values are used, but errors are larger with the lower third. Coefficients estimated from the full sample will still be unbiased, but their standard errors could be understated. With these qualifications, diversified firms appear to have higher market-to-book-value ratios, and the ratios are unaffected by regulatory climate, whereas climate affects the ratios for undiversified firms. This pattern is consistent with the view that diversification allows better financial performance in less favorable regulatory climates.

Social Costs of Private Benefits and Complications for Regulation

When more than one activity is included within a rate-of-return regulated enterprise, that enterprise has more scope to circumvent regulation. This point was made by Averch and Johnson (1962) in their original analysis of input bias under rate of return regulation, in which they discussed the complaint of Western Union that AT&T could charge low prices while leasing lines in competition with them because capital devoted to line leasing was used by AT&T to justify high rates in other more protected areas of business. Peles and Sheshinski (1976) developed this argument more generally. They demonstrated that, by integrating, two regulated firms could use more capital in one area and then, under rate-of-return regulation, take advantage of that capital to obtain higher prices in another area where monopoly power was greater. A general distortion of this sort can be expected under rate-of-return regulation when there is scope for multi-product pricing (Sherman, forthcoming).

In view of these difficulties, which may arise with greater scope of regulated enterprise, separation into constituent parts, insofar as that is possible, might limit them. For example, dividing an electric utility into subsidiaries might improve the opportunity for sound regulation, by clearly defining each activity with an organizational and accounting unit (Rappaport and Lerner 1969). Each part of the enterprise could then be controlled, and attention could be focused on transfer pricing to eliminate cross-subsidization or similar practices which shift profit from a regulated subsidiary to an unregulated one. Quite complicated arrangements have been coordinated across public utilities (Gegax and Tschirhart 1984). Payments to affiliates have been limited in several ways, most often by an overall limit on the affiliate's return (Flippen 1982). If it is too strict, however, such a division of the firm into subunits can prevent achievement of genuine scope economies that might be available (Baumol and Willig 1985; Mac Avoy and Robinson 1985).

Crew and Crocker (1987) analyze a case where economies of scope exist and output proportions can be determined by choice of technology, with only one of the outputs being regulated. When an overall rate-of-return constraint is imposed on the entire firm in this situation, the firm may be able to appropriate the scope economies through its technological choices. Indeed, consumers may then have to pay more for the regulated good if it is jointly produced with an unregulated one. Results can be efficient if the technological choice is imposed by the regulator, but such control would be very difficult to exercise. In other cases, where the return of only the regulated subsidiary is controlled and cost allocation rules are employed, Crew and Crocker find that the benefits of economies of scope often still may be absorbed by the firm rather than reaching consumers. Efficiency can be reliably obtained only with the extreme cost allocation rule that assigns all common cost to the regulated subsidiary. This result is consistent with Sweeney (1982), who found output distortions were motivated under revenue and output rules for cost allocation.

In a special case, where profit opportunities in an unregulated market are positively correlated with costs in the regulated one, Lewis and Sappington (1988) offer a very clever argument for improving regulated firm performance through diversification. In these conditions, it is possible to offset somewhat the firm's tendency to exaggerate its costs, because claims of high costs in the regulated market also mean high profit in the unregulated market. Thus, in claiming high cost in its regulated market, the firm implies that there is high profit in the unregulated markets, which can warrant lower regulated prices. Therefore, the regulated firm has less incentive to claim high cost in its regulated market. Lewis and Sappington stress that their argument focuses on solving only the informational asymmetry between the firm, which knows its cost, and the regulator, who doesn't, and that their analysis does not attend to the many other issues that diversification may raise.

There is another practical problem: regulating the subsidiary of a holding company. If subsidiary organizations are wholly owned by a holding company, the latter's shares may be the only ones publicly traded. Just one cost of capital can then be observed, and it may not be appropriate as a guideline for the allowed return in any single subsidiary. If the subsidiary operates in a well-defined line of business, it still may be possible to observe returns of other firms there and to use that cost of capital in setting a return on assets to be used in setting prices for the subsidiary. Several methods have been used to create a reference capital structure for the subsidiary as basis for allowing it a rate of return (Flippen 1982). These procedures are more feasible when separate subsidiary organizations exist than when operations in other industries remain part of the larger organization.

The process of regulation is handicapped also when one enterprise carries on activities across more than one regulatory jurisdiction. Then each regulatory agency will have difficulty identifying the consequences of its own regulatory policies because outcomes are affected by another regulatory agency. Wherever feasible, it probably is better to have the boundaries of regulated units contained within one regulatory agency's jurisdiction. Forming subsidiary organizations may help to comply with this principle by letting separate subsidiaries be included in the jurisdictions of separate regulatory agencies. As we noted, however, cost allocation rules will not reliably induce efficient results (Crew and Crocker 1987; Sweeney 1982). It is also possible for complicated assemblies of subsidiaries that cut across many regulatory jurisdictions to enter into activities which the Public Utility Holding Company Act was created to prevent nearly 50 years ago. Thus subsidiaries are not bad per se, but on a very large scale they may make unwanted manipulations difficult to prevent, even today.

The desire of the firm to form a holding company with separate subsidiaries primarily to avoid state regulation is necessarily a concern, though it is an issue that can be separated from that of diversification itself. Forming subsidiaries of a holding company, when it serves to separate utility and nonutility activities, sometimes will remove the latter from state regulation, although state regulators may consider the performance of the holding company when setting rates on utility services (Gies and Comment 1982). As mentioned earlier, however, reorganization can cause more sales to occur at wholesale levels and, thereby, become subject to FERC rather than state regulation (Pfeffer and Lindsay 1984). To the extent that this allows public utilities to choose between regulators, it may have undesirable effects.

Diversification in its most complete form arises when a public utility enters into an unregulated market. Here the problems for regulation also become more serious, if the regulatory agency can control effectively only some portion of the resulting firm. In 1972, the National Association of Regulatory Utility Commissioners urged stricter control of diversification into unregulated fields, because they saw no need for it and because failure in some other field could endanger a utility's credit and earnings (National Association of Regulatory Utility Commissioners 1972). Organization as subsidiaries might reduce this problem by confining financial effects more within each subsidiary's boundaries. An evaluation 10 years later (National Association of Regulatory Utility Commissioners 1982) was less pessimistic. It urged that policies on the subject be prepared in advance, to arrange statutory changes were necessary and so that firms would know ground rules on which to operate. It made many recommendations, but it took no strong stand on the issue.

The 1972 position of the commissioners against diversification into unregulated industries is understandable, in part because the task of regulation is much greater when utilities also engage in unregulated activities. For we know that anytime an unregulated subsidiary can sell an input to the regulated firm at a higher-than-competitive price, which the regulated firm can pay by drawing on its monopoly power, the effect is to subvert regulation. This potential for perversion of regulation has long existed for a number of utilities that supply their own coal or other fuel, and appears to have been controlled. Full oversight of intersubsidiary transactions,which most regulatory commissions have statutory power to enforce, should prevent cross-subsidization and related sins. Nevertheless, the expansion of utilities into unregulated areas does require more regulatory effort, and one naturally wonders what its social advantages can be.

None of the issues we raise here would seem to warrant closing off the diversification option for public utilities. It should be undertaken only with organizational distinctions, probably through separate subsidiaries, with clear regulatory responsibilities (National Association of Regulatory Utility Commissioners 1982) and reliable oversight of intersubsidiary transactions and cost allocations (Mirman, Tauman, and Zang 1985; Rappaport and Lerner 1969). By drawing upon experience in various jurisdictions, a set of practices can be refined for this purpose (Flippen 1982). The rate-of-return constraint is not a means of regulation that is well designed, and it creates new risks for public utilities that diversification might moderate. So, if economies of scope are available, we should not arbitrarily give up all efforts to achieve them.

Conclusion

Firms that operate in more than one line of business can generally provide a more diversified and therefore usually more attractive expected profit stream from which to pay lenders. There may also be a specific desire in utilities that have seen diminished growth in their markets to find alternative kinds of internal investments, so that they can invest retained earnings rather than pay them in dividends to shareholders with attendant greater tax obligations. Current United States tax laws, which make interest expense deductible before taxes, further enhance this advantage, because a diversified firm may be able to use relatively more debt, with its tax deductible interest (Sherman 1972). Indeed, most goods and services are provided by firms that operate in more than one industry (U.S. Bureau of the Census 1981). To the extent that this conveys a tax advantage, refusing to allow diversification in one industry essentially imposes on it a higher tax, which would be difficult to justify. But the general movement to more conglomerate organizational forms need not affect electric utilities and seems tenuous as explanation for the utilities' recent interest in diversification.

Closer relation of public utility services to unregulated market activities where economies of scope can exist, such as telecommunications to computing, may cause an even stronger motive for diversification. Regulating the resulting enterprise so that consumers of regulated services receive benefits may be difficult, but it is desirable in part so that competition can function fairly in the unregulated activities. And it is desirable to pursue the economies of scope where they appear to be substantial.

That diversification may have raised market-to-book-value ratios, at least in less favorable regulatory climates, indicates that private financial benefits are possible. Such benefits could arise, at least in part, from weakened regulation, although we have no real evidence of that. The revenue per KWH was essentially the same, for instance, across diversified and nondiversified utilities in our sample. Although the favorable financial effects of diversification that we found must be regarded as tentative because data are limited, they indicate there may be advantages to public utilities and to their consumers in the form of lower capital cost. This possibility, combined with known means of control over most serious abuses, suggests that efficiency advantages of diversification by public utilities are worth pursuing.

Notes

1. The House considered the Public Utility Financial Reform Act, H.R. 5220 and the Senate considered Diversification Amendments to the Public Utility Holding Company Act of 1935, S. 1870.

2. See Senate Report No. 621, 74th Congress, 1st Session 11 (1955).

3. Id., Sec. 3.

4. Letter from John S.R. Shad, Chairman of S.E.C., to Senator Alfonso D'Amato of 21 December 1981.

5. *Federal Power Commission v. Hope Natural Gas Co.*, 320 U.S. 591 (1944).

6. The debt/equity mixture need not affect the allowed rate of return if the historical interest rate equals the current interest rate. When those rates differ, regulators might try to emulate investor evaluations, making equity more valuable when the historical interest rate is below the current level and less valuable when the historical rate is above the current level. If they succeeded, the allowed rate of return might be independent of the firm's capital structure, but they would have to consider the current interest rate. The Hope decision urged the use of the historical interest rate as cost of debt, not the current interest rate.

7. Montana Public Service Commission Order No. 5051C, Docket No. 83.9.67, August 1984.

8. New York State Public Service Commission decision in Case No. 26798, April 1979.

9. The offering of conservation services was required of electric utilities under the Energy Policy and Conservation Act (Public Law 94-163, 22 December 1975), and the Public Utility Regulatory Policies Act (Public Law 95-617, 9 November 1978), although, of course, a separate entity for that activity was not required.

10. The Cabot study also examined debt-to-equity ratios and pretax interest coverage and found them very similar for the two groups. The diversified sample was found at the 0.05 level of significance (two-tailed test) to have a lower average stock yield. The regulatory climate data in the tables will be explained below.

11. Navarro converted the ratings into a common three-category set of very favorable (3), favorable (2), and unfavorable (1), and used majority rule among other ratings to determine his composite rating.

References

Archer, S.H. 1973. "Risk: The View of the Public Utility Analyst." In *Risk and*

Regulated Firms, edited by R.H. Howard. East Lansing, MI: Michigan State University Press.

Averch, H., and L.L. Johnson. 1962. "Behavior of the Firm under Regulatory Constraint." *American Economic Review* 52 (December): 1053-1069.

Baron, D.P., and R.R. De Bondt. 1979. "Fuel Adjustment Mechanisms and Economic Efficiency." *Journal of Industrial Economics* 27 (March): 243-269.

Baumol, W.J., and R.D. Willig. 1985. "Telephones and Computers: The Costs of Artificial Separations." *Regulation* 9 (March/April): 23-32.

Cabot Consulting Group. 1982. "Diversification in the Utility Industry." Washington, D.C.

Crew, M.A., and K.J. Crocker. 1987. "Diversification and Regulated Monopoly." Working Paper, Pennsylvania State University.

Delano, M.S., and R.H. Howard. 1973. "Regulatory Risk and Public Utilities." In *Risk and Regulated Firms*, edited by R.H. Howard. East Lansing, MI: Michigan State University Press.

Dublin, J.A., and P. Navarro. 1982. "Regulatory Climate and the Cost of Capital." In *Regulatory Reform and Public Utilities*, edited by M.A. Crew. Lexington, MA: Lexington Books.

Edison Electric Institute. 1981. "Investor-Owned Electric Utility New Business Ventures." Washington, D.C.: Economics Division of E.E.I.

Flippen, E.L. 1982. "Regulation and the Wholly-Owned Public Utility." *William and Mary Business Review* 4 (1): 33-37.

Gegax, D., and J. Tschirhart. 1984. "An Analysis of Interfirm Cooperation: Theory and Evidence from Electric Power Pools." *Southern Economic Journal* 50 (April): 1077-1097.

Geis, T.G., and R. Comment. 1982. "Restructuring Ownership to Escape Regulation." In *Deregulation: Appraisal Before the Fact*, edited by T.G. Geis and W. Sichel. Ann Arbor, MI: University of Michigan Press.

Hagerman, R.L., and B.J. Ratchford. 1978. "Some Determinants of Allowed Rates of Return on Equity to Electric Utilities." *Bell Journal of Economics* 9 (Spring): 46-55.

Joskow, P.L. 1972. "The Determination of the Allowed Rate of Return in a Formal Regulatory Hearing." *Bell Journal of Economics* 3 (Autumn): 632-644.

Keran, M.W. 1976. "Inflation, Regulation and Utility Stock Prices." *Bell Journal of Economics* 7 (Spring): 268-274.

Lewis, T.R., and D.E.M. Sappington. 1988. "Controlling the Activities of Regulated Firms in Unregulated Markets." Paper given at ORSA/TIMS Conference in Washington, DC (April 26).

Mac Avoy, P.W., and K. Robinson. 1985. "Losing by Judicial Policymaking: The First Year of the AT&T Divestiture." *Yale Journal on Regulation* 2 (2): 225-262.

Mirman, L.J., Y. Tauman, and I. Zang. 1985. "On the Use of Game-Theoretic Concepts in Cost Accounting." In *Cost Allocation: Methods, Principles, Applications*, edited by H.P. Young. Amsterdam: North-Holland.

Modigliani, F., and M.H. Miller. 1958. "The Cost of Capital, Corporation Finance and the Theory of Investment." *American Economic Review* 48 (June): 261-297.

National Association of Regulatory Utility Commissioners. 1972. "Report of the Ad Hoc Committee on Nonutility Investments." Washington, D.C.: NARUC.

National Association of Regulatory Utility Commissioners. 1982. "Report of the Ad Hoc Committee on Nonutility Diversification." Washington, D.C.: NARUC.

Navarro, P. 1980. "Public Utility Commission Regulation: Performance, Determinants, and Energy Policy Impacts." Harvard Energy and Environmental Policy Center Discussion Paper E-80-05.

Peles, Y.C., and E. Sheshinski. 1976. "Integration Effects of Firms Subject to Regulation." *Bell Journal of Economics* 7 (Spring): 308-313.

Pfeffer, J.L., and W.W. Lindsay. 1984. "The Narragansett Doctrine: An Emerging Issue in Federal-State Electricity Regulation." N.R.R.I. Occasional Paper No. 8, Ohio State University.

Pierce, R.J., Jr. 1984. "The Regulatory Treatment of Mistakes in Retrospect: Canceled Plants and Excess Capacity." *University of Pennsylvania Law Review* 132 (March): 497-560.

Rappaport, A., and E.M. Lerner. 1969. *A Framework for Financial Reporting by Diversified Companies*. New York: National Association of Accountants.

Scott, F.A., Jr. 1980. "Fuel Adjustment Clauses and Profit Risk." In *Issues in Public-Utility Pricing and Regulation*, edited by M.A. Crew. Lexington, MA: Lexington Books.

Sherman, R. 1972. "How Tax Policy Induces Conglomerate Mergers." *National Tax Journal* 25 (December): 521-529.

Sherman, R. 1977. "Financial Aspects of Rate-of-Return Regulation." *Southern Economic Journal* 44 (October): 240-248.

Sherman, R. forthcoming. *The Regulation of Monopoly*. Cambridge, MA: Cambridge University Press.

Sherman, R., and M. Visscher. 1982. "Rate-of-Return Regulation and Two-Part Tariffs." *Quarterly Journal of Economics* 97 (February): 27-42.

Srinagesh, P. 1986. "Nonlinear Prices and the Regulated Firm." *Quarterly Journal of Economics* 101 (February): 51-68.

Sweeney, G. 1982. "Welfare Implications of Fully Distributed Cost Pricing Applied to Partially Regulated Firms." *Bell Journal of Economics* 13 (Autumn): 525-533.

Taggart, R.A., Jr. 1981. "Rate-of-Return Regulation and Utility Capital Structure Decisions." *Journal of Finance* 36 (May): 383-393.

Wellisz, S.H. 1963. "Regulation of Natural Gas Pipeline Companies: An Economic Analysis." *Journal of Political Economy* 55 (February): 30-43.

Westfield, F. 1965. "Regulation and Conspiracy." *American Economic Review* 55 (June): 424-443.

5

EFFICIENT INCOME MEASURES AND THE PARTIALLY REGULATED FIRM
Shimon Awerbuch

Introduction

Utility company managers (and most business people) are often surprised to learn that accounting income and rate-of-return measures have little economic significance and do not offer much insight into the profitability of a venture or firm. Why the serious shortcomings of the accounting earnings measure are not more widely recognized is quite puzzling in view of the fact that the academic literature has been dealing with this problem for at least 25 years.[1] So significant are the errors associated with the accounting rate of return (ARR), according to some researchers, that it "provide[s] almost no information about the [true] economic rates of return" of American corporations (Fisher and McGowan 1983, 82). Nonetheless, the ARR continues to be widely followed, and, in the regulatory context, forms the basis for ratemaking, a role for which it was certainly never intended and for which it is poorly suited (Awerbuch 1986, 20-21).

Accounting rules for the determination of income and rate of return are promulgated by the Financial Accounting Standards Board (FASB), whose criteria and objectives for income measurement are largely driven by a need to provide fair and accurate "information for investment and credit decisions" (FASB 1978, 14). This "investor orientation" of financial reporting, which can be traced to the "full and fair" disclosure requirements of the Securities

Acts of 1933 and 1934 (Beaver 1981, 13), results in an income measurement system that does not have the economic properties needed for the ratemaking process. This outcome is not accidental: FASB carefully defines its primary user group (FASB 1978, 11) to include investors, suppliers, creditors, and financial analysts, while specifically excluding regulators who, FASB notes, have the capability to obtain required information independently (*Ibid.*, p.12).

In attempting to meet its financial reporting objectives, FASB and its predecessors have grappled with the question of how best to define and report income. This question raises a variety of research issues, including the information content of accounting reports and the cost-benefit of additional (or more complex) reporting requirements. While the issues are not entirely resolved, the resulting dialogue has elevated the level of investigation and understanding.

Although a similar line of inquiry would appear to be essential in the regulatory practice, the question of how best to define and report income has not been addressed in the field of regulation, where, ironically, accounting decisions probably have greater impact on economic well-being (i.e., efficiency) than in any other setting. Clearly this is an area that has "fallen through the cracks," with FASB essentially disowning it, and regulators feeling that they cannot or would rather not exercise policy control. As a consequence, the regulatory process indiscriminantly uses accounting concepts that were designed for different purposes.

Accounting-based ratemaking is bad enough under an assumption of strict monopoly, where its use distorts price signals, leading to inefficient consumption and investment patterns over time (Bidwell 1985). Given the case of a firm operating in a partially unregulated market, however, prices that are based on the ARR will lead to entirely uneconomical results which detrimentally affect the firm and its customers. Rather than simply affecting the time-pattern of consumption, for example, such regulated rates can, if set too high, drive customers needlessly to unregulated competitors. This deprives the firm of potentially profitable business, which in turn may increase rates for remaining customers. The bypass problem in telecommunications is partially a consequence of such accounting-based rates. On the other hand, accounting-based ratemaking that yields rates that are "too low" relative to economically based or market-driven rates, will result in "unnecessary" barriers to competition.

The case of partial regulation has received particular attention recently, in view of the concern that the firm will cross-subsidize from inelastic (monopoly) markets to the more elastic (unregulated) markets (see, for example,

Crew and Kleindorfer 1986). Traditional accounting measures are not helpful in determining the extent to which such cross-subsidization exists:[2] the ARR is of little help in determining whether the firm, or its subsidiary, is earning "too much" or "too little" (for discussion see Fisher and McGowan 1984; Fisher 1985), and earnings comparisons will, likewise, not be helpful (Kolbe, Read and Hall 1984, 52).

The rest of this chapter reviews the accounting and economic definitions of income and illustrates the effects of accounting-based ratemaking under various assumptions of inflation and technology. The analysis seems to show that accounting concepts are particularly ill-suited to pricing in the case of a regulated firm attempting to meet unregulated competitors.

Accounting Versus Economic Return

A considerable body of evidence indicates that the accounting return is a poor proxy for a firm's true economic rate of return.[3] Although there is no clear consensus, the evidence does suggest that the biases are systematic (Salamon 1985, 496-497). Partly as a consequence of design and partly as the result of usage, the accounting definition of income is quite different from the economic notions of income and return. These differences have a considerable impact on the regulatory process.

The accounting definition of income can be stated as the difference between the "realized revenues" of the period and the "corresponding historical costs" which includes an arbitrary allocation of historic capital costs in the form of accounting depreciation (Belkaoui 1981, 141). Gordon illustrates the practical significance of the concept:

Income . . . is sales revenue less the cost of labor employed two to three months earlier, the materials purchased three to nine months earlier, the equipment that may have been purchased ten years earlier and a building purchased up to thirty years earlier (1967, p. 69).

In addition, changes in value of any asset from the point it is considered "purchased" are only recognized at the point it is considered "sold." The rate of return is taken as the net income divided by accounting book value which can be written as:

$$ARR_t = \frac{NCF_t + AFC_t - DEP_t}{OC - ACCDEP_t}$$

where NCF_t is the net cash flow in period t (cash revenues minus all expenses except for depreciation); OC is the original cost of assets, expressed in the nominal dollars in which they were purchased; AFC_t is the non-cash allowance for funds used during construction; DEP_t is accounting depreciation (i.e., the arbitrary but "systematic" allocation of OC to each period over some expected life, n) and $ACCDEP_t$ is the sum of DEP_j for $j=1$ thru $(t-1)$. DEP_t is not related to the economic concept of depreciation (i.e., a change in asset value) but merely reflects the accountant's attempt to "match" historic outlays to present revenue generation. The allocation process is quite arbitrary, thus resulting in considerable intra- and interpractitioner inconsistency (Sterling 1970, 255).

The economic income definition, by comparison, represents a considerably different "expectational" approach[4] under which income is a measure of the change in present value expectations. The notion is elegantly expressed in the well-known Hicks (1946, 172) definition, according to which income can be taken as:

> The maximum value (a person) can consume during a week and still expect to be as well off at the end of the week as he was in the beginning.

This definition clearly shows the intricate relationship between income and depreciation—the consumption of capital. And, while the use of accounting depreciation contributes significantly to the difference between accounting and economic returns, this difference is attributable to a number of additional factors, including inflation, the effects of tax deferrals, and the fact that accounting treats returns to debt capital in a manner that is conceptually different from its treatment of returns to equity capital (see Anthony 1986).

Ironically, Hicks seems uncomfortable with the entire notion of income but feels that its role "in practical affairs is to give people an indication of the amount they can consume without impoverishing themselves" (1946, 172). The expectational approach to income definition correctly reflects the economic (i.e., marginal) costs of doing business and hence provides the proper (i.e., efficient) signals for dividend distribution,[5] future investment, and, in the case of regulation, pricing. Based on this approach, the correct economic framework for measuring the return on investment, r^*, involves finding the yield or discount rate which equates the present value (PV) of an asset's future cash flows to its cost. We can express this relationship as:

$$W_O = \sum_{t=1}^{n} \frac{CF_t}{(1+r^*)^t} \qquad (5.1)$$

where W_O is the cost or value of the asset at time period $t=0$; CF_t is the net cash flow in period t, for $t=1,n$; $CF_t=0$ for $j>n$; and r^*, the discount rate that satisfies (5.1), is the investment's internal rate of return (IRR).

By redefining cash flow slightly to include the investment outlay made at $t=0$, we can rewrite (5.1) to yield the net present value (NPV) of the investment. As an illustration, consider an asset with a six-year life that produces an annual after tax net cash flow of $229.61 with an initial cost of $1,000 and no salvage. This cash flow stream satisfies equation (5.1) at $r^*=.10$, which is the asset's economic return or IRR.

ARR Versus IRR as the Basis for Regulated Rates

The Case of Constant Technology

We can now consider how prices and returns are determined given an environment of certainty and perfect regulation.[6] We assume that regulators have properly estimated the cost of capital, k, through the use of divisional costs of capital (see Brealey and Myers 1984, 172-173; for applications in regulation see Melicher 1987), so that it correctly reflects the risk of the competitive service in a manner similar to what would be experienced by the unregulated competitors.

We begin by considering the investment of the previous section, (IRR=10 percent, Wo=$1,000, n=6 years), with the additional assumptions of all-equity financing, no operating expenses, and constant technology and productivity. Table 5-1 shows the cash flow, capital recovery, accounting return,

Table 5-1. Net Income and ARR for a 10%, Six-Year Project

Year	Cash Flow	Depreci- ation	Net Operating Income	After-Tax Net Income	After-Tax Cash Flow	Beginning Year: Assets	ARR
1	$271.57	$166.67	$104.90	$62.94	$229.61	$1,000.01	6.3%
2	271.57	166.67	104.90	62.94	229.61	833.34	7.6%
3	271.57	166.67	104.90	62.94	229.61	666.67	9.4%
4	271.57	166.67	104.90	62.94	229.61	500.00	12.6%
5	271.57	166.67	104.90	62.94	229.61	333.33	18.9%
6	271.57	166.67	104.90	62.94	229.61	166.66	37.8%
TOTALS							
	1629.42	1000.02					
PV	1182.76			1000.01			
EAC[a]							
	$271.57		IRR = 0.10		TAXRATE = 0.40		

[a] Equivalent (Levelized) Annual Charge with PV = $1182.76.

net income, and asset balances. The figures include the effects of a 40 percent tax rate, but have been set up so that the after tax net cash flow is still $229.61 in each of the six years, consistent with the earlier example.[7] Net operating income is $104.90 ($271.57 less $166.67), and the net asset balance is reduced by the straight line depreciation (SLD) amount of $166.67 each year.

From (5.1) we know that the after-tax cash flow in table 5-1 produces an economic return of 10 percent for an asset whose original cost is $1,000. Yet the ARR gives a considerably different, and misleading, indication, rising from an initial 6.3 percent in year 1 to 37.8 percent in year 5. This table illustrates a fact first pointed out by Solomon (1970) and restated by Myers (1972): with level cash flows (CF) and SLD, ARR significantly understates IRR early in an asset's life while overstating profitability later. These errors do not "average out" (Navarro, Petersen, and Stauffer 1981, 404; Fisher and McGowan 1983, 85-86) as commonly believed.

This "accounting measurement error" (Beaver 1981, 77-82) is of particular importance in regulation, where choice of accounting policy directly affects the regulated "revenue requirement" and, hence, the rates charged. This is in contrast to the unregulated environment, where the impact of depreciation and other choices is far less significant, affecting primarily the reported income. Since the competitive firm can be viewed as a "price-taker," accounting policy, including choice of depreciation, will not affect pricing or cash flow (Brealey and Myers 1984, 276).[8]

Given conditions of perfect information, a potential entrant can evaluate the investment illustrated in table 5-1 using standard capital budgeting criteria. Indeed any investor, whether regulated or not, with a cost of capital (hurdle rate) of 10 percent would improve its wealth by undertaking the investment. Accounting-based ratemaking, however, leads to a time profile of rates that makes it difficult for the regulated firm to compete.[9]

Table 5-2 illustrates how the competitive market may provide for pricing and capital recovery for the previous example, given ACRS tax depreciation as provided by the Tax Reform Act of 1986 (a 40 percent marginal tax rate is assumed). We again assume no operating expenses and a constant technology, so that any learning or productivity gains will appear with the next vintage of assets in the seventh year. This assumption results in a level after-tax cash flow of $229.61 (IRR=10 percent) although taxes now alter the time-shape of prices. As table 5-2 shows, the use of accelerated depreciation results in a generally decreasing competitive price (Pc) (see Salamon 1985, 499).[10] Also, while the sum of the Pc stream is identical to that of the SLD-generated cash flow requirement (table 5-1), the present value of the Pc charges ($1166.83) is lower than the PV of the cash flow required with

Table 5-2. Unregulated Cash Flow, Net Income, and ARR for a 10 Percent Six-Year Project

Year	Cash Flow (Pc)	Depreci- ation (ACRS)	Net Operating Income	After-Tax Net Income	After-Tax Cash Flow	Beginning Year: Assets	ARR
1	$282.68	$150.00	$132.68	$79.61	$229.61	$1,000.01	8.0%
2	236.02	220.00	16.02	9.61	229.61	850.01	1.1%
3	242.68	210.00	32.68	19.61	229.61	630.01	3.1%
4	242.68	210.00	32.68	19.61	229.61	420.01	4.7%
5	242.68	210.00	32.68	19.61	229.61	210.01	9.3%
6	382.68	0.00	382.68	229.61	229.61	0.01	– –
TOTALS							
	1629.43	1000.00					
PV	1166.83				1000.01		
EAC[a]							
	$267.91		IRR = 0.10	TAXRATE = 0.40			

[a] EAC (Equivalent Annual Charge) is the level price stream with PV = $1629.43.

SLD (table 5-1: $1182.76).

The accounting "measurement error" is not without impact in the case of an unregulated firm and, if not recognized and compensated for, can severely distort realization of correct expectations. Consider the unregulated firm that invests in the project of table 5-2 with the expectation of a 10 percent (IRR) return, only to subsequently discover from its accountants that the investment generated a mere 8.0 percent (ARR) return in its first year and 1.1 percent the next! Were expectations too optimistic or is the accountant wrong? As Ijiri (1980) has already observed, the differences between economics (i.e., capital budgeting) and accounting may simply be "irreconcilable." In addition, management incentive plans based on accounting results may lead to inefficient investment decision (see Solomons 1986; and Sherman 1972).

Such problems, though perplexing, may have only minor impact on the unregulated firm, since the evidence suggests that markets are quite efficient (see Brealey and Myers 1984, 266-280) so that investors and analysts can "see through the accounting veil" (Benston and Krasney 1978, 163). In the case of the regulated firm operating in a less than strict monopoly setting, however, the discrepancies between accounting and economics could produce serious consequences, as we now discuss.

Consider the situation of the regulated entrant in a market whose technology and costs are already described by tables 5-1 and 5-2. Table 5-3 shows how accounting-based ratemaking would provide for pricing and capital recovery under a regime of perfect regulation.[11]   A significant difference between the competitive after-tax CF (table 5-2) and the regulated after-tax CF (table 5-3) is the "saw-tooth" regulatory profile under which ratepayers pay more for a new asset than an equivalent older asset.[12]   Clearly, the illustrated project meets the criteria for a 10 percent IRR investment: observe that the present value of the after-tax cash flow is $1,000 at 10 percent. Moreover, use of SLD now results in an ARR of 10 percent each year as well. This result follows because the perfect regulation assumptions of the table yield that particular CF profile for which ARR=IRR. No other CF profile will yield this result for the case of SLD.[13]

The dilemma facing the regulated firm operating in this competitive marketplace is clearly seen in table 5-3. We have established that the project meets the economic criteria for a 10 percent investment. Still, the regulated firm seems unable to compete since the regulatory rates (Pr) imposed for the first four years are higher than the competitive market prices (Pc).[14] In addition, the Pc vector has a lower present value ($1,166.83) than does the Pr vector ($1,182.76), so that an informed customer would do business with the unregulated firm, notwithstanding the fact that the Pr vector has a smaller

Table 5-3. Regulated Cash Flow, Net Income, and ARR for a 10 Percent, Six-Year Project

Year	Revenue Require- ment, (Pr)	Depreci- ation (SLD)	Net Operating Income	After-Tax Net Income[a]	After-Tax Cash Flow	Beginning Year: Assets	ARR
1	$333.34	$166.67	$166.67	$100.00	$266.67	$1,000.01	10.0%
2	305.56	166.67	138.89	83.33	250.00	833.34	10.0%
3	277.78	166.67	111.11	66.67	233.34	666.67	10.0%
4	250.00	166.67	83.33	50.00	216.67	500.00	10.0%
5	222.22	166.67	55.55	33.33	200.00	333.33	10.0%
6	194.45	166.67	27.78	16.67	183.34	166.66	10.0%
TOTALS							
	1583.35	1000.02					
PV	1182.76				1000.01		
EAC[b]							
	$271.57		IRR = 0.10		TAXRATE = 0.40		

[a] For Ratemaking only.
[b] EAC (Equivalent Annual Charge) is the level price stream with PV = $1,182.76.

nominal sum ($1,583.35) than the Pc vector ($1,629.43). These differences would tend to become more pronounced as asset lives increase. The analysis therefore suggests that under a constant technology scenario the regulated firm will find it difficult to be competitive except, perhaps, as each equipment vintage matures.[15]

The Effect of Using Market Prices in Regulation

The foregoing discussion illustrates how accounting-based ratemaking leads to situations under which the regulated firm may be unable to compete because the time-profile of prices imposed permits unregulated competitors to increase market share. To make matters still worse, the regulated firm that proposed using market rates for a competitive service would be viewed with considerable suspicion by regulators and intervenors, since a stream of charges based on the competitive cash flow will make it appear that the company is attempting to cross-subsidize.

Consider a firm represented by table 5-3, that seeks a tariff structure (for a competitive service) equal to the competitive price (Pc) shown in table 5-2. When regulators evaluate the firm's proposal they will observe, not without distrust, that the resulting annual values of ARR (table 5-4) are only 7.0 percent, 5.0 percent, 6.8 percent, and 9.1 percent for the first four years. Since the regulator incorrectly assumes that the ARR is a true reflection of the economic (IRR) return, these rates, when compared to the expected 10

Table 5-4. Net Income and ARR for a Regulated Firm Charging Pc

Year	Cash Flow	Depreci- ation (SLD)	Net Operating Income	After-Tax Net Income	After-Tax Cash Flow	Beginning Year: Assets	ARR
				-1000			
1	$282.68	$166.67	$116.01	$69.61	$236.27	$1,000.00	7.0%
2	236.02	166.67	69.35	41.61	208.28	833.33	5.0%
3	242.68	166.67	76.01	45.61	212.27	666.67	6.8%
4	242.68	166.67	76.01	45.61	212.27	500.00	9.1%
5	242.68	166.67	76.01	45.61	212.27	333.33	13.7%
6	382.68	166.67	216.01	129.61	296.27	166.67	77.8%
TOTAL		1000.00					
PV	1186.82				990.44		
				(irr)	9.7%		
		IRR = 0.10	TAXRATE = 0.40				

percent cost of capital, will make it seem as if monopoly profits are (or will be) used to support predatory practices[16] (i.e., "Why else would a regulated company propose a rate structure that yielded an ARR less than k and how will the the 'shortfall' in equity return be made up if not from monopoly services?")

Misleading indicators of "cross-subsidization" as shown above could become chronic for a growing company, where investments for the competitive service are increasing rapidly. In such circumstances, new assets could outvalue older vintage assets, thus generating an ARR that consistently understates IRR (Solomon 1970), thereby supporting (incorrectly) the regulator's hypothesis of cross-subsidization.[17] Indeed this situation will never "average out" as previously discussed, making it appear that the competitive service is not producing sufficient return for the regulated firm. While this may not be the precise situation described by Sherman (1972), certainly it, too, must contribute to "schizophrenic" utility managers.

Annuity Depreciation

The front-loaded regulatory CF profile that contributes to the regulated firm's competitive difficulties can be alleviated, to some extent, through the use of annuity depreciation (AD).[18] Table 5-5 illustrates the use of AD, a special case of general economic depreciation (Hotelling 1925; Anton 1952;

Table 5-5. Cash Flow, Net Income, and ARR Under Annuity Depreciation Ratemaking

Year	Regulated Cash Flow (Pr)	Depreci- ation (AD)	Net Operating Income	After-Tax Net Income	After-Tax Cash Flow	Beginning Year: Ratebase	ARR
1	$296.28	$129.61	$166.67	$100.00	$229.61	$1,000.01	10.0%
2	287.64	142.57	145.07	87.04	229.61	870.40	10.0%
3	278.13	156.83	121.31	72.78	229.61	727.83	10.0%
4	267.68	172.51	95.17	57.10	229.61	571.01	10.0%
5	256.18	189.76	66.42	39.85	229.61	398.50	10.0%
6	243.53	208.74	34.79	20.87	229.61	208.74	10.0%
TOTALS	1629.43	1000.01					
PV	1195.38				1000.01		
EAC[a]	$274.47						
	IRR = 0.10		TAXRATE = 0.40				

[a] EAC (Equivalent Annual Charge) is the level price stream with PV = $1,195.38 .

Bower 1985;) in ratemaking. Annuity depreciation, which is analogous to the schedule under which principal is repaid in a simple, self-amortizing mortgage, equalizes ARR and IRR whenever the cash flow profile is exactly level. Under conditions of level cash flow, AD also yields annual net book values that are equal to the present value of all remaining cash flows. For example, the fourth year ratebase in table 5-5 is equal to the present value of remaining net cash flows:

$$\$571.01 = \frac{\$229.61}{(1.10)^1} + \frac{\$229.61}{(1.10)^2} + \frac{\$229.61}{(1.10)^3}$$

Given perfect regulation and no taxes, AD results in a stream of net (after-tax) cash flows that are levelized (table 5-5), thereby eliminating intergenerational subsidies when inflation is zero, while equalizing ARR and IRR. This is an important result in the strict monopoly case, where AD will substantially eliminate inter-temporal pricing distortions and the "rate shock" associated with new plant.[19] As a consequence, rates will be lower with new plant in the rate base, which sends the correct signals to encourage consumption—a desired outcome when capacity is ample (Bidwell 1985).

Corporate income taxes alter the level after-tax profile provided by AD, since the increasing depreciation charges provide an increasing tax shelter, which enables the firm to reduce its rates and still maintain the same net cash flow. As a result, the required rates (Pr in table 5-5) show a somewhat declining pattern. Although Pr is still generally higher than the Pc vector (table 5-2), the differences are now considerably less than under SLD (Table 5-3), at least initially. While it improves the CF time-shape, AD yields an after-tax benefit stream that is quite decelerated. As a consequence, the Pr vector has a higher present value (\$1,195) than it did for ACRS or even for SLD.[20]

The emerging picture seems to suggest that regulated firms cannot compete in a static technology environment, even though both types of firms—regulated and unregulated—share the same technology and hence the same costs. Unlike the competitive environment, however, regulation uses distorted accounting costs as a basis for pricing.

We next examine pricing and return in a regime of technological progress. While this case has been ably analyzed by Bower (1985), Crew and Karen (1984), and others, there are implications for regulatory policy that deserve further attention.

Table 5-6. Pc, Net Income, and ARR for a Technology with Short Diffusion Time

| Year | Cash Flow (Pc) | Depreci- ation (SYD) | Operating Income | Tax Net Income | After-Tax Cash Flow | Beginning Year | |
						Assets	ARR
1	$188.93	$286.00	(97.17)	($58.30)	$277.70	$1,000.00	-5.8%
2	357.40	238.00	119.40	71.64	309.64	714.00	10.0%
3	420.62	190.00	230.62	138.37	328.37	476.00	29.1%
4	328.23	143.00	185.23	111.14	254.14	286.00	38.9%
5	163.21	95.00	68.71	41.23	136.23	143.00	28.8%
6	63.21	48.00	15.21	9.13	57.13	48.00	19.0%
TOTALS							
	1522.01	1000.00					
PV	1114.58				1000.02		
EAC[a]							
	$262.80						
		IRR = 0.01		TAXRATE = 0.40			

[a] EAC (Equivalent Annual Charge) is the level price stream with PV=$1,144.58.

The Case of Technological Progress

The rate of diffusion of a technology through the market can be modeled as a proportional birth-death process (Fisher and Pry 1971). Under this approach, a new product or technology will at first generate increasing cash flows as it becomes adopted, after which they decline as newer, lower cost technologies are introduced. Table 5-6 illustrates how pricing and cash flows may occur in the competitive market given a technologically driven "Q-Profile" of cash flows originally suggested by Fisher and McGowan (1983). This time-shape of cash flows may be appropriate for such technologies as semi-conductors which have relatively short diffusion times.

The "Q-Profile" has been scaled in table 5-6 to yield an after-tax IRR of 10 percent, consistent with our other examples, while depreciation is shown as sum-of-the-years digits (SYD), consistent with the application suggested by Fisher and McGowan. In this case, the regulated firm faces a competitive situation that is not entirely clear, with Pr (table 5-3) lower than Pc (table 5-6) in years 2 through 4, but higher in the other years. This leads to an indeterminate situation in which it may be possible for the regulated firm to maintain market share, although, once again, the present value of Pr adjusted for normalization ($1,172.24) is greater than that of Pc ($1,144.58, table 5-6), with the sum of Pr also exceeding the sum of Pc. Use of AD for ratemaking will not significantly improve the situation in the case of the Q-Profile, although "correct" depreciation schedules can be developed (Awerbuch 1988).

We can now turn to the case of technological progress in the presence of inflation and taxes. This case has recently been examined (in the absence of taxes) through the use of an ingenious example that reflects the decisions of various entrants into the market, each of whom is exposed to a new vintage of technology (see Bower 1985, 15-17).

The example involves market entrants who purchase a unit of capacity that can produce one unit of output for three years, after which it expires— "one-hoss shay" style. Prices of capacity and other inputs rise over the period and productivity increases as well. The industry faces a downward sloping demand, and all entrants expect a return of exactly 12 percent—i.e., "There are no unhappy or overjoyed entrants" (*Ibid.*, p. 16). The capital and operating costs of each vintage of equipment are given in the table below: e.g., in

Capital and Operating Costs for Each Technology Vintage

Vintage	Capacity Price	Operating Cost in Year:		
		1	2	3
1	$3.30	$1.00	$1.10	$1.20
2	3.60	1.05	1.15	1.25
3	3.90	1.10	1.20	1.30
4	4.20	1.15	1.25	1.35
5	4.50	1.20	1.30	1.30
6	4.80	1.25	1.25	1.25

year 3 vintage 1 entrants are in their last year, with operating costs of $1.20; vintage 2 entrants are in their second year and experience operating costs of $1.15; while vintage 3 entrants are in their first year with operating costs of $1.10.

Table 5-7a shows the cash flows of each market entrant, based on the market-derived price. Economic depreciation is implicit, since it reflects the yearly changes in equipment values in an efficient market, although the economic values in the table (i.e., equipment value, economic return, cash flow, and operating cost) are unaffected by depreciation, and any allocation of the original cost will suffice.

Any potential entrant, regulated or not, will find that cash flows in this industry permit a 12 percent (IRR) return in all cases (i.e., the 12 percent discounted value of each cash flow stream is equal to the cost of the associated

Table 5.7a. Unregulated Market Entrants with Technology, Inflation, and No Taxes

| | YEAR | | | | | | | |
	1	2	3	4	5	6	7	8
Industry Price	$2.31	$2.43	$2.71	$2.83	$2.94	$3.25	$3.25	$3.25
Vintage 1								
Equipment Value	$3.30	$2.89	$1.35					
Operating Cost	1.00	1.10	1.20					
Economic Depreciation	.91	1.04	1.35					
Return (B.V.*0.12)	.40	.29	.16					
Net CF (PV=$3.30)	1.31	1.33	1.51					
Price (PV=$5.93)	2.31	3.43	2.71					
Vintage 2								
Equipment Value		$3.60	$2.65	$1.41				
Operating Cost		1.05	1.15	1.25				
Net CF (PV=$3.60)		1.38	1.56	1.58				
Price (PV=$6.34)		2.43	2.71	2.83				
Vintage 3								
Equipment Value			$3.90	$2.76	$1.46			
Operating Cost			1.10	1.20	1.30			
Net CF (PV=$3.90)			1.61	1.63	1.64			
Price (PV=$6.77)			2.71	2.83	2.94			
Vintage 4								
Equipment Value				$4.20	$3.02	$1.69		
Operating Cost				1.15	1.25	1.35		
Net CF (PV=$4.20)				1.68	1.69	1.90		
Price (PV=$7.18)				2.83	2.94	3.25		
Vintage 5								
Equipment Value					$4.50	$3.30	$1.75	
Operating Cost					1.20	1.30	1.30	
Net CF (PV=$4.50)					1.74	1.95	1.95	
Price (PV=$7.53)					2.94	3.25	3.25	
Vintage 6								
Equipment Value						$4.80	$3.38	$1.79
Operating Cost						1.25	1.25	1.25
Economic Depreciation						1.42	1.59	1.79
Return (B.V.*0.12)						.58	.41	.21
Net CF (PV=$4.80)						2.00	2.00	2.00
Price (PV=$7.81)						3.25	3.25	3.25

Table 5.7b. Regulated Market Entrants with Technology, Inflation, and No Taxes

	YEAR							
	1	2	3	4	5	6	7	8
Vintage 1								
Book Value	$3.30	$2.20	$1.25					
Operating Cost	1.00	1.10	1.20					
Depreciation (SL)	1.20	1.10	1.10					
Return (B.V.*0.12)	.40	.26	.13					
Net CF (PV=$3.30)	1.50	1.36	1.23			(IRR=0.12)		
Rev. Req. (PV=$5.92)	2.50	2.46	2.43					
Vintage 2								
Book Value		$3.60	$2.40	$1.20				
Operating Cost		1.05	1.15	1.25				
Depreciation (SL)		1.20	1.20	1.20				
Return (B.V.*0.12)		.43	.29	.14				
Net CF (PV=$3.60)		1.63	1.49	1.34				
Revenue Req. (PV=$6.34)		2.68	2.64	2.59				
Vintage 3								
Book Value			$3.90	$2.60	$1.30			
Operating Cost			1.10	1.20	1.30			
Depreciation (SL)			1.30	1.30	1.30			
Return (B.V.*0.12)			.47	.31	.16			
Net CF (PV=$3.90)			1.77	1.61	1.46			
Revenue Req. (PV=$6.76)			2.87	2.81	2.76			
Vintage 4								
Book Value				$4.20	$2.80	$1.46		
Operating Cost				1.15	1.25	1.35		
Depreciation (SL)				1.40	1.40	1.40		
Return (B.V.*0.12)				.50	.34	.17		
Net CF (PV=$4.20)				1.90	1.74	1.57		
Revenue Req. (PV=$7.18)				3.05	2.99	2.92		
Vintage 5								
Book Value					$4.50	$3.00	$1.50	
Operating Cost					1.20	1.30	1.30	
Depreciation (SL)					1.50	1.50	1.50	
Return (B.V.*0.12)					.54	.36	.18	
Net CF (PV=$4.50)					2.04	1.86	1.68	
Revenue Req. (PV=$7.53)					3.24	3.18	2.98	
Vintage 6								
Book Value						$4.80	$4.80	$4.80
Operating Cost						1.25	1.25	1.25
Depreciation (SL)						1.60	1.60	1.60
Return (B.V.*0.12)						.58	.38	.19
Net CF (PV=$4.80)						2.18	1.98	1.79
Revenue Req. (PV=$7.80)						3.43	3.23	3.04

Table 5-8. Regulated and Unregulated Market Entrants: Technology, Inflation, and Taxes

	YEAR		
	1	2	3
Vintage 1			
Unregulated			
Book Value	$3.30	$1.65	$0.55
Net CF (Table 5-7a) PV=$3.30	1.31	1.33	1.51
Depreciation (SYD)	1.65	1.10	.55
Operating Cost	1.00	1.10	1.20
Tax Inclusive Price*(Pc) PV=$6.30	2.08	2.58	3.35
N.O.I	-.57	.38	1.60
Income Taxes at 40%	-.23	.15	.64
Regulated			
Book Value	$3.30	$2.20	$1.10
Net CF (Table 7b) PV=$3.30	1.50	1.36	1.23
Depreciation (SL)	1.10	1.10	1.10
Operating Cost	1.00	1.10	1.20
Revenue Req.* PV=$6.36	2.76	2.64	2.52
N.O.I.	.66	.44	.22
Income Taxes at 40%	.26	.18	.09
Normalization adjustment	-.02	-.02	
Adjused Revenue Req. (Pr) PV=$6.33	2.74	2.62	2.52

* Revenue Needed = [Net CF − (Dep.)(Tax Rate)]/(1 − Tax Rate) + Operating Costs.

equipment vintage). The regulated firm that wishes to enter the market, however, is constrained by the regulatory rate-setting formula as previously shown. While regulation allows for the same 12 percent IRR (table 5-7b), the revenue requirement is quite different from Pc (table 5-7a), although the present values in each case are the same. Comparing revenue requirements with Pc indicates that, under our assumptions of technological progress, inflation, and no taxes, there are periods when the regulated firm may be able to successfully enter the market, although these are limited to the last half of each vintage life. This may make the task of increasing market share strategically difficult.

Given accelerated tax depreciation and normalization accounting, one would expect that taxation would widen the revenue gap between tables 5-7a and 5-7b, especially for long-lived assets. Table 5-8 shows Pc and Pr for vintage 1 equipment when the effects of taxation are included. As can be seen, taxes cause the Pc to rise more steeply over time, since the tax shelter is nominally greatest at the outset of the vintage. In fact, during the first year, Pc is lower in the presence of taxes, than without taxes (figure 5-1). On the other hand, taxation causes Pr to decline more steeply over time, so that the differences between Pr and Pc are heightened at the beginning and the end of the vintage (figure 5-1). Pr is considerably greater than Pc in year 1 and significantly smaller in year 3, although the present value of Pr and Pc are nearly equal.

Tables 5-7 and 5-8 suggest that, without greater pricing flexibility, regulated firms may not be able to increase market share in the presence of inflation and technological progress. Further, as table 5-9 shows, the situation does not improve when the technology produces monotonically decreasing real costs and the assets are longer-lived: Pc in table 5-9 is consistently lower than Pr throughout the asset's life (with the exception of the half-year effect in year 1), even though technological progress imposes a declining pretax cash flow.

With little exception, it therefore appears that changing technology only worsens the competitive problems of the regulated firm. Regulation leads

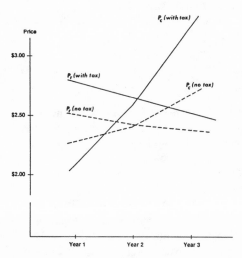

Figure 5-1. The Effects of Taxation on P_c and P_r

Table 5-9. Pc and Pr for Longer-Lived Assets with Cash Flow Decay, Inflation, and Taxes

	1	2	3	4	5	6	7	8
	Market	Regulated			Depreci-	Market	Market	Regulated
	Cash	Asset	Income	Cash	ation	Oper.	Price	Rev.Req.
Year	Flow	Value		Flow	(ACRS)	Income	(Pc)	(Pr)
1	375.22	1000.00	237.60	337.60	80.00	295.22	572.03	495.99
2	327.92	900.00	213.84	313.84	140.00	187.92	453.20	456.39
3	286.59	800.00	190.08	290.08	120.00	166.59	397.65	416.79
4	250.46	700.00	166.32	266.32	100.00	150.46	350.77	377.19
5	218.89	600.00	142.56	242.56	100.00	118.89	298.15	337.60
6	191.30	500.00	118.80	218.80	100.00	91.30	252.17	298.00
7	167.19	400.00	95.04	195.04	90.00	77.19	218.65	258.40
8	146.11	300.00	71.28	171.28	90.00	56.11	183.52	218.80
9	127.70	200.00	47.52	147.52	90.00	37.70	152.83	179.20
10	111.60	100.00	23.76	123.76	90.00	21.60	126.00	139.60
PV		1000.01		1000.00			1410.19	1419.37
TOTALS	2202.98				1000.00		3004.97	3177.95
	TAXRATE = .40			IRR = 0.237595				

Column 1: This after-tax CF profile is taken from Crew and Karen (1984, Table 2) and reflects the following conditions: Inflation 4%; real rate of technological progress, 19%; nominal rate of cash flow decay, 12.6%; real IRR, 19%; nominal IRR = nominal regulated return of 23.76%.
Column 2: Original cost ($1,000) less regulated (SLD) depreciation.
Column 3: (Column 2)*23.76%
Column 4: Column 3 + SLD
Column 6: Column 1 - Column 5
Column 7: (Column 6)/(1-TAXRATE) + ACRS DEPREC.
Column 8: (Column 3)/(1-TAXRATE) + SLD

to perverse results: at the point in time when price needs to be low so additional demand can be induced (i.e., during the early years of a new product or technology), the regulatory constraint forces a price that is needlessly high, thus leading to inefficient results.[21]

Conclusion

Regulation has traditionally relied on the ARR to measure performance. This previously unreliable indicator becomes especially misleading where, as in the case of partial regulation, the "time-path" of revenues that a regulated company earns from a service will be not be the same as the time-path of cash flows that an unregulated firm obtains from that same service (Kolbe 1985, 30; see also Myers, Kolbe, and Tye 1986). The implication of accounting "measurement error" in an unregulated setting is primarily informational: financial reports must be carefully analyzed in order to gain an insight into the firm's economic profitability.[22]

In regulation, the accounting "error" has a considerably greater economic impact. While ARR and IRR will be equal for the unrealistic case of perfect regulation, accounting-based ratemaking will, in practice, yield sizable pricing distortions, whose effects will vary depending on the degree of monopoly power. If we make the traditional strict monopoly assumptions, these distortions will lead to inefficient investment and consumption levels. Yet, because of the presence of market power, the viability of the firm is not at issue, at least in the short run. In the long run, incorrect pricing has more serious consequences for the firm itself, since it encourages the quest for substitutes, which eventually erode even the strongest monopoly.

When the regulated firm faces competition, the problems produced by ARR-based ratemaking could be severe. In the presence of taxes and constant technology (no inflation), the front-loaded regulated price makes it easy for unregulated competitors to expand market share with each new equipment vintage. Moreover, use of accelerated depreciation in the competitive environment results in a present value of Pc lower than that of Pr.

The results are not much more encouraging for the case of technological progress, and they indicate that, in the presence of taxes, Pc will be lower than Pr most of the time. The findings are less conclusive in the case of a technology with a short diffusion cycle, represented by the Q-Profile. Here the increasing nature of the competitive price stream provides several "windows" during which the regulated firm may be able to increase market share. The specific timing requirements probably make this outcome unlikely (and strategically unattractive) in practice.

Analysis of the various scenarios generally indicates that accounting-based ratemaking (which prices on the basis of fully distributed costs) does not provide sufficient flexibility for the regulated firm facing unregulated competition. In addition, regulators seem to feel that SLD is obligatory, although its desirability in regulation is "not obvious" (Bierman 1974, 454). A more sensible regulatory approach would be to develop cash flow objectives and depreciation schedules that implement such objectives (*Ibid.*; see also Kraus and Huefner 1972).

If regulated firms are to survive in the current environment of partial regulation, regulators must learn the secret codes of accounting reporting and the art of "removing the nails from the soup" (Treynor 1972). While the competitive markets seem to understand the meaning of accounting data, one "should not assume" that regulators can do likewise (Winn 1976; 1978, 3). Continued reliance on accounting-based ratemaking, to the exclusion of economic based measures of cost and return, will hurt the regulated firm and limit its viability.

Notes

1. The literature comparing accounting and economic income concepts is too voluminous to list here; a good overview can be found in Beaver (1981), Sterling (1970), and D. Solomons (1986); for illustrations of the problem as it affects regulation see E. Solomon (1970), Kolbe, Read, and Hall (1984), and Awerbuch (1985; 1986)

2. Solomons (1986, 16) provides an interesting example which illustrates how efforts to allocate overhead or joint costs may be contrary to the firm's interests.

3. In addition to the references of note 1, see Brief (1987), Fisher and McGowan (1983), Salamon (1985), and Harcourt(1965).

4. Which is generally attributed to I. Fisher (1906), Lindahl (1939), and Canning (1929); see Edwards and Bell (1961, 24-25).

5. Hicks (1969, 74) extends the income definition to serve as a guide for dividend distribution: "Income derived from a business would be the *maximum* that could be *safely* taken out . . . without damaging the prospects of the business."

6. A regime of perfect regulation is defined as one in which: prospective rates go into effect each January 1st; regulated firms purchase completed assets ("turnkey") each January 1st and immediately place them in service; there is precise foreknowledge of inflation; and there is an equivalence of allowed and achieved returns, of actual income taxes and those assumed for ratemaking purposes, and of actual and accounting useful lives.

7. An assumption of level cash flows is reasonable in the absence of technological or productivity improvement since new market entrants have the same technology vintage and hence face the same costs; see Bower (1985), Crew and Karen (1985), and Griffith and Robinson (1984).

8. This should not be confused with the matter of tax depreciation, which involves a set of choices independent of those made for reporting purposes. It is reasonable to expect that tax depreciation will be taken as rapidly as permitted, since this maximizes the firm's wealth.

9. The accounting measurement problems highlighted by table 5-1 do not go unnoticed in the unregulated firm, as is discussed subsequently.

10. In table 5-2, ACRS allows for recovery over five years, so that pretax cash flow rises in the sixth year. Under certain circumstances the market could levelize Pc; i.e., the price vector of table 5-2 could be replaced with a constant Equivalent Annual Charge (EAC) of $267.91 per year, since this stream has the same present value.

11. For definition, see Awerbuch and Boisjoly (1988). One of the assumptions of perfect regulation is that regulators will permit capital recovery over the economic life of the asset, although experience indicates that regulators favor useful lives that are longer than the economic lives (see Crew and Karen 1984), which reduce rates early in the assets' life, but which ultimately produce higher rates of financial distress, if technology progresses at a sufficient pace.

12. It has been argued that the saw-tooth profile produces results that are not all-too inequitable given the proposition that increasing maintenance costs serve to more or less level the gross cash flow (Bower 1985, 10). The life cycle of new technology, however, is often limited more by economic obsolescence than by a gradual "wearing out" which requires more maintenance (e.g., telecommunications switching equipment).

13. Stauffer (1980), Kay (1976), and others have used illustrations such as table 5-3 to argue incorrectly that rate-base regulation yields an equivalence of accounting and economic returns.

Such is clearly not the case in reality, since significant distortions in the ARR appear when the cash flow profile is altered by as little as 5 percent per year from that shown in table 5-3 (Awerbuch 1988). Even if all of these factors were corrected, the use of unadjusted, historic costs makes the resulting ARR "uninterpretable" in the presence of inflation and technological progress (Beaver and Landsman 1983, 26).

14. If Pc (Table 5-2) were replaced by an EAC of $267.91 as discussed previously, the regulated cash flow becomes competitive one year earlier—sometime during the fourth year. However, since accelerated depreciation enables Pc to have a lower present value than Pr, the unregulated competitor should always be able to design a vector of prices that is strictly lower than the regulated rate; this situation may be offset to some extent by normalization accounting as is discussed subsequently.

15. One of the assumptions of perfect regulation is that regulators will permit capital recovery over the economic life of the asset, although experience indicates that regulators favor useful lives that are longer (see Crew and Karen 1984), which reduces rates early in the asset's life, but ultimately produces higher rates or financial distress if technology progresses at a sufficient pace.

16. Normalization accounting alters the Pr vector slightly ($334.01, $304.09, $274.58, $245.07, $215.55, $194.55) and reduces its PV from $1,182.76 (table 5-3) to $1,172.24, thus not significantly improving the time-shape or the PV relative to Pc.

17. Regulators will observe an IRR of 9.7 percent for the after-tax CF of table 5-4. Actual IRR will be 10 percent using ACRS (as in table 5-2).

18. The problem of partial regulation aside, this has interesting regulatory implications. Early in an asset's life, the firm, believing it is "underearning" because its ARR<k, will seek rate increases until ARR=k, at which point IRR will be greater than ARR over the asset's life (see Awerbuch 1985, 348-350).

19. The statement is equivocal because the problem illustrated can not be corrected entirely using the traditional accounting approach to ratemaking (Awerbuch and Boisjoly 1988).

20. Consider the self-amortizing mortgage which recovers principal on the annuity schedule—small amounts at first, large amounts near the end, and hence considerably lowers cost in the initial years. If straight-line concepts were used, a $100,000, 20-year, 10 percent mortgage would cost approximately $15,000 (100,000*(.10)+100,000/20) the first year as compared to the $11,750 required under annuity concepts.

21. Normalization reduces the rates further ($295.46, $283.72, $272.09, $260.14, $247.83, $243.53) to a total of $1,602.77 and present value of $1,176.53, still not as low as the PV of table 5-2.

22. As Bidwell (1985) observes, marginal costs also tend to be low during the initial years of a project, which provides economic rationale for rates lower than those provided by the traditional regulatory practices.

23. Techniques for estimating the firm's IRR on the basis of publicly available accounting information are available. A good survey of the literature in this area can be found in Luckett (1984) or Brief (1987).

References

Anthony, Robert N. 1986. "Accounting Rates of Return." *American Economic Review* 76 (1): 244-246.

Anton, Hector A. 1956. "Depreciation, Cost Allocation and Investment Decisions." *Accounting Research* (April): 117-134.

Awerbuch, Shimon. 1985. "Return on Equity Ratemaking: Biased Earnings and Market-to-Book Ratios Due to Obsolescence and Excess Capacity." In *The Impact of Deregulation and Market Forces on Public Utilities*, edited by Patrick V. Mann and Harry M. Trebing. East Lansing, MI: Michigan State University.

Awerbuch, Shimon. 1986. "Accounting Traditions and the Determination of Regulated Return." Presented at the Advanced Workshop in Regulation and Public Utility Economics, Rutgers University.

Awerbuch, Shimon. 1988. "Accounting Rate of Return." *American Economic Review* (June).

Awerbuch, Shimon, and Russel Boisjoly. 1988. "The Use of Accounting Rates of Return in Regulation." Working Paper, College of Management Science, University of Lowell.

Beaver, William H. 1981. *Financial Reporting: An Accounting Revolution*. Englewood Cliffs: Prentice Hall.

Beaver, William H., and Landsman, W.R. 1983. *Incremental Information Content of Statement 33 Disclosures*. Stamford, CT: FASB (November).

Belkaoui, Ahmed. 1981. *Accounting Theory*. New York: Harcourt.

Benston, George J., and Krasney, M.A. 1978. "The Economic Consequence of Financial Accounting Statements." In *Economic Consequence of Financial Accounting Standards*. Stamford, CT: FASB (July): 161-252.

Bierman, Harold. 1974. "Regulation, Implied Revenue Requirements and Method of Depreciation." *Accounting Review* (July).

Bidwell, Miles O. 1985. Direct Testimony Before the N.Y. State P.S.C. in the *Matter of the Niagra Mohawk Power Corp.* Case No. 29069/70 (August).

Bower, Richard S. 1985. "The Capital Recovery Question." *Resources and Energy* 7:7-42.

Brealey, Richard, and S.C. Myers. 1984. *Principle of Corporate Finance*. 2d ed. New York: McGraw Hill.

Brief, Richard P. (ed.) 1987. *Estimating the Economic Rate of Return From Accounting Data*. New York: Garland Press.

Canning, J.B. 1929. *The Economics and Accountancy*. New York: Roland.

Crew, Michael A., and Nancy P. Karen. 1984. "Proposal for Reforming Depreciation Schedules in the Regulated Telecommunications Industry: The Case of New York Telephone." Advanced Workshop in Public Utility Regulation and Economics, Rutgers University, Newark, NJ.

Crew, Michael A., and Paul R. Kleindorfer. 1987. *The Economics of Public Utility Regulation*. London, Macmillan Press.

Edwards, Edgar O., and P.W. Bell. 1961. *Theory and Measurement of Business Income*. Berkley: University of California Press.

Financial Accounting Standards Board (FASB). 1978. "Statement of Financial Accounting Concept No. 1: Objectives of Financial Reporting by Business Enterprises." Stamford, CT: FASB (November).

Fisher, Franklin M., and J.J. McGowan. 1983. "On the Misuse of Accounting Rates of Return to Infer Monopoly Profits." *American Economic Review* 73 (No. 1, March): 82-97.

Fisher, Irving. 1906. *The Nature of Capital and Income*. New York: MacMillan.

Fisher, J.C., and Pry, R.H. 1971."A Simple Substitution Model of Technological Change." *Technological Forecasting and Social Change*: 75-88.

Gordon, M.J. 1967. "An Economist's View of Profit Measurement." In *Profits in the Modern Economy*, edited by H.W. Stevenson and J.R. Nelson. Minnesota: University of Minnesota Press.

Griffith, Mark, and Terry Robinson. 1985. "Economic Value and Capital Recovery: A Regulatory Economic Model." Presented at the Avanced Workshop in Regulation and Public Utility Economics, Rutgers University, Newark, N.J.

Harcourt, G.C. 1965. "The Accountant in a Golden Age." *Oxford Economic Papers*, Series 2, 17 (March): 66-80.

Hicks, John R. 1946. *Value and Capital*. 2d ed. London: Oxford University Press.

Hicks, John R. 1969. "The Measurement of Capital." Proceedings of the 37th Session, London, *Bulletin of the International Statistical Institute* 43:253-263; Reprinted in Brief (1987).

Hicks, John R. 1979. "The Concept of Income in Relation to Taxation and to Business Management." *Proceedings of the 35th Congress of the International Institute of Public Finance*; Reprinted in Brief (1987).

Hotelling, Harold. 1925. "A General Mathematical Theory of Depreciation." *Journal of the American Statistical Association* 20 (September): 340-353.

Ijiri, Yuji. 1980. "Recovery Rate and Cash Flow Accounting." *Financial Executive* (March): 54-56.

Kay, J.A. 1976. "Accountants, Too, Could be Happy in a Golden Age: The Accountants Rate of Profit and the Integral Rate of Return." *Oxford Economic Papers* 28 (November): 447-460.

Kolbe, Lawrence. 1985. "How Can Regulated Rates—and Companies—Survive Competition?" *Public Utilities Fortnightly* (April).

Kolbe, A. Lawrence, James A. Read, Jr., and G. Hall. 1984. *The Cost of Capital*. Cambridge, MA: MIT Press.

Kraus, A., and R.J. Huefner. 1972. "Cash-Flow Pattern and the Choice of a Depreciation Method." *Bell Journal of Economics and Management Science* 3 (Spring): 316-34.

Lindahl, Erik. 1939. *Studies in the Theory of Money and Capital*. London: Allen and Unwin.

Luckett, Peter F. 1984. "ARR vs. IRR: A Review and Analysis." *Journal of Business Finance and Accounting* 2 (No. 2, Summer): 213-231.

Melicher, Ronald W. 1987. "The Unbundling of Traditional Measures of Rate of Return by Regulated and Unregulated Services." In *New Regulatory and Management Strategies in a Changing Market Environment*, edited by H. Trebing. East Lansing, MI: Institute for Public Utilities, Michigan State University.

Myers, S., L. Kolbe, and M. Tye. "Inflation and Rate of Return Regulation." *Research in Transportation Economics*, Vol. 2.

Myers, Stewart C. 1972. "The Application of Finance Theory to Public Utility Rate Cases." *Bell Journal of Economics* 3 (Spring): 59-97.

Navarro, Peter, B.C. Peterson, and T.R. Stauffer, "A Critical Comparison of Utility-

Type Ratemaking Methodologies in Oil Pipeline Regulation." *Bell Journal of Economics* 12 (No. 2, Autumn): 392-412.

Salamon, Gerald, L. 1985. "Accounting Rates of Return." *American Economic Review* 75 (No. 3, June): 495-504.

Sherman, Roger. 1972. "The Rate of Return Regulated Public Utility Firm is Schizophrenic." *Applied Economics* 4 (March): 23-31.

Solomon, Ezra. 1970. "Alternative Rate of Return Concepts and Their Implications for Utility Regulation." *Bell Journal of Economics and Management Science* 1 (No. 1, Spring): 65-81.

Solomons, David. 1986. *Making Accounting Policy*. New York: Oxford University Press.

Stauffer, Thomas R. 1980. *The Measurement of Corporate Rates of Return*. New York: Garland Press.

Sterling, Robert R. 1970. *Theory of the Measurement of Enterprise Income*. Lawrence: University of Kansas.

Suelflow, James E. 1973. *Public Utility Accounting*. East Lansing, MI: Institute of Public Utilities, Michigan State University.

Treynor, Jack L. 1972. "Discussion." *Empirical Research in Accounting: Selected Studies*. Graduate School of Business, University of Chicago, 42-44.

Winn, Darryl. 1978. "The Potential Effect of Alternative Accounting Measures on Public Policy and Resource Allocation." In *Economic Consequences of Financial Accounting Standards*, FASB Research Report, Stamford, CT (July).

6

DECENTRALIZED PRICING IN NATURAL MONOPOLIES

William A. Hamlen, Jr.
Susan S. Hamlen

Introduction

In this chapter we present the case for and examine the possibilities of using decentralized pricing schemes in the situation of natural monopoly (decreasing marginal and average costs). To some extent, we will be offering an alternative view to that recently espoused by William Baumol in his new book, *Superfairness* (1986). Baumol finds little to recommend in pricing schemes based on "full cost allocation" (FAC) methods. These methods have been considered extensively in the accounting literature and are commonly used in all types of firms. However, as an economist, Baumol regards them as clearly second or third best in respect to the primary goals of natural monopoly firms which are to either maximize profits (unregulated) or maximize social welfare subject to a profit constraint (regulated).

In the next sction we summarize the arguments by Baumol and offer the justification for the use of FAC methods given by accountants. After that, we examine, analytically, the use of marginal and incremental cost charges in the case of both profit- and welfare-maximizing natural monopolists.

The Discussion

The concept of Pareto optimality has been the primary guide recommended by economists for judging efficiency in economic policies. It is a simple concept which requires that some gain and none lose in order to justify a change in the status quo. However, it seems to be an inadequate guideline for many policy recommendations. Baumol recognizes this in his motivations for investigating concepts of "fairness" (1980, 308):

> Perhaps the most plausible explanation for noneconomists' resistance to our most cherished instruments of micro policy . . . is the economists' determined disregard of their implications for distributive justice. . . . Recently matters have begun to change. There is a growing literature on the economics of equity in welfare theory, in public finance and in a number of areas.

In Baumol's work on fairness, there is a basic, underlying assumption that the notion of "envy" must be included in the analysis. An individual examines the levels of goods or services (or money) received by others and may offer political resistance to any policy in which he envies the gains of others. This concept of envy can work in public utility pricing when consumer groups take action to reduce "unfair" prices facing their group or "unfair" profits obtained by the monopolist.

Unfair prices, according to Baumol, are largely associated with perceptions of "cross-subsidies" between prices. Cross-subsidies are said to occur when a firm purposely subsidizes prices in relatively competitive markets by charging higher prices in less competitive markets. However, for an unregulated profit maximizing monopolist seeking to equate some form of marginal revenue and marginal cost, Baumol feels the term cross-subsidization is inappropriate (1986, 112). In essence, then, it is the preaccepted (Paretian) concept of fairness found in the profit maximization motive which excludes it from the accusation of cross-subsidization. For regulated monopolists, however, the accusation is given more credence, since the alternative goals under regulation are a deviation from the status quo and therefore require acceptance. In order to gain acceptance, the joint cost and pricing scheme used by the monopolist should be based on well-accepted principles. Baumol favors the idea of maximizing consumer surplus subject to a normal profit constraint (zero excess profits).

Thus only the two polar cases, maximizing profits and a constrained maximization of consumer surplus, represent acceptable objectives of the natural monopolist and yield optimal output and pricing solutions that mitigate the claims of unfairness based on their accepted underlying principles. This is true even if the goals are not ultimately sought. For example, Baumol recommends that the profit-maximizing solution be used to set prices under a normal profit constraint.

On the other hand, Baumol has little regard for the various FAC methods proposed in the accounting literature (see Hamlen, Hamlen, and Tschirhart 1977, 1980; Moriarity 1981). He specifically examines the simple Shapley value, the nucleolus and the concept of the core (1986, 136-137). He believes that because they are based solely on cost information and not on demand considerations, they cannot have useful welfare implications. In addition, because they are based on preselected output and cost levels, they cannot be efficient. We quote Baumol in his conclusion on these FAC methods (p. 149):

> In the last analysis most of the allocation procedures constitute exercises in arithmetic processes such as those one normally associates with cost accounting. . . . Those can hardly be interpreted as the embodiment of fairness.

This view, expressed by Baumol and shared by many economists, continues to dismiss too easily the realities of large multi-product and multi-market firms, including those characterized by natural monopoly conditions. In an award-winning article, Zimmerman (1979), building on the similar findings of others, concluded that it is the overwhelming need to use decentralized decisionmaking that keeps firms using FAC methods.

> The important point emerging from this analysis is that cost allocations appear to be a proxy for certain hard-to-observe costs that arise when decision making responsibilities are assigned to and vested in various individuals (i.e., decentralized) within the firm (p. 519).

In a recent accounting article, Bruegelman et al. (1985) found that 83 percent of the 500 firms they interviewed used some form of FAC pricing methods. We must conclude, then, that there is a definite need to rely on decentralizd pricing schemes and that firms find useful net benefits in the FAC methods. Restricting our interest here to natural monopolies, we then consider the important attributes sought in a decentralized pricing scheme. For the unregulated monopolist, incremental (marginal) cost charges offer a practical decentralized charge scheme which will yield the maximum profits. By submitting the respective incremental cost charges (more rigorously described below) to their divisions, the division leaders are then motivated to maximize divisional profits. Assuming the divisions face demand curves that are independent across divisions, the optimal solution, after some iterations, will be exactly that which would have resulted under a centralized profit-maximizing goal. Why, then, might unregulated natural monopolies consider any alternative decentralized charge scheme? We believe that there are two reasons. First, the literature contains two related theories, "limit pricing" theory and "contestable market" theory (see Baumol 1982). Both of these suggest that a firm with monopolistic powers might not take full advantage of these powers in pricing because it significantly increases the incentive for other firms to enter the industry. Within the contestable market theory, it is common to find predictions that prices might even equal those which produce zero excess profits.

The second reason why a monopolist might not take full advantage of its position to maximize profits is that the perception of "unfairly" high monopoly process could lead to future public regulation. This argument compliments the traditional arguments, which suggest that monopolies do have incentives to advertise and innovate, although not to the same extent as in less monopolistic situations. Thus, besides being relatively easy to use and guaranteeing at least normal profits, the FAC methods have the property of mitigating excess profits, which in turn can be explained as a way of reducing the threat of competition or increased regulatory intervention. For the regulated monopolist, the use of FAC methods is even easier to accept, since there is a greater political response to perceived unfair prices and less of a motivation to maximize profits.

In order to compare the FAC approaches to decentralized pricing under natural monopoly conditions, it is useful to first form a reasonable categorization of problems. First we classify the decentralized firms by their profit or constrained welfare motives. While there are obvious alternatives, these represent the two basic motivations of private and public natural monopolies. The profit-maximizing, decentralized firm will submit some "form" of joint cost charge to each division and require that each division seek to maximize its divisional profit which consists of total revenues less the joint cost charge. In the constrained welfare maximization situation, the divisions are directed to set prices equal to the per unit charges. These charges must cover total costs in order to provide at least normal profits. In both types of firm objectives, an equilibrium solution requires that the total amount demanded by divisions and consumers equal the total amount supplied.

Charges e_i are assumed to be submitted to divisions in three "forms." These are: (1) $e_i = \bar{e}_i$, (2) $e_i = a_i + b_i q_i$, and (3) $e_i = e_i(q_i)$. In the first form, divisions do not expect their output level to have an impact on the charge. In the second form, divisions are faced with a linear charge scheme with respect to output. This is the most familiar form of a charge scheme. The third form represents a nonlinear charge scheme. This could either be the case either if management submits a nonlinear charge formula or if the divisions understand the underlying computation of the charges. In this chapter we will assume that all divisions hold a "conjectural variation" of zero. This term is borrowed from the early Cournot work in which firms base their output decisions on the assumption that other firms won't react. In the current context it rules out charges of the form $e_i = e_i(q_i, q_j)$.

In constructing and examining specific charge schemes, there are several considerations that have to be dealt with. First, assuming that the divisions are not given instruction in rationing techniques, it is necessary to seek the equilibrium solutions to charge schemes. This is where the demand for the joint cost supplies by all divisions equals the demand for final products by consumers. A major complaint, including Baumol's, directed against the FAC methods is that the divisional demands were taken as inelastic and were obtained from *a priori* considerations, which might be inconsistant with the divisional reactions to the charge schemes. Second, there is a degree of mutual welfare between the division receiving a specific charge and the consumers of that divisions products. Given the specific, directed objective of the division, a higher charge is going to imply a higher consumer price and vice versa. Thus, it is consistent throughout the rest of the chapter to identify the relative treatment of the division with that of its consumers.

In order to begin our analysis in a more analytical fashion, we re-examine the traditional concept of marginal cost pricing.

Incremental and Marginal Cost Charges

We examine here the somewhat traditional rule for charging joint costs to divisions in order to maximize profits. We will assume in this, and in the rest of the analysis of the chapter, that each division of the corporation has a single demand which is independent of the other demands. This allows us to concentrate on the cost side rather than on the demand side. It is well known, of course, that decentralized pricing methods are less efficient when there are interdependent demand curves. In addition, we will set up a small example problem which can be used to compare the results of alternative charge schemes that are discussed in the following sections. The comparative results are summarized in table 6.1.

Rather than work with n-dimensional analysis, we use, for simplicity in exposition, a three-division problem as our standard. Assume that there is a natural monopolist that sells goods in three independent markets but produces them in a single facility with cost function $C(Q)$ where $dc/dQ > 0$, and $d^2C/dQ^2 < 0$. The amounts sold in the individual markets, q_i, $i = 1,2,3$, should equal the total amount produced, $\Sigma q_i = Q$. In essence this is the familiar discriminating monopolist problem applied to a decentralized natural monopoly setting. The objective function is:

Table 6.1. Comparative Results of Alternative Charge Schemes

	q_1	q_2	q_3	q_{123}	e_1	e_2	e_3	p_1	p_2	p_3	π	cs	W
1. $MR_i= 0$													
	1	.5	.75	2.25	2.25	1.0	2.8	4.	2.	3.	1.13	6.63	4.78
2. $e_i=a+bq_i$													
	.66	.16	.41	1.24	1.78	.43	1.10	5.34	3.34	4.34	2.36	1.28	3.64
3. $e_i= e_i(q_i)$													
	.69	.17	.43	1.29	1.73	.45	1.11	5.25	3.32	4.29	2.35	1.37	3.73
4. $p_i= MC$													
	1.42	.42	.92	2.76	3.28	.97	2.13	2.31	2.31	2.31	-.96	6.11	5.15
5. Ramsey, λ^*													
	1.13	.33	1.05	2.5	—	—	—	3.49	2.70	1.82	0	4.94	4.94
6. Shapley Form 2													
	.75	.19	.47	1.41	1.56	.82	1.61	5.0	3.24	4.11	2.32	1.64	3.96
7. Shapley Form 3													
	.66	.16	.41	1.24	1.39	.72	1.43	5.34	3.34	4.34	2.36	1.27	3.64
8. Shapley Welfare Max													
	1.37	.40	.89	2.67	2.69	1.56	2.86	1.96	3.87	3.21	0	4.89	4.89
9. Nucleolus Form 2													
	.92	.40	.66	1.98	.98	.5	.74	4.34	2.38	3.36	1.71	2.87	4.58
10. Nucleolus Form 3													
	.65	.14	.40	1.19	1.87	.38	1.13	5.40	3.44	4.42	2.35	1.20	3.55
11. Average Cost Form 2													
	.64	.14	.39	1.18	2.00	.45	1.22	5.43	3.42	4.42	2.35	1.18	3.53
12. Average Cost Form 3													
	.65	.15	.4	1.2	1.86	.42	1.14	5.38	3.42	4.4	2.35	1.22	3.57
13. Average Cost Welfare Max.													
	1.33	.33	.83	2.48	3.55	.88	2.23	2.69	2.69	2.69	0	2.44	2.44

$$\underset{q_i,\ i=1,2,3}{Maximize}\ \pi = \sum_{i=1}^{3} p_i(q_i)q_i - C\left(\sum_{i=1}^{3} q_i\right). \qquad (6.1)$$

The necessary conditions for an optimal solution are:

$$MR_i(q_i) = MC(Q),\ i=1,2,3,\ for\ q_i>0\ and\ \sum_{i=1}^{3} q_i = Q. \qquad (6.2)$$

The second order conditions require that each marginal revenue curve be more negatively sloped than the negatively sloped marginal cost curve at the optimal solution. In addition, it is required that each division pass a positive profitablity rule; total revenue must be greater than or equal to total cost. In a decentralized setting, the relevant charge, e_i, i=1,2,3, is submitted to each division and divisional managers maximize the following profit functions:

$$Maximize \ \pi_i = p_i(q_i)q_i - e_i, \ i=1,2,3. \qquad (6.3)$$

As described in the previous section there can be three forms of charges to be considered; $\bar{e}_i=e_i$, $e_i=a_i+b_iq_i$, and $e_i=e_i(q_i)$. The most familiar, traditional scheme is the second of these, where $a_i=0$ and $b_i=MC(Q_t)$. As shown in the Appendix, the true optimal solution, Q^*, need not be known, since it is locally stable for linear demand and marginal cost curves. If the corporation sets a charge equal to the current marginal cost, then an excess demand (supply) by all divisions would imply that output should be increased (decreased) and the charge decreased (increased).

If we use the first form of charge, with $e_i=\bar{e}_i$, i=1,2,3, and direct each division to maximize divisional profits, they will each produce at the levels where $MR_i = 0$, i=1,2,3, which will yield a lower profit level than the second form. Finally, assume that the divisions understand the basis of $b_i=dc/dQ$, i=1,2,3, and act with a conjectural variation equal to zero. The necessary condition for profit maximization by each division is then:

$$MR_i = dc/dQ + q_i(d^2c/dQ^2), \ i=1,2,3. \qquad (6.4)$$

This would yield a solution which is approximately equal to the optimal centralized solution only in the case where q_i is very small. Since the second derivative of the cost function is negative under natural monopoly conditions, the right side of (6.4) would be less than that under the naive charge scheme given by form (2). Thus, we would expect a higher output and lower price charged by the division.

In order to illustrate these differences, assume that three linear demand curves and a quadratic cost function have been estimated. These are given by

$$p_1= 8-4q_1, p_2=4-4q_2, p_3=6-4q_3,$$
$$and \ C(Q) = 3Q-.125Q^2 \ for \ Q=q_1+q_2+q_3. \qquad (6.5)$$

In addition it will be useful later to define the various coalition cost functions as:

$$c1 = c(q_1), \ c12 = c(q_1 + q_2), \ etc., \ with \ c(Q) \ replaced \ by \ c123. \quad (6.6)$$

Table 6.1 shows the equilibrium solutions to decentralized marginal cost charges under the three forms and under profit maximization. As predicted, total welfare is highest, but profits are lowest, when the charge is regarded as fixed by the divisions. Profits are roughly equal in this example for both the second and third forms of charge schemes, with total welfare highest under the third scheme with $e_i = e_i(q_i)$.

Under contemporary microeconomic theory, the concept of incremental cost (IC) has replaced marginal cost (see Baumol 1986, 126; 1982, 280).

Define the long-run total cost function by $c(Q) = c123$, using the notation described above. The incremental cost of division 1 becomes $IC(1) = c123 - c23$. It should be noted that this includes both long-run variable and fixed-cost terms (see Baumol 1982, 280). If division 1 is given a charge equal to its incremental cost, its problem is the following:

$$Maximize \ p_i(q_i)q_i - (c123 - c23). \quad (6.7)$$

The first order conditions in this case require that $MR_1(q_1) = dc123/dq_1$, which is exactly what is desired by the corporate management. An additional test for positive profitability of the division would be that the price charged p_1 be greater than the average incremental cost (AIC), $AIC1 = IC1/q_1$.

We find that the solution is exactly the same as that under marginal cost pricing and form two with $b_i = dc/dQ$, $i = 1,2,3$. The advantage, however, in giving the division the incremental cost, instead of an optimal linear cost charge, is that in the latter case the division might second-guess the corporate management and realize the underlying effect it has on the rate b_i. This would result in the solution $e_i = e_i(q_i)$ yielding potentially lower profits and higher total welfare. As described in the previous section, this result might be the desired goal if the firm is attempting to mitigate excessively high profits or prices for some self-protection reasons. However, it is not desirable if unintended.

Before turning to the alternative FAC charge schemes, we will verify the expected results when the decentralized natural monopolist requires that the divisions set prices equal to marginal cost. The equilibrium results for our example problem are shown in table 6.1. Prices are exceedingly low, with a high consumer surplus. Of course, the firm is experiencing losses, as marginal cost pricing does not cover average costs. Nevertheless the net total welfare, (consumer surplus plus profits) is higher than under the profit-maximizing objective.

In the next section, we consider some of the alternative FAC methods under both profit-maximization goals and welfare-maximization goals.

FAC Charges

Ramsey Prices

We begin with the one FAC charge scheme which Baumol distinguishes from all others. It is the Ramsey pricing rules. Their difference from the others emanates from the fact that they are not meant to seek full joint cost allocation as a goal, but only as a constraint. The objective is to maximize total welfare, given by consumer surplus plus profits. In the current problem this becomes

$$Maximize \sum_{i=1}^{3} \int_{o}^{b_i} p_i(q_i)dq_i - c123 \qquad (6.8)$$

$$s.t. \sum_{i=1}^{3} p_i(q_i)q_i = c123.$$

The first order conditions for optimization are given by:

$$p_i - MC(Q_T) = \lambda[MR_i(q_i) - MC(Q_T)] \quad i=1,2,3 \qquad (6.9)$$

where λ is the Lagrangian multiplier which yields the marginal welfare value of including the break-even constraint. As one can soon determine, when in working with (6.9) there is no practical way to use the Ramsey price solutions in a decentralized manner. The value of the Lagrangian is unknown to the corporate management.

In table 6.1, we find that the equilibrium Ramsey solution with optimal λ^* does indeed yield the highest total welfare of all methods. The optimal value of the Lagrangian multiplier in this case was approximately -.33; a value which would have been impossible to choose, *a priori*. Choice of an arbitrary value $\lambda=0$ reproduces the marginal cost pricing discussed in the previous section, along with its associated losses. A choice of $\lambda=1$ would require $p_i = MR_i$, $i=1,2,3$ which only occurs at $q_i = 0$, $i=1,2,3$.

Given that the Ramsey prices do not provide useful decentralized charge schemes, we turn to the FAC methods that can be used. Basically this includes the Shapley allocations, the nucleolus allocations, and average cost methods. However, before examining these, we should note that Baumol lists another approach, the "core" allocation scheme (1986, 136). This is not actually an allocation, but a condition which any allocation might be required to meet (see Hamlen et al. 1977). It requires that the charges to any grouping or coalition of divisions within the firm never exceed the "stand-alone" costs of that coalition. Baumol (1986, 120) includes this condition, via his discussion on prices, as one of the important attributes of fair prices in natural monopoly pricing. The nucleolus is known to satisfy the core condition, and it has been shown that some member of the class of generalized Shapley allocations (see Hamlen et al. 1980) will always satisfy the core conditions. The core condition is important for several reasons other than for perceived fairness. First, failure to meet core conditions entices divisional managers to purchase their supplies external to the firm, but to the detriment of the firm. Second, it encourages the development of competing firms made up of the coalitions which were overcharged their respective stand-alone costs. The competing firms could under price the monopolist in this set of products.

The Shapley Allocations

The "simple" Shapley allocation (Shapley 1953) is an FAC solution which yields a unique joint cost allocation. However, it has been generalized by Loehman and Whinston (1974) and then by Hamlen, Hamlen, and Tschirhart (1980). These generalizations are accomplished by maintaining the crucial "Shapley decomposition principle" while relaxing less important assumptions. In the current natural monopoly context, there is a cost savings to being larger. This is based on increasing returns to scale conditions. Under the decomposition principle, the total cost savings of including all divisions in the corporation can be decomposed into the savings attributable to each coalition of divisions, including the individual divisions themselves and the grand coalition of divisions. For example, in the three-division problem there would be potentially seven coalitions. These are given by the cost savings of $s1, s2, s3, s12, s13, s23, s123$. However, in the current context, the decomposition principle does not attribute any cost savings for being alone, so $si=0$, $i=1,2,3$. The cost savings for any two-division coalition i,j are $sij=ci+cj-cij$. The cost savings of the grand coalition $s123$ is given by $s123 = (c1+c2+c3-c123)-s12-s13-s23$ which, in turn, yields $s123=(c12+c13+c23 -c1-c2-c3-c123)$. It can then be shown by substitution that allocating all of the cost savings terms will exactly allocate the joint costs. The "simple Shapley" allocation results when two "fairness" rules are added to the allocation process. The cost savings attributable to any coalition i,j must be allocated only to divisions i and j and, in fact, must be allocated equally. Thus, division i would receive half of sij and half of sik. On the other hand, it would receive only one-third of $sijk$. Division i's charge e_i can be directly related to the savings scheme by the formulae

$$e_i = c_i - \sum_{R \in N} w_i(R)s_R. \qquad (6.10)$$

In the current three division-problem this becomes

$$e_1 = c1 - [w_1(12)s12 + w_1(13)s13 + w_1(123)s123]$$

$$e_2 = c2 - [w_2(12)s12 + w_2(23)s23 + w_2(123)s123]$$

$$e_3 = c3 - [w_3(13)s13 + w_3(23)s23 + w_3(123)s123] \qquad (6.11)$$

here in the "simple Shapley" solution $w_1(12) = .5$, $w_2(23) = .5$, etc. and $w_1(123)$ $= .333$, etc. By substituting the values for the allocative weights, w_i, and cost savings terms, sij, these charges can be transformed to yield the general solution (see Baumol 1986, 140):

$$e_i = (1/3)ci + (1/6)(cij\text{-}cj) + (1/6)(cik\text{-}ck) + (1/3)(cijk\text{-}cjk),$$
$$i \neq j \neq k, i=1,2,3. \qquad (6.12)$$

In this form, the interpretation has traditionally been that the charge to division i is equal to one-third of its stand-along cost, ci, plus one-sixth of its incremental cost to each of the other two divisions j,k plus one-third of its incremental cost to the coalition j,k. Sometimes these fractions are further interpreted as the "naive" probabilities of the arrival of division i to the grand coalition.

There are again four cases we should consider with respect to the use of the simple Shapley allocation in setting decentralized charges. The three forms of profit-maximization charges and the constrained welfare-maximization problem of setting prices equal to the per unit charge. The first case in which $e_i = \bar{e}_i$ yields an optimal solution for each divisiion of $MR_i = 0$ and results in the same solution considered for marginal cost charges. Under form (2), the corporation would calculate the simple Shapley allocation and submit the average charge per unit to each division. This yields a stable equilibrium under reasonable conditions. The solution to our example is given in table 6-1. The third profit-maximization charge assumes that divisions will react with a conjectural variation of zero. For example, in the simple Shapley solution with three divisions this results in an optimal solution of:

$$MR_i(q_i) = (1/3)\frac{\partial ci}{\partial qi} + (1/6)\frac{\partial cij}{\partial qi} + (1/6)\frac{\partial cik}{\partial qi} + (1/3)\frac{\partial cijk}{\partial qi},$$

$$i=1,2,3 \qquad (6.13a)$$

The right side of (6.13) is a weighted marginal cost of division i's quantity. In a decreasing marginal cost situation, it would be greater than $\partial cijk/\partial q_i$ for the same quantities $q_i + q_j + q_k$. Thus, we would expect lower outputs, higher prices, and, possibly, higher monopoly profits under the third form of the Shapley allocation than under the third form of the marginal cost pricing. This can be seen to occur in the example problem by comparing rows 3 and 7.

There are several generalized Shapley allocations that have intuitive appeal. For example, Whinston and Loehman (1976) chose to divide the residual savings attributed to each coalition (as described above) by the relative demands of the divisions rather than on the bases of equal divisions. In other words, division i would receive $[q_i/(q_i + q_j)]$ of sij, etc. The resulting decentralized charge for division i in a three-division problem would be:

$$e_1 = a_1c_1 + b_1[c12 - c2] + d_1[c13 - c3] + g_1[c123 - c23] \quad (6.13b)$$

where $a_1 = 1 + (q_1/(q_1 + q_2 + q_3)) - (q_1/(q_1 + q_3)) - (q_1/(q_1 + q_2))$
$b_1 = (q_1/(q_1 + q_3)) - (q_1/(q_1 + q_2 + q_3))$
$d_1 = (q_1/(q_1 + q_2)) - (q_1/(q_1 + q_2 + q_3))$
$g_1 = (q_1/(q_1 + q_2 + q_3))$.

Similar charges can be derived for divisions 2, 3. By setting $q_1 = q_2 = q_3$, the simple Shapley charges are obtained. It is fairly easy to see that the larger divisions in equilibrium are given a relatively higher weight of the last term of (13). In other words, larger divisions are given weights which are closer to the pure incremental cost, such as c123 - c23.

Another way of using the generalized Shapley solution is to transform other charge schemes, when possible, into the generalized Shapley form using the cost savings residuals. This allows us to determine which coalitions are being more selectively overburdened. This, in turn, might invoke both claims of unfairness by the consumers of these respective products or entrance of competitors in these particular markets. For example, the incremental charge scheme which is the best for unconstrained profit maximization transforms to an interesting generalized Shapley form. It acts as if every division were to receive the total cost savings of any coalition to which it belongs. For example, division 1 would receive all of s12, s13, and s123. The fact that this promise is made to all divisions is only feasible in monopoly situations, since the redundant promises are paid for by monopoly profits.

The Nucleolus Schemes

The nucleolus scheme of allocation was proposed by Schmeidler (1969). It has its roots in the Rawlsian or minimax criterion which seeks to minimize the worst treatment received by any member of a group. In this case each coalition of divisions is accounted membership including individual divisions. In the current context, the nucleolus solution in the three-division joint cost-charge problem could be obtained through the linear programming (LP) problem (see Hamlen et al. 1977):

$$Maximize \ r(min) \tag{6.14}$$

$$s.t. \ (a) \ r + e_i \leq ci, \ i=1,2,3$$
$$(b) \ r + e_i + e_j \ cij, \ i,j=1,2,3, i=j$$
$$e_i + e_j + e_k = cijk.$$

Once this problem is solved, the charges can be used in any of three profit-maximizing forms for profit maximization listed above or prices can be set equal to the average charge in the case of constrained welfare maximization. Again, form 1 yields the case of $MR_i = 0$ as described above. The forms 2, 3 and the constrained welfare-maximization solutions are given in rows 9 and 10 in table 6.1. As stated above, the nucleolus has the very convenient property of being in the core when it exists. However, it has an inconvenient property in requiring the LP solution prior to submitting the charges. After the solution to (6.14) is obtained, a set of functional charges can be derived. For example, assume that it was found from the solution to (6.14) that $r > 0$ and the first series of constraints (a) were binding. Then the functional form of the decentralized charge is:

$$e_i = (2/3)(ci + .5(c123-cj-ck)), \ i,j,k. \tag{6.15}$$

On the other hand, if the constraints given by (6.14b) were binding, the charges would be given by

$$e_i = (1/3)(c123 + cij + cik - 2cjk), \ i=1,2,3. \tag{6.16}$$

Of course, other variations of these binding constraints can occur and the problem becomes increasingly complex as more divisions are added. Like the generalized Shapley allocation, there are variations of the nucleolus solution. Hamlen et al. (1980) derived a "relative" version of the nucleolus in which they maximize the minimum relative attainment. This was found always to satisfy the core condition in the current context with three-division problems, but not necessarily for larger problems (see Hamlen 1982). The charge scheme in this case is given in the current three-division problem as:

$$e_i = (1-k)ci + k(cijk - cjk) \qquad (6.17)$$

where $k = (ci+cj+ck-cijk)/(ci+cj+ck+cij+cik+cjk-3cijk)$.

This allocation can also be shown to be a member of the generalized Shapley allocation wherein k is the unique equal share of all cost savings going to the divisions, subject to costs being fully allocated.

Average Cost Allocations

The last allocations method under discussion is probably the most familiar and well-used FAC method. This method allocates the total costs by the use of uniform average cost charges, where $e_i = c123/(q_1+q_2+q_3)$, i=1,2,3. As in the other methods, the average cost can be used in conjunction with profit-maximization motive by allowing prices to ration the final supplies using the three forms. Table 6-1 (rows 12 and 13) contains the results of forms 2 and 3 in our example problem. Alternatively, the welfare-maximizing monoplist can set prices equal to average cost and, through numerous iterations, reach an equilibrium where total supply and demand are equal. The solution to this problem is also given in table 6-1 (row 13).

The average cost method has many attributes such as requiring the least amount of computation and information. As seen in our example problem, it comes close to the profit maximization level of profits. However, most of the alternatives are able to do better in terms of total welfare. This is primarily due to the uniform nature of the charge to all divisions in average cost pricing. In essence it acts like an additional constraint to the allocation. In the Shapley and nucleolus methods, the equilibrium solutions where total supply and demand are equal permit one more degree of freedom by allowing unequal per unit charges.

The average cost charge scheme can be put into the generalized Shapley form with a fixed share. In the three division case the share of every cost savings allocation sij, sik, sijk going to division i is $1/(q_1+q_2+q_3)$ with each division obtaining an additional fixed share of $(c1+c2+c3)/(q_1+q_2+q_3)$. In this way the average cost would appear quite "fair" in the same sense as the simple Shapley allocation. On the other hand, it is easy to find average cost allocations that do not meet the core conditions.

Summary of Alternative Approaches

We have considered the four alternative joint cost charge methods, each with three forms. In addition, we have examined a three-division example with linear demand curves and a quadratic cost curve. Each method requires only information on the cost function. The incremental cost charge scheme would require only the cost function approximated at the current output. The average cost charge scheme requires only the current level of cost and total output levels. It is easy to see why this is so popular. However, in our example we found it to be relatively weak on total welfare maximization while fairly strong in profit maximization.

The nucleolus is the only solution that guarantees that the core conditions be met for divisional problems larger than three. It was the only solution to meet the core conditions in our example. Also, in our example it yielded a relatively high total welfare. However, the nucleolus is more difficult to implement because of the need for an LP subproblem.

The Shapley allocation provided the highest total welfare, other than Ramsey pricing, when the prices were set equal to the average Shapley charge. It is fairly easy to compute given the estimated cost function and has allocation properties which are generally regarded as "fair."

Incremental cost pricing maximizes profits (in form (2)) as expected, but it yields less total welfare in our example than either the Shapley or nucleolus approaches. This reinforces our contention in the introduction that these alternative FAC methods can act as a fair constraint on profits, when it is deemed desirable to do so, without the fear of less than normal profits.

Finally, the action of allowing or encouraging divisions to take the basis of the charge scheme into consideration with a zero conjectural variation has uncertain implications on profits and welfare, after equilibrium is reached. In the incremental and average charge schemes, shifting from form (2) with a linear charge to form three with a nonlinear charge causes profits to slightly decrease and total welfare to increase. The opposite effect occurs for the Shapley and nucleolus approaches.

Appendix

In the body of this chapter, we allude to stable equilibriums in the decentralized cost schemes. In other words, one need not begin with the equilibrium solution to have the solution iterate over time. Here we offer the proof of just one of these stability conditions. We show that marginal cost charges will be stable if the marginal cost function is less negative than the average demand function.

Assume the inverse demand functions are given by $p_i = a_i - bq_i$ and the marginal cost function is given by $MC = A - BQ$. The excess demand function $E(e')$ will be given by

$$\sum_{i=1}^{n} [(a_i - e')/2b_i] - [(A - e')/2B]$$

where e' is the uniform per unit charge.

Then

$$de'/dt = -kE(e') = -[k(1/2) \Sigma a_i/b_i - k(1/2) \Sigma(1/b_i)e' - kA/2B + ke'/2B].$$

Therefore,

$$e' = -R + S,$$

where

$$R = [e'_0 + .5(\Sigma(a_i/b_i) - A/B)/.5(\Sigma 1/b_i) - (1/B))] - [exp(k(.5)(-(1/B) + \Sigma(1/bi)))],$$

$$S = .5[-(a_i/b_i) + (A/B)]/.5\{-\Sigma(1/b_i) + (1/B)] \text{ as } t \to \infty,$$

$$e' \to [-(a_i/b_i) + (A/B)]/[-(1/b_i) + (1/B)]$$

$$if -(1/B) + \Sigma(1/b_i) < 0.$$

Assume all b_i are the same, then the condition is $-B > -b/n$. Thus, the charge scheme will be stable as long as the slope of the marginal cost curve is greater in value than the average slope of the demand curves facing the divisions. This, of course, is only approximately the answer for unequal b_i. All of the stability requirements in this chapter require similar conditions, which can reasonably be assumed to hold.

References

Baumol, W.J. 1980. "Theory of Equity in Pricing for Resource Conservation." *Journal of Environmental Economics and Management* (December): 308-320.

Baumol, W.J. 1982. "Contestable Markets: An Uprising in the Theory of Industry Structure." *American Economic Review* 72 (March): 1-15.

Baumol, W.J. 1986. *Superfairness*. Cambridge, MA: MIT Press.

Baumol, W.J., J.C. Panzar, and R.D. Willig. 1982. *Contestable Markets and the Theory of Industry Structure*. New York: Harcourt, Brace, Jovanovich.

Bruegelmann, M., G. Haessly, C. Wolfangel, and M. Schiff. 1985. "How Variable Costing is Used in Pricing Decisions." *Management Accounting* (April): 58-61.

Hamlen, W. 1982. "The Output Distribution Frontier: A Comment and Further Consideration." *American Economic Review* (March): 247-255.

Hamlen, S., and W. Hamlen. 1981. "The Concept of Fairness in the Choice of Joint Cost Allocation Methods." Proceedings of the Joint Cost Allocation Conference, University of Oklahoma (April).

Hamlen, S., W. Hamlen, and J. Tschirhart. 1977. "The Use of Core Theory in Evaluating Joint Cost Schemes." *Accounting Review* (July): 616-627.

Hamlen, S., W. Hamlen, and J. Tschirhart. 1980. "The Use of the Generalized Shapley Allocation in Joint Cost Allocation." *Accounting Review* (April): 269-287.

Loehman, E.T., and A.B. Whinston. 1974. "An Axiomatic Approach to Cost Allocation for Public Investment." *Public Finance Quarterly* (April): 236-251.

Loehman, E.T., and A.B. Whinston. 1976. "A Generalized Cost Allocation Scheme." In *Theory and Measurement of Economic Externalties*, edited by S. Lin, 87-101. New York: Academic Press.

Moriarity, Shane, ed. 1981. *Joint Cost Allocations, Proceedings of the Univ. of Oklahoma Conference on Cost Allocations*. University of Oklahoma Press.

Schmeidler, David. 1969. "The Nucleolus of a Characterisitic Function Game." *SIAM Journal of Applied Mathematics*: 1163-1170.

Shapley, L.S. 1953. "A Value of N-Person Games." In *Contributions to the Theory of Games*, edited by H.W. Kuhn and A.W. Tucker, 307-317. Princeton, NJ: Princeton University Press.

Takayama, A. 1974. *Mathematical Economics*. Hinsdale, IL: Dryden Press.

Zimmerman, J.L. 1979. "The Costs and Benefits of Cost Allocations." *Accounting Review* (July): 504-521.

7

NEW TECHNOLOGIES AND DIVERSIFIED TELECOMMUNICATIONS SERVICES: POLICY PROBLEMS IN AN ISDN ENVIRONMENT
Almarin Phillips

Introduction

It is commonly recognized that the "seeds of [the] struggles" that unraveled the Bell System "were sown by the revolution in electronic technology that occurred during and after the Second World War."

The development of this technology, much of it from the fertile genius of Bell Laboratories, enabled other firms to supply customers with products and services in competition with Bell. The only barrier was regulatory . . . [1]

The changes in industry structure and regulation wrought by these struggles have been thoroughly chronicled. There remains, however, a vitally important aspect of the revolution in technology to which little attention has been paid. That is the question of whether the new regulatory approaches and the new structural arrangements are conducive to promoting the development and use of yet newer technologies. It is arguable that the old system was put in place precisely because an integrated structure was essential for the provision of nationwide telecommunications services based on the technologies of the time. In the same vein, it is at least questionable whether the "competitive," multiple seller approach now being pursued is compatible with the use of current and foreseeable technologies in ways that will "make available, as far as possible, to all the people . . . a rapid, efficient, nationwide . . . communication service with adequate facilities at reasonable charges."[2]

This chapter is an exploration of that question. The next section traces briefly the paths to the present regulatory and structural conditions in the industry, with emphasis on enhanced and diversified services. The third section contains an analysis of possible shortcomings inherent in these arrangements. This includes consideration of scale and scope economies, efficient pricing, transactions costs, and standards setting. The final section examines policy options, with a critique of the present posture of the Federal Communications Commission and the recently modified Modified Final Judgment (MFJ).

Background

The 1956 Consent Decree

The case brought against Western Electric and AT&T in 1949 concerned the monopolization of telephones, telephone apparatus, equipment, materials, and supplies. Telecommunications services, as such, were not the focus. Nonetheless, the 1956 Consent Decree terminating the case enjoined AT&T and its subsidiaries from engaging "in any business other than the furnishing of common carrier communications services." Western Electric was enjoined from manufacturing for sale or lease "any equipment which is of a type not sold or leased . . . to Companies of the Bell System, for use in furnishing common carrier communications services." Thus, the Decree effected a split between regulated telecommunications services, on the one hand, and the computer industry—data processing, information processing, and information services—on the other hand, except as the latter might be "incidental" to the furnishing of common carrier communications services.

Specialized Common Carriers, Terminal Equipment, and the First Computer Inquiry

As technology advanced, distinctions between communications, data processing, and information services became more blurred. The growth of the computer industry—particularly after the introduction of distributed processing in the middle and late 1960s—caused rapidly increasing demand for the transmission of data among the nodes at which it was generated, used, stored, or processed. This gave rise to ideas for data networks and "computer utilities," the implementation of which required terminal equipment and network services that AT&T was unable or unwilling to provide. Specialized common carriers (SCCs, now Other Common Carrier or OCCs) were envisioned, and data transmission was prominent among the services proposed by the SCCs in their initial applications.[3]

While the *Carterfone* case represents the important turning point, the pressures for change in the carriers' terminal equipment policies are not well depicted by the facts of that case. Data processing and transmission required new kinds of terminal equipment. The "foreign attachment" provisions of existing tariffs prevented others from providing that equipment so that the new services could be carried on the network. Market reality, as well as the 1956 Decree, made it clear that the carriers could not provide the required array of devices. Yet it was equally clear that entry by the SCCs and interconnect terminal equipment suppliers was inevitable if the growing needs for data transmission could not be accommodated on the networks of the existing common carriers.

The Federal Communications Commission (FCC) began its *Computer Inquiry (CI-I)* in 1966. The MCI application was before the Commission at the time and the Commission was cognizant of the *Carterfone* matter. In a 1973 *CI-I* ruling, the FCC distinguished between regulated communications services and unregulated data processing services in the same way as had been done in the 1956 Decree. Regulated common carriers were permitted to engage in unregulated data processing services only through separate corporate entities. This ruling was of no avail to AT&T, however, because of the provisions of the 1956 Decree.

The Second Computer Inquiry

It was soon apparent that the distinctions between regulated telecommunications and unregulated data processing were far from clear. This was particularly true of so-called "hybrid data processing" services that included aspects of message switching and "hybrid communications" services that included aspects of data processing.

In an effort to clarify policy, the *Second Computer Inquiry (CI-II)* was opened in 1978. A 1980 *CI-II* ruling produced a dichotomy of "basic services" and "enhanced services." "Basic service" was defined as the offering of transmission capacity to move information from one place to another; "enhanced services," those that utilize computer technology to alter the content or to provide subscriber interaction with stored information. Three types of enhanced services were defined—those that: "(1) act on the format, content, code, protocol or similar aspects of the subscriber's transmitted information; (2) provide the subscriber additional, different or restructured information; or (3) involve subscriber interaction with stored information." All of the latter—along with all customer premises equipment (CPE)—were deregulated. The FCC also used the rationale that AT&T was subject to potential regulation in an attempt to circumvent the restrictions of the 1956 Consent Decree. The latter aspects of the rulings were on appeal at the time the MFJ was entered.

The Modification of Final Judgment

The 1982 agreement between AT&T and the Department of Justice (DOJ) presented the Court with a document that barely considered enhanced services, ongoing technology, and the role of network carriers in providing information services. The events on which the MFJ was based took place in the 1950s, 1960s, and 1970s and were primarily concerned with ordinary telephone service and the terminal, transmission, and switching equipment involved in producing that service.

The DOJ's Competitive Impact Statement and the Court recognized that changes in technology might in time alter the economic significance of the Bell Operating Companies' (BOC) apparent access bottleneck. And the Court, it appears, was less concerned than the DOJ about the BOCs providing both regulated and unregulated services so long as there was no significant adverse competitive effects. Even so, there were severe restrictions against BOC offerings of information services, particularly electronic information services, in the MFJ as entered in 1982. No service involving the "generating, acquiring, storing, transforming, processing, retrieving or making available information . . . conveyed via telecommunications" could be offered by the BOCs. Further, the telecommunications services of the BOCs would make no changes "in the form or content" of information "as sent and received."[4] In short, while the MFJ removed the vestiges of the 1956 Decree for AT&T, the BOCs could neither provide the generic interfacing which would facilitate others' use of the network to deliver information services nor themselves provide such services.

The ISDN Inquiry

The FCC released a *Notice of Inquiry into Integrated Services Digital Networks* (ISDN) in Docket No. 83-841 in August 1983.[5] A First Report was released in April 1984, largely in the context of the policies enunciated in *CI-II*. The report reviews FCC actions on basic and enhanced services up to that point and juxtaposes these against ongoing activities of the International Telegraph and Telephone Consultative Committee (CCITT) and the International Standards Organization. The latter include the development of the Open System Interconnection (ISO/OSI) model. The FCC concluded that, in contrast to the other worldwide cooperative efforts, its competitive policies are appropriate for the planning and design of ISDNs in the United States. While it was recognized that continued United States representation at the CCITT was desirable, the FCC indicated that it was likely to become actively involved in ISDN development only if the latter moves in directions inconsistent with the policy approach expressed in *CI-II*. That is, the Commission wants ISDNs to "evolve under a structure which accommodates [its] mulitiple vendor telecommunications market and [its] pro-competitive policies."[6]

The Third Computer Inquiry

The *Third Computer Inquiry (CI-III)* Notice and Proposal appeared in August 1985. In a May 1986 Phase I Order, the FCC recognized that the inefficiencies and costs associated with structural separation for carrier provision of enhanced services may often outweigh the benefits. While maintaining the basic/enhanced service definitions of *CI-II,* the Commission adopted new regulations to govern the offerings of enhanced services.

Dominant carriers (i.e., AT&T and the BOCs) are required to provide comparably efficient interconnection (CEI) to apparent competitors for any enhanced services the carriers are permitted to offer. They were also required to file plans for open network architecture (ONA) by February 1988. Any basic service used in the offering of an enhanced service must be tariffed and available to others on any "unbundled and functionally equal basis." Beyond this, the carriers were required to file detailed accounting plans and to receive approval for the methods used in allocating joint and common costs. A *Report and Order* under Docket No. 86-111, released in February 1987, provides guidelines for that purpose. Cross-subsidization is again the underlying issue; the order aims at inhibiting "carriers from imposing on ratepayers for regulated . . . services the costs and risks of unregulated ventures."

Phase II orders under *CI-III* established that protocol processing is an enhanced service which, if offered by AT&T or a BOC, must satisfy nonstructural safeguards set forth by the Commission. The latter specify types of access to end offices, interfaces, transmission, and transport networks that must be made available to value-added network (VAN) competitors and the network rate elements (NRE) for which tariffed rates must be available. AT&T and the BOCs have petitioned the FCC for substantially less restrictive and more equal rules for protocol processing, but no basic changes in the original Phase II order have thus far been made. At least one Commissioner recognizes that the "regulatory cleavage between basic and enhanced services is a relic of the past."[7] At the same time, a new docket has been opened to consider the carriers' ONA plans.

Modifying the Modified Final Judgment

The 1983 MFJ requires a triennial report to the Court by DOJ concerning the line of business restrictions imposed on the BOCs. The first such report was filed in February 1987 and made what many regarded as rather startling recommendations.[8] These include a lifting of the ban on BOC provision of interexchange services for areas outside their own local exchange areas, removal of all restrictions on BOC manufacturing and distribution of telecommunications equipment and customer promise equipment (CPE), removal of restrictions on non-telecommunications businesses, and—most relevant to this discussion—removal of the ban on BOC provision of information services. Not surprisingly, the BOCs joined the DOJ in these recommendations to the Court. AT&T concurred in the view that the ban on information services should be eliminated but opposed the other recommendations. Depending on their own business interests, some other parties strongly supported and some opposed the recommendations in whole or in part.

The DOJ position on the provision of information services by the BOCs was based on efficiency, practicality, and competitive considerations. It was argued that:

> ... What is most significant, from the perspective of the United States' Report and Recommendations, is that information services vary widely in technical and market characteristics. They also vary in the extent to which they are likely to be integrated with or dependent on local exchange telecommunications facilities. Information services not only are varied, they are constantly changing. New services are being developed, as are new and more efficient ways of providing existing services.
>
> There is no bright line, in either a technical or a definitional sense, that distinguishes information services, which the BOCs may not provide, from "exchange" and "exchange access" services, which they are allowed to provide. On the contrary, today's basic exchange networks perform many storage, retrieval and processing functions identical to those involved in some information services. ... Similarly, there is no clear or competitively rational dividing line between information services and CPE. Most PBXs and other sophisticated CPE perform some information services functions, but the MFJ permits the BOCs to provide all types of CPE.[9]

Judge Greene's initial reaction to the DOJ/BOC proposals was distinctly negative. While he was prepared to exempt the transmission of information generated by others and did repeal the restriction on BOC entry into non-telecommunications businesses, his September 1987 opinion emphasized the pervasiveness of local exchange bottlenecks and the dangers that these would be used anticompetitively if the restrictions on information services were much relaxed. If he recognized that functions closely analogous to voice messaging, call returns, call forwarding, call blocking, delayed call completion, and emergency announcements had been performed by switchboard operators from the earliest days of telephony, it was not then obvious.[10]

Six months later, Judge Greene clarified the meaning to be attached to the exemption for the "transmission of information generated by others." It was made clear that the BOCs are foreclosed from the "generation of information content." The Court reaffirmed, however, that data transmission, address translation, protocol conversion, billing management, and introductory information content are "transmission functions." These the Court saw as necessary to permit development of a United States counterpart of the French Teletel. The restriction against "electronic publishing," as defined in the MFJ, was explicitly continued. The Court literally encouraged the BOCs to develop an audiotext system within the constraint banning their own generation of information. Extensions of "976" services were used as illustrations.

The definition of "electronic white page" information services was clarified to make more evident what the Court regarded as permissable "gateway service" transmission of introductory information content. Similarly, the Court indicated that it is now prepared to accept "kiosk" billing by the BOCs, so long as nothing more than minor and "technical" revenue sharing is involved. The adoption of any sort of protocol conversion services would be allowed so long as they do not involve manipulation of content. In this connection, the Court appears to have concluded that the generic capability to convert individual users' protocols to X.400 for electronic mail services does not constitute a change in content.

Perhaps the most surprising of the recent modifications to the MFJ are those concerning voice storage and retrieval, voice messaging, and, more particularly, electronic mail services by the BOCs. After a careful probing of alternatives, the Court concluded that "the risk of anticompetitive activity is small" and permitted the BOCs to participate in these markets—again subject to the prohibition against their providing or manipulating information content. In other places in the opinion, the Court indicates a willingness to defer to FCC decisions pertaining to enhanced services and to accept the procedural safeguards set forth by the Commission. Still, "if it appears [to the Court] that the Regional Companies are abusing the authority granted ... and that FCC control is insufficient to curb violations, the Court will take the requisite enforcement action."

Remaining Policy Problems

Despite Judge Greene's recent opinion, there are many remaining problems in United States telecommunications policies. This section will focus on those related to enchanced service offerings, but others—some of them interrelated with problems concerning enhanced services—will be noted as well.

Economies of Scale and Scope

An extremely difficult set of problems arises because of the probable existence of significant economies of scale and scope in the switched network. While some have argued that these economies are limited to size ranges much below those of the United States network, the bulk of the credible evidence points to the existence of economies of scale throughout the network sizes thus far experienced.

There are numerous econometric studies of the United States and Canadian networks that attest to such economies. Problems associated with the data and a number of technical difficulties make the conclusions of the econometrics less than unassailable, however, and the best evidence of the scale and scope economies continues to come from market facts.

Of the several facilities-based interexchange carriers, AT&T is the only one persistently able to generate profitable operations. AT&T has done this despite its early obligations to pay differentially high carrier access charges, its continuing and unique regulatory burdens as a dominant carrier, the relatively large volume of service it provides on low-density routes, and its providing carrier-of-last-resort service to the other carriers. Few would suggest that AT&T's ability to outperform the OCCs is due to superior management, better technology, or lower labor and capital costs. The only plausible reason seems to be economies deriving from its size.

The economies of scale in the old system were not restricted to interexchange services. They undoubtedly arose in part from the integral provision of local exchange and interexchange services. Here again the new arrangements entail inefficiencies in the forced and arbitrary separation of functions. Indeed, the provision by the BOCs of equal trunk-side access to an indefinite and changing number of interexchange carriers is far from costless. The costs of providing CEI (or ONA) for the multiple vendors of enchanced services in an ISDN environment may reach such proportions that the general public will benefit little from them.

Costs of Sustaining Multiple Vendors

A brief review of the FCC's concerns in making decisions under its *CI-III* rules makes it clear that there are enormous problems inherent in maintaining multiple vendor offerings of enhanced services. The conditions attached to the Commission's recent approval of voice mail services (VMS) by Pacific Bell[11] make one wonder whether the non-structural safeguards of *CI-III* are not worse than the structural separation required by *CI-II*.

Under the Phase I Order, Pacific had to offer a CEI plan showing that it would "provide interconnection opportunities to others . . . to insure that basic facilities are available to other enhanced service providers and users on an unbundled and functionally equal basis." The CEI plans must cover "interface functionality, unbundling of basic services, resale, technical characteristics, installation, maintenance and repair, end-user access, CEI availability, minimization of transport costs, and recipients of CEI."

To comply with CEI requirements, Pacific will provide its VMS "competitors" with a variety of tariffed incoming and outgoing access lines to the VMS system. The "competitors" will also be provided with tariffed data lines for signal information about the calls and tariffed central office hardware-software-supplied services, such as multi-line hunt groups and automatic call distribution. To satisfy the equal interface functionality requirement, Pacific's own VMS offering will interconnect with the network "in the same way and on the same terms and conditions available to all voice mail providers."

The basic services that support Pacific's VMS are "unbundled from other basic service offerings and are associated with a specific rate element. . . . Pacific . . . will not use network functions that are not available to all providers in an unbundled tariffed form." Indeed, Pacific will itself "purchase" the CEI elements "at the same tariffed rates, terms, and conditions as other voice mail providers," thus making resale of its services easily possible. An installation, maintenance and repair system is set up to prevent discrimination. Any end user access system (e.g., abbreviated dialing) made available to Pacific's VMS subscribers must be made available to "competitors."

In gaining approval for its VMS offering, Pacific sacrificed "certain efficiencies . . . since it [gave] no recognition to cost reductions in furnishing dial access to its own collocated enhanced service." These are precisely the sort of efficiencies that led the Commission to abandon its earlier *CI-II* "separate facilities" requirement. Here, however, since Pacific agreed to "charge itself the same tariffed rates as it charges all other VMS providers," the Commission's view was that "it achieves the pro-competitive goals" of the CEI requirements.

The idea of preserving competition—really, preserving competitors—by requiring that Pacific not price its VMS offerings in ways that might reflect its greater efficiency is carried into the criteria used for approval of its rates.[12] For example, the fact that VMS access lines within a local central office area are tariffed at flat, non-distance-sensitive rates appears to have been a favorable factor. Distance-sensitive tariffs might favor Pacific's own VMS and require the collocating of competitors' equipment with that of Pacific.[13]

The Commission also set requirements for non-discriminatory BOC access and use of customer proprietary network information (CPNI). Quarterly reports attesting to the non-discriminatory treatment of installation, maintenance, and repair services must be submitted. Approval must also be given for the billing arrangements for VMS, particularly since competitors may have few realistic alternatives to having the carrier perform at least the record-keeping aspects of the billing functions. At a minimum, Pacific is required to follow the guidelines of the *Joint Cost Order* for VMS billing for itself and other providers and to assure that none of the costs associated with its VMS offering are borne by its basic service offerings.

The import of this particular ruling can be appreciated only when it is extrapolated to the vast array of other services that Pacific and the other BOCs are petitioning to offer under the general *CI-III* Phase I and Phase II Orders. The fact that the MFJ will now be modified means that interstate equal access (CEI/ONA) will also have to be provided. That is, AT&T, MCI, GTE, Sprint, and interstate VAN carriers must be provided with the same sort of enhanced service opportunities. Regulatory and other governance costs promise to grow, perhaps to unmanagable proportions.

Pricing Inefficiencies

Quite apart from the *Joint Cost Order*, standard economic theory for pricing the services of a multi-product natural monopoly consists of the familiar Ramsey-Boiteux "inverse elasticity rule." The markups of prices over the respective marginal costs should vary inversely with demand elasticity. In the absence of external subsidization, all prices must be high enough so that total revenues cover total cost. In addition, there are two widely accepted limits on rates. At the lower bound, every price should be "subsidy free" and, on the upper side, prices should satisfy the "stand-alone" cost test.[14]

A service is subsidy free when the incremental revenues generated from its sales at least cover the amount by which costs are increased due to that service being provided. More specifically, where demands are independent, a particular service is subsidy free so long as the incremental revenue it generates is equal to or greater than the (long-run) incremental cost of the service.

When the demand for the service in question is not independent of demands for other services, the test for subsidy-free pricing must consider cross-demand effects. If the service is a substitute for another of the carrier's services, lowering the price of the first will increase its output but simultaneously reduce the demand for the substitute service. The fact that the price of the focal service exceeds its own incremental unit cost does not suffice. There may be a more than offsetting loss in contribution from the fall in output of the second substitute service. If the service is complementary to one or more others, lowering the rate charged for it tends to increase the demand for the others. Here the test for subsidy free prices must consider the gain in contribution from the increased demand for the others as well as the direct relationship between the incremental revenues and costs of the good in question.[15] Complementarity in demands—as, for example, that between the demand for access and the demand for usage—may mean that the set of optimal rates includes at least one for which the rate is less than unit long-run incremental costs (LRIC).

There is, as well, the classic externality rationale for violating the subsidy-free price test. The most obvious case is when there is a strong adoption (universal service) externality and when service penetration rates are low. Conceptually, the externality means that the prices paid by individual subscribers fail to reflect the full social value of their being subscribers. Each additional subscriber confers a benefit to all of the others.

Historically, the prime example of pricing to capture externalities and demand complementary in telephone services appeared in connection with basic subscription (access) and toll (usage) rates. It was early recognized that low access rates made subscription more attractive, led to an increase in the proportion of households having telephones, and, consequently, increased the demand for telephone usage. Thus, despite low price elasticity in the demand for access, the more profitable and publicly acceptable strategy for the carriers was to keep those rates relatively low. This rate structure also served to produce near-universal service.

The present situation is more complicated. A large array of interactive telecommunications services can be provided with the networks now in place and the potential is even larger with ISDN technologies. In addition to improved telephone service, new networks services may include voice storage and retrieval, centrex, interactive data-based videotex, telefax, teletex (electronic mail), fast and slow moving picture services (picture phone), high resolution picture services, general protocol and speed conversion services, and services based on fast and slow packet switching. And, as has been evidenced, both the FCC and the Court now see merit in permitting the BOCs to provide at least the broadly defined transmission services on which these are based.

While below-cost rates for access to ordinary voice telephone service are now less easy to justify because of near-universality in service, universality obviously does not extend to enhanced services. Indeed, with respect to most enhanced services, penetration rates are as low as they were for telephone services in the very early years of this century. The multiplicity of possible services and the complexity of the demand interrelationships among them make coordinate pricing strategies even more relevant, however. In the context of modern technology, the demand for one service by one class of customers depends not just on the price of that service, but as well on the menu of available services—that is, the number and type of service providers—and on the number of other subscribers to those services. And as was the case for the telephone years ago, low rates for access may initially be necessary to stimulate demand growth, greater universality, and a broader array of service.[16] Without such pricing, the new services may be available only to large users and then largely through specialized terminal equipment rather than through the network and Central Office Switching Equipment (COSE).

Pricing, Regulations, and Transactions Costs

Despite Judge Greene's recent liberalization in the permissable enhanced service offerings of the BOCs, the modified MFJ still prevents the patterns of pricing necessary to bring a wide array of enhanced services to the general public. And this is not oversight. While the Court lauded the French Teletel system, lamented the lack of "consumer-oriented," "home videotex" services in the United States, and noted that the "kiosk [revenue-sharing] system appears to have been a key factor in the growth and expansion of Teletel," it denied use of the essential feature of access pricing that underlies the success of the French system.

The French Minitel terminal was specifically developed for use in the Intelmatique videotex system. It is small, lightweight, attractively packaged, and extremely easy to learn to use. It has no intelligence save that needed to signal the central office. A Minitel terminal was provided to each residence without charge as a substitute for the paper telephone directory as videotex was introduced according to a nationwide plan beginning in 1983. Additional terminals could be rented or purchased, including the areas in which the free terminal was not yet available. Software is available to facilitate adaption of privately purchased PCs so that they can incorporate the functions of Minitel. The French videotex system is largely integrated into the rest of the nationwide network. The Minitel accesses the local exchange through the regular local loop facilities. The local exchange serves as the video access point, switching traffic onto the nationwide Transpac, packet-switched data network. The latter provides protocol conversion based on CCITT X.25 standards and is in turn accessed by the data bases of information service providers (ISPs) and their proprietary computer networks. Both economies of scope and scale are thus realized.

In addition to the free Minitel, subscriber use is encouraged through a novel pattern of revenue-sharing tariffs. Directory use is free for the first three minutes. There are several other tariffs, including the popular Kiosk. Charges for the communications services provided by the telephone authority and charges for the services of the ISPs are divided between the subscriber and the ISP depending on the nature of the service. Where the ISP derives value from its reaching large numbers of subscribers (e.g., advertising), the ISP pays for the bulk (or all) of the usage. Where the subscriber derives value from using a service (e.g., video games, "chat lines"), the user pays for the use of the network and for the service.

It is not only the modified MFJ that prevents this kind of output-augmenting, welfare-enhancing rate discrimination in the United States. The FCC's *CI-III* requirements are formidable obstacles as well. The unbundled offering of each element involved in each enhanced service of a BOC, with rates based on fully distributed costs, simply obviates the possibility of efficient pricing.[17] Scope economies will necessarily be foregone, and, indeed, the whole purpose of permitting the integrated use of COSE and the network in providing enhanced services will be thwarted.

Unfortunately, even if the MFJ were further modified and even if the FCC adopted an explicit net revenue test (with revenue sharing) for enhanced services, there would be enormous difficulties in establishing nationwide (or areawide) service systems in the United States. The unified structure of the French PTT permits it to internalize the sharing of costs and revenues. It need not set rates and share costs and revenues in ways that assure the profitability of arbitrarily separated components of the system. More specifically, the revenues from local exchange and transport services in each of the many exchange areas need not cover some arbitrary measure of the full costs of the system assigned to those services in those areas. The same thing is true across services as well as across geographic areas.

In the United States, given the now fractionalized structure, contractual and regulatory means would have to be developed to share costs and revenues among large numbers of participants. This was not easy to do in the former settlements and division of revenues process for plain old telephone service; it appears hopelessly complicated in the new structure with new services. There are the 22 BOCs, 1,500 other local exchange companies, three substantial facilities based, nationwide interexchange carriers, and an indeterminant and changing number of resale carriers. Literally tens of thousands of ISPs would have to be accommodated, some with only local reach and others with regional, national, and international orientations.

The transactions costs involved in the combined regulation of and contracting among these parties in order to create the nationwide, consumer-oriented enhanced service system Judge Greene wants are prohibitive. Even if contracts (within the context of a permissive regulatory system) could be defined, the idiosyncratic nature of some of the investments as well as the number and heterogeneity of the participants would expose the parties to the dangers of post-contractual opportunistic behavior. *Ex ante* commitments for participation would lack full credibility. Free-riding among the interexchange carriers would be possible, particularly in the light of MFJ and other regulatory requirements mandating equal access, CEI and ONA.

Standards and the Transition to the ISDN Technology

While many new services can be added within the basic technology of today's networks, ISDN technologies will provide even greater opportunities for service innovations. A typical network planning scenario is first to digitize the interoffice trunks, with common channel interoffice signalling. Existing analog subscriber loops are used for a new and wider variety of narrowband services, including videotex. In a second stage, the present local loops are to be digitized. As this occurs, the entire network moves to an ISDN system, fully digitized and capable of handling switched narrowband services. Open systems interconnections (OSI) using non-proprietary interfaces, protocols, and functions would be adopted, permitting communications among otherwise incompatible terminals and sub-networks. Finally, optical fiber technology would be introduced to realize switched broadband as well as narrowband services by the end of this decade.

In order to accommodate all sorts of users and ISPs, the network carrier must offer communications services using parallels to what are called the applications layers of the ISO/OSI reference model, in addition to transport functions. This allows advanced communications processing in the network and provides a truly open network architecture. If the carrier is restricted to the transport layers, it can do no more than carry VAN traffic and interconnect the local area networks (LANs) and local ISDNs laid down by others for their own defined needs. Some of the latter may be services designed for resale to the general public, but failure to integrate these into the carriers' tariffed offerings will mean that they will be available only for large customers in areas where traffic density is high. The carrier could not in these circumstances assume its obligations to provide "to-whom and from-whom-it-may-concern" enhanced services to the general public.

The development and use of international standards are critical. Without well-defined ISDN specifications in the equivalent of ISO/OSI layers 5 through 7, users will necessarily turn to proprietary protocols. If, alternatively, the carriers are providing public services with non-proprietary standards and open architecture, they will aid in establishing standards which others can use. Such standardization would promote universal service in the ISDN framework and permit the network to play a larger role in information-processing activities.[18]

Through their role in standardization and the provision of network services, the network carriers can provide interfaces among all users, maximizing the ability of any one information end-user to access or be accessed by any other. The carriers' non-proprietary standards thus ought to enlarge the opportunities for user group applications, creating a larger CPE market, broader choices among manufacturers whose equipment can be used compatibly, and, consequently, lower costs to users. This role in promoting standardization and in providing protocol and speed conversion services is a very important one. Without non-proprietary standards for information transmission and communications processing, proprietary data processing standards developed for computer networks, with intelligence centered in CPE's, will increasingly be used. The latter are not conducive to the spread of universally available new technology services.

Conclusions

Despite the modifications made to the MFJ, telecommunications policies in the United States continue to warp the introductions of new technologies in ways that are inconsistent with the broad public interest. The transition to the "information society" in the United States may be a rapid one for a small number of select, high volume users; it will not be rapid in the putting into place of a nationwide network available to the general public. Indeed, the failure in the United States to recognize the infrastructural importance of a modern telecommunications system, including the need for integrated pricing decisions and non-proprietary standards for ubiquitous user interfacing, may slow progress not only in the use of information itself but also in the other industrial, commercial, and service sectors that will be increasingly dependent on information processing and information flows.

The shortcomings in United States policy in this regard arise for several related and fundamental reasons. Both the divestiture of AT&T and FCC policies assume that competition is the best means for bringing about socially desirable results. The local exchange carriers are required to facilitate competition among interchange carriers by providing equal access to their regulated services, including CEI or ONA, for whatever enhanced services the interexchange carriers may offer.

Current policy requires that each element of local exchange service be unbundled and priced at or above its own costs, including some allocations of common costs in the latter. Unbundling is actually at odds with the ISDN concept, where the integrated use of information among services is the most important aspect of the new arrangements. It is also difficult to see how the economies of scope inherent in ISDN are to be realized when unbundling and tariffs based on fully distributed cost are required.

Beginning with the 1956 Consent Decree and continuing through *CI-I*, *CI-II*, the BOC divestiture, and even now under the *CI-III* policies and the modified MFJ, distinctions have been drawn between basic and enhanced services. The BOCs will now be permitted—indeed, perhaps encouraged—by the FCC to develop capabilities in the transmission of data for utilization by defined user groups, but they will continue to be handicapped in offering what are defined as enhanced services to the general public. A distinction between regulated and unregulated services must be made, but it cannot be based on technical criteria. Attempts to do so deny the use of new technology in the regulated areas. Drawing distinctions on the basis of the historically derived legal criteria now in existence is equally fruitless. The only proper way to distinguish between regulated and unregulated services is through a consideration of a variety of pertinent market facts and social infrastructural needs.

There is no obvious way to organize efficient nationwide enhanced, full service networks in the United States. The regulations governing access and pricing severely limit the ability of the BOCs to participate effectively. The interexchange and other non-BOC carriers have fewer restrictions, but they lack the local distribution facilities necessary for a mass subscriber base. Distribution by the BOCs could be obtained as a tariffed service, but an arrangement external to the BOCs would be needed to supply terminal equipment and to price that equipment and subscriber use in an efficient and attractive way. Moreover, with equal access, CEI, and ONA requirements, great ingenuity will be required of the enterprise undertaking the subsidization of subscriber access to prevent others from "cream skimming" the profitable parts of enhanced service network operations. The arrangements for cost and revenue sharing and the technical arrangements for switching and local distribution are just too complex to imagine the private undertaking of such a network with current structural and regulatory conditions.

Another way of looking at the United States situation—and this is the way many do now see it—is to maintain that there is inadequate overall demand for enhanced services to justify a nationwide, multi-service network. This view is currently correct, but it is correct only because the present and foreseeable size and scope of such networks in the United States are limited by the structural and regulatory milieu. With the costs and services feasible in that environment, rates would be high, and service offerings would be sparse; there is little likelihood of growth. Most of the general public will not soon experience most enhanced services. With appropriate pricing for subscribers, information-providers, and advertisers, however, demand would be self-generating as the networks developed. This is, of course, just the story of telephone service itself but in a bit more complicated scenario. If innovations in telecommunications, as in other areas, were held back because of the lack of preexisting, unfilled consumer demand, few innovations would indeed occur.

The telecommunications policies that have developed in the United States during the past two decades will not result in intolerable inefficiencies in plain old telephone service. The big problems will emerge in connection with new telecommunications technologies. If the policies continue to insist and enlarge on competitive solutions, including competitive solutions to problems of standardization, and if the services and pricing policies of local exchange carriers continue to be restricted as they now are, a public network for new services operating on common carrier principles for the benefit of the nation at large will not become available.

Putting AT&T back together again is not the answer. We must, nevertheless, appreciate that proposals for various forms of integrated service offerings may rebound to the public benefit. We need recognize, too, that competition and efficiency are incompatible in many telecommunications services, particularly when the concept of efficiency pays proper attention to the bestowing of benefits to the general public.

Notes

1. Faulhaber (1987, p. xvi).

2. Federal Communications Act, 47 U.S.C. para. 151.

3. AT&T's rates for MTS and private line services encouraged entry by the SCCs for ordinary voice services as well as for data services.

4. These restrictions were very broad, limiting both the provision of information to subscribers and technical changes to the physical signals which contain the information. They applied even if those changes were transparent to the subscriber. For example, a BOC could not deliver a signal sent by a Wang personal computer to an Apple computer even if the carrier changed only the technical characteristics of the transmission so that the owner of the Apple did not need to own translating devices. And the restriction applied even if the translation merely permitted the Apple owner to display the same information that was typed by the Wang owner.

5. As used here, ISDN refers to the integrated use of digitized information among several services. For example, information such as speech text, data, and pictures are transmitted simultaneously and where desired, for coordinated use on a single line. ISDN includes both broadband and narrowband services, although discussions of longer term developments stress switched broadband services carried at high bit rates on optical fibers.

6. Notice of Inquiry, 94 FCC 2d 1289, at 1305. For discussion, see Frieden (1986).

7. Commissioner Patricia Diaz Dennis, as quoted in *Telecommunication Reports* 54 (no. 2, January 18, 1988): 5.

8. "Report and Recommendations of the United States Concerning the Line of Business Restrictions Imposed on the Bell Operating Companies by the Modification of Final Judgment," *U.S. v. Western Electric Co.*, Civil Action No. 82-0192 (February 1, 1987). The DOJ position is based in large measure on *The Geodesic Network: 1987 Report on Competition in the Telephone Industry*, prepared by Peter Huber, a consultant to DOJ.

9. "Report and Recommendations. . .," loc. at., pp. 106-107, 133.

10. See remarks of Commissioner Patricia Diaz Dennis, as reported in *Telecommunications Reports* 53 (no. 50, December 14, 1987): 10.

11. In the Matter of Pacific Bell and Nevada Bell Plan for Voice Mail Services, Memorandum Opinion and Order, FCC 88-11 (Released: February 18, 1988).

12. The FCC has not preempted the states in the matter of rates for intrastate enhanced services, but has indicated that it may condition approval of the offering of such services on the acceptability of rates and other conditions imposed by state regulations.

13. A 1987 Bell Atlantic proposal that incorporated lower, cost-based charges for the carriers' own "short loop" connections were amended prior to its gaining approval for its CEI plans. See Bell Atlantic Telephone Companies' Offer of Comparably Efficient Interconnection to Enhanced Service Providers, Memorandum Opinion and Order, FCC 88-12 (Released: February 18, 1988).

14. For theoretical detail, see Faulhaber and Levinson (1981).

15. The FCC calls this approach the "net revenue test." See In the Matter of Guidelines for Dominant Carriers' MTS Rates and Rate Structure Plans, Memorandum Opinion and Order (Released: October 17, 1985).

16. With non-zero cross-demand elasticities, the inverse elasticity rule becomes:

$$\frac{p_i - mc_i}{p_i} = k\left(\frac{1}{z_i} + \sum_{j=1}^{m} r_{ji} e_{ji}\right),$$

Where p_i is the price i^{th} service, mc is its marginal cost, z_i is the own-elasticity of demand for the ith service, r_{ji} is the ratio of revenue from sales of the jth service to revenue from sales of the ith service, and e_{ji} is the cross-flexibility of demand between the jth and i^{th} services. The latter measures the percentage change in the market-clearing price of the jth service that results from a 1 percent change in the price of the ith service.

In the case of complementary relations between i^{th} and j^{th} services, a lowering of p_i raises the market-clearing p_j. Since e_{ji} is negative, the optimal p_i-mc_i ratio is lower than would be the case with zero cross-elasticities. A $p_i < mc_i$ may even be optimal (and profit-maximizing). Note, however, that as r_{ji} increases (i.e., as penetration rates rise for the jth service), a more than proportional (absolute) decrease in e_{ji} tends to occur, thus mitigating the incentive to maintain the low p_i to add to revenues from the jth service.

17. See Baumol, Koehn, and Willig (1987).

18. For an interesting comment along these lines, see Horwitt (1987). An opposing view appears in Lera (1986).

References

Baumol, W.J., M.F. Koehn, and R.D. Willig. 1987. "How Arbitrary is 'Arbitrary'?—Or, Toward the Deserved Demise of Full Cost Allocation." *Public Utilities Fortnightly* (September 3).

Faulhaber, Gerald R., 1987. *Telecommunications in Turmoil: Technology and Public Policy*. Cambridge, MA: Ballinger.

Faulhaber, Gerald R. and S.B. Levinson. 1981. "Subsidy-Free Prices and Anonymous Equity." *American Economic Review* 71 (no. 5, December).

Frieden, Robert M. 1986. "Making ISDN Work: Practical Policy Considerations." *Telematics* 3 (no. 1, February).

Horwitt, Elisabeth. 1987. "Ma Bell, We Miss You." *Computerworld* 21 (no. 2, January 12): 29.

Lera, Emilio. 1986. "Uncertain Prospects for ISDN." *Telecommunications Policy* (December): 313-324.

8

CONTESTABLE MARKETS AND TELECOMMUNICATIONS
Richard E. Simnett

Introduction

This chapter[1] provides an economic analysis of the post-divestiture inter-LATA (Local Access and Transport Areas) telephone business. The analysis shows that the industry is not now competitive in its structure, and is unlikely to become more so. Competitive industries used to be defined in terms of the number of competing firms and their relative sizes. However, Baumol and others have introduced and refined the concept of contestability. An industry might have only one participating firm, but if the market were contestable there would be no adverse impact on economic efficiency. In an economically efficient industry, no firm can long sustain prices greater than economic costs. The number and relative sizes of firms does not matter. If the marginal cost structures of actual and potential competitors are similar, and sunk costs are unimportant, then new entry or the expansion of existing firms will destroy the incentives for any firm to set prices above competitive levels.

The analysis shows that the firms in the United States interLATA telephone business do not have similar cost structures. This means that prices could be set above economic costs and rents might be earned if the industry were deregulated. The necessary condition for this is the continuation of the present regulatory rules governing the behavior of participating firms. The argument does not depend upon significant network scale or scope economies among the long distance carriers.

Under present arrangements only users with very large demands can realize the benefits of competition among carriers. These customers have had the opportunity to adopt private networks for more than 20 years, so the change in their circumstances may not be very great.

The chapter begins with a brief outline of the changes in the telephone industry created by the divestiture of the Bell Operating Companies and some telephone assets by AT&T. The new regulatory regime created by this action is described. User and carrier options created by these events are then analyzed and compared to the ideals of contestability or competition. The differences between the ideal and the reality suggest the infeasibility of thoroughgoing competition.

The Restructuring of the Industry at Divestiture

On January 1, 1984, the formerly AT&T-owned telephone network was split into two segments with eight owners. Seven of these owners are the divested regional holding companies whose Bell Operating Companies (BOCs) are limited to the provision of local and long-distance telephone service within geographic areas (LATAs). The BOCs also provide connections between end-users and interLATA carriers. These are now called Access services and provided under tariff. Before divestiture the revenues from the AT&T interstate services were divided among the joint providers of the service based on agreed rules. The Other Common Carriers (OCCs) paid for access and did not participate in the division of revenues process. AT&T is now a smaller company which retained the manufacturing and interLATA telephone businesses. AT&T also retained the terminal equipment sales, leasing, and manufacturing business. The regional holding companies have been allowed to enter the retailing stage of this business through new corporate subsidiaries, separate from their BOCs.

Post-Divestiture Regulation

In general, the BOCs are subject to rate regulation by the Federal Communications Commission (FCC) and the public utility commissions of the states in which they operate. Their activities are also subject to the restrictions contained in the antitrust decree which broke up the Bell System. This decree is enforced by the Department of Justice and the Federal courts. It is this regulatory regime that has governed the post-divestiture evolution of the industry.

The popular view at the time of divestiture was that the interLATA business would soon become, or was already, workably competitive. Rate-of-return regulation for interLATA carriers (AT&T was the only fully regulated carrier) was no longer necessary and was expected to be abandoned. However, AT&T is still subject to FCC regulation of its interstate business. The rate of return limitations are still being enforced and are binding AT&T (i.e., AT&T has approached its rate-of-return ceilings and been obliged to reduce rates). The OCCs are not subject to rate-of-return regulation, but are forced by the market to follow AT&T's actions. The FCC thus controls the interstate tariff structures and rate levels of all carriers, whether directly or indirectly.[2]

At present the FCC has two regulatory regimes for carriers. The basic regime is a fully distributed cost (FDC) standard applying the rate of return ceiling to services or groups of services. The second regime allows regulated firms some relaxation of the FDC rules if sufficient cause is shown. The local exchange companies have not been very successful in getting the full cost standard relaxed. Under the FDC standard, each service, or in the extreme case, each rate element (i.e., any item with a price attached), is priced so that it demonstrably covers its direct costs and its share of all joint and common costs. The allocations are performed according to an FCC-approved cost allocation manual.

AT&T can now justify new optional services or rate plans if it can show that they will increase corporate earnings over a reasonable time horizon. The basic idea behind this relaxation is a sound one from the efficiency standpoint. If the new service or rate plan is optional to customers, they cannot be worse off than if the service were not available. If it raises AT&T's earnings in the short run it is not predatory, so AT&T's efficient rivals need no regulatory protection. This allowed AT&T to use marginal rather than average costing and was a significant change of policy. Much less detailed information has to be made public now, and AT&T can operate more flexibly than before.

AT&T's principal rivals, the other common carriers such as MCI and Sprint, are effectively unregulated. They may change tariffs without any case being made. They may also provide service without tariffs if they so choose, although an FCC attempt to force them not to file tariffs was unsuccessful. There are also private carriers, who need no regulatory permission to provide service.

Some states have moved from rate-of-return regulation to rely on the market, or on other rate adjustment criteria. The rest of the chapter will focus only on current federal regulatory rules.

Equal Access Regulatory Requirements

The economies of scale inherent in networking were thought, at divestiture, to have been exhausted or to be of no further economic significance. AT&T had asserted their significance in its defense to the antitrust case, but with its agreement to a consent decree, ceased to press the point. AT&T's rivals, the OCCs, held that they were more efficient than AT&T and could compete successfully, if given the same treatment as AT&T, in the long distance business.

The OCCs argued that their growth had been impeded by their inability to obtain access to end-users that was technically equal to the access which AT&T enjoyed. Users of OCC Message Telephone Service (MTS)-like services had to dial more digits per call than AT&T users, had to use more costly touch-tone telephone service, and allegedly received noisier connections. The antitrust decree contained explicit timetables binding the BOCs to offer equal access services to all carriers, and to offer their end-user customers the chance to choose a carrier as their primary interLATA carrier.

Let us look at equal access from the end-user point of view. After the conversion to equal access, an end-user dialing 1+415-567-8900 will be connected to his chosen carrier, while in the old arrangement all 1+ calls would have been retained in the Bell/AT&T network. End-users in equal access exchanges can reach other carriers by dialing a carrier selection code 10XXX+ if the carrier is willing to accept such "casual" calling. In unconverted areas, the OCC user first dials a seven-digit number for his carrier. After a second dial tone he dials his personal identification code and the number being called. This process may take as many as 12 digits more than is needed for AT&T (and for all carriers in equal access areas). It also takes longer to establish calls, as the extra dialing stages take time. The carrier has to check the customer identification code to bill for the call. This adds to the setup time, too.[3]

In effect, the equal access requirements allow the telephone industry to offer end-users similar service to the predivestiture Bell System. The difference is that more carriers can be involved, and users can choose whichever long distance carrier they wish, without a change in dialing. If the analysis in this chapter is correct, this is the single most important policy driving the future course of competition in the industry. Competition between carriers is for a (single line) customer's account. Once a single line customer has presubscribed to a carrier, all his interLATA calls are routed to that carrier, unless he dials a carrier code with the call to override the presubscription. Customers do not need to make any further decisions after they have decided on a carrier.

Rate Regulation of Access Charging

The FCC regulates interstate access charges and has continued the subsidy from long distance to local service, albeit at reduced levels. The vehicle for doing this has been a Carrier Common Line (CCL) charge to the interLATA carriers for each minute of use of the access networks. This charge is wholly unrelated to economic costs, but is intended to raise a fixed sum (the residual, after deducting all the federal subscriber line revenues, of 25 percent of the fixed costs of local loops) each year. The charge is averaged across all local carriers.

The important feature of this arrangement is the use of per minute charges to recover a fixed cost. The more minutes of use there are, the lower the rate per minute will be. Any interLATA carrier can stimulate the market by reducing his charges for service. However, all interLATA carriers benefit from the CCL rate reduction that the stimulation entails. Since AT&T has the largest share of the market, roughly 75-80 percent according to press reports, it will capture most of the value of the per minute cost reduction and can plan accordingly. It is also reasonable for AT&T to expect its rivals to follow any reduction in its rates, so AT&T may assume that its market share will be unchanged by a price reduction. AT&T would then not include any of this subsidy component in its marginal cost for access. Its average costs do include the subsidy flow, but in general AT&T will pay additional subsidy amounts in only two circumstances. The first is if it increases its overall share of the market. Its share of the total subsidy will then rise accordingly. The second is during the interval between access rate revisions, when volume growth leads to increased subsidy flows. AT&T can press for speedy rate action if it can make the case that the subsidy flow is larger than it need be.

Contrast this with AT&T's smaller rivals' position. Any of these firms can make a rate reduction, but cannot be sure that AT&T will follow it. An OCC's ability to stimulate the whole industry is very limited. Most of the access rate reduction would be received by AT&T, and so an OCC's marginal access cost is close to the tariff rates. The CCL rate currently stands at around 4 cents per conversation minute. AT&T's expected marginal cost would be less than 1 cent per minute, if its share were 80 percent and if it assumed that OCC volumes would not change.[4]

Inter exchange carriers (IXCs) must also pay traffic-sensitive access charges, probably equal to about 5 cents per conversation minute. The same effect occurs here, too. Local exchange carrier (LEC) regulation sets limits to these rates, and, although the revenue requirement does vary with usage, the marginal revenue requirement per minute is lower than the tariff rates. I have seen no published estimates of this effect, but it is reasonable to suppose that AT&T's marginal cost is at most half the tariff rate, or 2.5 cents per minute.

The OCCs receive access charge discounts where they are obliged to use unequal access. As exchanges are converted to equal access this discount will disappear. Before divestiture it was officially a 55 percent discount from AT&T's equivalent interstate subsidy flow. In practice it may have been higher, since OCC use per flat-rated access line may have been higher than assumed in the rate-setting process. Currently, if 80 percent of their minutes come from areas where equal access conversions have been made, the effective OCC discount stands at about 11 percent.

The OCCs thus pay about 3.6 cents per conversation minute for the CCL charge and about 4.4 cents for traffic-sensitive access rates. Their marginal and average costs are similar.

Comparing AT&T with its rivals, AT&T has marginal access costs of 2.5-3.3 cents per conversation minute, depending on its assumptions about its rivals' behavior. AT&T's average access costs are around 9 cents per conversation minute. The OCCs have marginal and average access costs of around 8 cents. Thus AT&T has a marginal cost advantage of about 4.5 to 5.5 cents and an overall cost handicap of about 1 cent per minute. These differences between AT&T's costs and the smaller carriers' costs have been reduced since 1984, as the total carrier common line charge has been reduced. More of the cost is being borne by flat rate end user charges, and equal access is continuing to spread.

InterLATA Carriers' Options

In this section of the chapter, I will describe the basic options open to an actual or potential interLATA carrier. The differences between AT&T's options and those of largest of its rivals' are significant. The differences between larger OCCs and potential entrants are also significant. Regulatory policies cause much of the asymmetry between the carriers. The options facing an interLATA carrier can be briefly summarized as the answers to the questions "Where?," "What?," and "To whom?" I will deal with each of these in turn. The analysis focuses on demand and marketing cost considerations, although network design options will also affect the carriers' choices.
Where?

Where should an IXC offer service? AT&T offers service ubiquitously, "from anywhere to anywhere" within the mainland United States. This is an historical accident, derived from its former regulated monopoly status and the policy of universal service. AT&T has connections with all exchange carriers. The principal OCCs provide service to and from most urban areas in the United States over their own or leased facilities. They have not provided service from much of the rural United States, and so in some states there has been little competition between carriers.

The OCCs. The OCC's decisions are driven by traffic patterns and costs. Two kinds of costs are directly relevant. One is the cost of providing service, and the other is the cost of obtaining and retaining customers. The costs of providing service are access costs and network costs. Network costs are governed by the construction and maintenance expenditures necessary for the satisfactory handling of the anticipated traffic volumes. As is well known, there are economies of scale in trunking, so high capacity routes are more efficient than low capacity routes in carrying calls. In general, high capacity routes are also cheaper to construct and maintain (per circuit) than low capacity routes. This is because there is a substantial fixed cost involved with any construction project, regardless of the capacity installed. High capacity technologies (e.g., fiber optics) may also be inherently cheaper per circuit than low capacity (e.g., copper cables).

The costs of obtaining business also vary with the areas served. More efficient advertising media are available in denser areas. Other sales vehicles may offer similar savings in high density areas. Telemarketing may be cheaper, and representatives' traveling time between calls may be less, for example.

If we assume that telephone usage into and out of an area is dependent on the population and the concentration of business there, then both the economics of network design and the costs of obtaining customers drive an entrant to serve the highest density areas first. The first routes constructed should connect high density areas with each other. Low density areas lying along these routes might be served too, as a byproduct.

Some OCCs had deployed networks between major urban areas before the January 1984 Bell System divestiture. Since then the principal OCCs (MCI and US Sprint) have added fiber optic systems on some of these routes, as has AT&T. New entrants have also constructed fiber networks, usually along rights of way between major cities.[5] As time passes, the major OCCs are installing their own plant to replace the circuits they leased from AT&T. The AT&T circuits had been used to provide service to more locations, more quickly, and with less investment than new construction would have permitted.

The answers to the question "Where?" thus depend on the carrier asking the question. Major OCCs are filling in their networks, both in geographic coverage and by building their own plant. New entrants have generally sought high density areas and accessible rights of way. OCC coverage is still not universal, but the principal cities are served by many carriers. (At the time of writing, hundreds of carrier codes or 10XXXs have been issued.)

AT&T. AT&T already provides service ubiquitously. For AT&T the question can refer only to the deployment schedule for new technologies and services. AT&T has gradually expanded its digital network service availability, for example, but has committed to a nationwide digital network. AT&T has not announced its ultimate plans for Integrated Services Digital Network (ISDN) in detail, but has begun a limited service introduction. However, AT&T is the largest carrier by far and so should have the best information on market demands by area. It can build to actual needs.

What?

Carriers must decide what services to offer. The decision depends on the anticipated returns, and so on both cost and demand conditions. There are two basic kinds of telephone service offering. These are switched message services packaged in various ways, with more or fewer features; and private line services, where circuits are leased to customers on a dedicated basis for a period of time.

Private line services are of interest only to a small subset of the public, generally large businesses or public organizations with special needs. For this market, the divestiture and equal access policies have not really changed anything, except the service provisioning process. Firms have been allowed to provide their own facilities for many years, and the initial thrust of the OCCs was to serve this market. New entrants are still pursuing this strategy, it appears, by targeting their sales efforts for fiber optic capacity at private line customers first. This is also the cheapest service for an entrant to provide, because the carrier avoids the investment in switches and in the complex billing and recording systems needed to provide switched telephone services.

Switched telephone service is used by almost everyone. Many different pricing and feature packages are provided by the existing vendors. In this section, the focus is on one particular characteristic of AT&T's services. AT&T offers terminating ubiquity to its customers. An AT&T call can be made to anywhere in the United States and to nearly everywhere else.

An OCC or a new entrant must decide whether to match AT&T's ubiquity. If he decides to restrict service to that set of places actually on his network, then his service is perceived as inferior to AT&T's, and perhaps as unfit for presubscription. If he decides to offer terminating ubiquity, then he is almost forced to resell AT&T's switched services. This is likely to mean a financial loss on off-network calling. The carrier must pay AT&T's tariff rates, and pay access charges at the originating LATA, too. He must price to compete with AT&T's tariff rates. AT&T's switched services offer volume discounts, but these are not designed to allow profitable resale. Service will be somewhat degraded too. When an AT&T switched service is resold, the reseller's own call set up process and its time must be added to AT&T's. The end user may not notice the increased delay or noise, but the carrier cannot truthfully claim to equal AT&T's service in these respects.

There has been a market response to this problem. A new class of carrier has emerged, the carriers' carrier. These firms construct networks and lease capacity to carriers or private customers who want relatively high capacity for a long time, but who could not individually justify construction on the routes in question. They thus provide a bulk private line service under contract, at lower rates than AT&T's normal tariff. The carriers' carriers extended non-AT&T facilities further than would otherwise have been possible. Nevertheless, many areas remain unserved by non-AT&T facilities, presumably because the anticipated revenues are insufficient. AT&T has responded to the carriers' carriers with its own high capacity offering (45 megabits per second, with rates dependent on the length of the contract) on some dense routes.

Summarizing the argument so far, the entrant must decide where to place his investments and what type of service to offer. Most of the traffic and revenue potential can be reached by linking major cities with each other and offering switched services. Switched services account for about 85 percent of AT&T's interstate revenues, according to its reports to the FCC. Rival carriers seeking to become or remain major players in this industry must compete with AT&T's switched services. AT&T's services are costly for a smaller rival to match, in at least one dimension of perceived quality—that is, the ability to call anywhere. The private line business is the easiest to enter, but may not provide a challenger with enough revenue to prosper.
To Whom?

Entrant Firms' Options. The entrant firm must choose the type of customers he seeks. Naturally every carrier would prefer to have customers who paid promptly, used high margin services, and spent enough to cover the costs of sales activity and account support. These characteristics are most likely to be found among business customers, for the business day rates are highest and there are more large business users than large residential users.

Business users do not use service outside normal working hours very much. If a carrier only attracts their business, his network will stand idle for the rest of the time. Residence customers have a complementary load pattern, with most calls in the evening or night and weekend periods. They are an attractive market to serve if load balancing can be made to pay.

Thus, a carrier would ideally like to attract high revenue business customers and balance his network load with a number of larger residence customers. The entrant, however, does not know who these desirable customers are. He must attract their business, without also attracting undesirable customers who spend too little or cost too much to serve. The tools available for this customer selection process are targeted marketing activities and price discrimination.

The economic literature on multipart tariffs[6] shows how they can be used to induce self-selection by customers with particular characteristics. An entrant must try to design services and rate structures that dominate other carriers' offerings for the particular class of customer he wants. In effect, each carrier hopes to provide some part of the optimal outlay/tariff choice schedule a user might compile. This is now no easy task. It was much easier with the predivestiture AT&T rate structure.

AT&T, before divestiture, had rates designed to encourage economically efficient use of its monopoly network. Wide Area Telephone Service (WATS) was AT&T's only volume discount service, and gave customers substantial volume discounts for high average use per line. Customers had reason to manage their traffic, by loading lines sequentially and using ordinary MTS for less heavily loaded overflow lines. In this way the average use per WATS line could be kept high. Other carriers had the opportunity to provide part of a customer's service while leaving most of it with AT&T.

There were two basic ways of doing this. Since large customers already managed traffic, a carrier could offer a non-ubiquitous service at low rates on routes where he had enough capacity. The customer would separate traffic into calls for this service and the rest. This approach would take traffic from AT&T based on geography, and is one of the few practical ways for a carrier with a very limited network to get started.

The other way to attract part of a customer's business is to offer a rate plan that beats AT&T's offerings, either for some part of the high volume per line WATS traffic or the low volume per line overflow traffic. Even before divestiture and equal access, the OCCs could offer WATS-like services apparently equivalent to AT&T's. Private line connections were used between the customer and the OCC switch. This way the carrier identifies the caller by the line used, and only one dial tone is needed. Competing for overflow traffic would be more difficult. WATS-like rates could be designed to do so, but, if only light line loadings were sought, the private line connection would be too expensive. Without equal access, the MTS-like service required the customer to dial additional digits. The carriers made a virtue of this necessity, by turning it into a vehicle for users to obtain costs allocated to different internal accounts. This is a feature which AT&T is only now beginning to offer.

What has changed since the divestiture? AT&T has restructured its services, as we shall see below. In general the restructuring makes customer traffic management less rewarding, and so may make it less likely for customers to mix services and vendors. The entrant's problem is still to take all or part of a customer's business, and the services offered are of the same kind. Now, though, traffic management is something the customer is not forced to do by AT&T's tariff structure.

AT&T's Options. AT&T, by contrast, serves nearly all customers already. Its decisions are constrained by this, and by regulation. AT&T cannot easily offer particular customers better terms if needed to retain business. It must offer the same terms to all, and almost any change in rates or services will hurt AT&T's returns from some individual customer. AT&T can respond to the loss of some broad class of business, but must always balance the reprice effects of its response with the effects in stemming competitive losses.

AT&T's response to the post-divestiture environment has been interesting. It has not reduced its margins in any general fashion.[7] However, it has introduced a series of new switched services for larger end users. These are all characterized by a fixed monthly charge and linear usage charges. That is, they are a classic series of two part tariffs whose envelope, in a perfect market, would be equivalent to a multipart tariff with a volume discount.

AT&T's predivestiture offering for these users, WATS, had a per line fixed monthly charge and a volume discount based on the average use per line per month. WATS offered users the incentive to level their offered load, because to earn the greatest discounts the average line had to be intensively used. This was only possible if the least used WATS line was itself heavily used, but this meant that the customer's peak-hour WATS use could not be much greater than his off-peak use. The WATS tariff thus encouraged users to place peak-hour calls at the higher MTS rates, and, in effect, provided a very load-sensitive marginal price for calls to this class of users. When other carriers entered the switched services market, they could compete for the overflow traffic from WATS lines. The target customers were already used to traffic management and prepared to overflow from the OCC's service to AT&T's MTS service as a last resort. The possible deficiencies of the OCC service were thus less important.

AT&T's new services (the Pro-America plans and Megacom) do not encourage overflow. Users can derive little benefit by managing their traffic. AT&T's fixed charge does not depend on the number of lines in service, and the usage charges do not drop with volume per line. Overflow to MTS or an OCC is thus no longer necessary. The customer can save by choosing the correct AT&T two-part tariff for his expected call volume. An entrant can make an attractive offer if he can become the user's primary carrier and offer volume discounts, but the overflow traffic market should be shrinking. An entrant can also offer a WATS-like service with volume per line discounts, so that he takes part of the customer's base load, and AT&T takes the overflow traffic.

AT&T has also reduced the benefit to users from using WATS lines intensively, so even WATS customers have less incentive to overflow to other carriers' services. The effective peak load sensitivity of pricing has also been reduced, so it is likely that network demand is somewhat less efficiently handled now than before.

To summarize, since 1984 AT&T and other carriers have, by their pricing and service introduction initiatives, sought to change the nature of competition in the multiline customer market. The user is less likely to find it advantageous to mix carriers serving a single location and more likely to decide on a single vendor. This is so even though equal access and presubscription had little effect in this market, and users were previously dealing with several carriers.[8]

Customers' Options

In an equal access environment the customer is asked to presubscribe to a carrier, who will receive all interLATA calls. However, if the customer has more than one access line, he can select more than one carrier. Carriers also offer many services which use access lines dedicated to that carrier. For services such as these, equal access is unimportant, because equal access only changed the way calls were handled in local exchange networks routing them to carriers. With two or more lines, then, the user can assign calls to carriers, in just the same way that users managed AT&T WATS and MTS services in the monopoly period. As discussed above, the carriers have introduced a number of services whose logic eliminates the need for customers to manage calls this way. Even large users might then make decisions primarily between carriers and service packages, rather than finding an optimal mix of carriers and services.

If the user is actually to optimize his call management, he needs to understand the carriers' tariffs and their structures, and his own usage patterns. Implementing the results of the analysis, if multiple vendors or services are chosen, involves either dialing rules for callers or software control of outward calling. This kind of call management would be unusual among small multiline customers and, in any event, is expensive. The user needs a private switch (or an equivalent service offering such as Centrex) with call control capabilities, and the information to use it properly. Every time a carrier changes rates, the user's analysis should be repeated to ensure optimal management. This should also be done every time the user's demand changes. Such variations as seasonal, monthly, or random changes in points called, call durations, call volumes, or time of day patterns all affect the optimum set of services. If a customer becomes aware of a new carrier offering, he may be uncertain about the ubiquity or quality of service he would actually experience and probably somewhat unsure about the actual cost of the service.

The appropriate framework in which to model a customer's decision making is choice under uncertainty, with substantial transaction costs. Customers are uncertain about their own future demand patterns and about the carriers' future offerings and prices. The fixed costs of seeking out and implementing an optimal solution must be recovered from an uncertain stream of savings, whose expected value will shrink with rate differentials.

User uncertainty of this kind has interesting consequences. AT&T, and to a lesser extent the other established carriers, are reasonably safe choices for many customers. Users who are satisfied with any of the vendors they currently use have little incentive to search for alternatives. Carrier price differences have narrowed enormously, and some studies have shown that AT&T is no longer the highest price carrier in all cases. They are continuing to narrow, so the user has steadily less reason to consider changing vendors. The number of vendors has risen, and new entrants have a difficult task if they are to stand out. US Sprint has sought to address this problem by new customer discounts, advertised as 10% off for a year. If this is enough to attract the customer, inertia and relatively small price differences may be enough to retain him.

AT&T's two-part tariff offerings can be an attractive solution. If they are close to the best service combination in monthly calling cost, the customer can avoid the need for sophisticated call management and its associated costs. The cost of adapting to changes in demand is also reduced, for with these plans new dedicated access lines will no longer be needed.

The Performance of the Market

The market is made up of both buyers and sellers. In earlier sections each has been looked at separately. Now we will look at the way the market can be expected to function.

AT&T began with a strong position, as the incumbent carrier for most customers. It was widely expected that it would lose share very quickly to its rivals, but it seems to have done better than that. If the analysis in this chapter is correct, there are fundamental economic explanations for its success. AT&T has a marginal cost advantage over its rivals in two areas. Its marginal access costs are lower than theirs, and its cost of information should be less. It should therefore be able to target its new services and marketing efforts more effectively than entrants. AT&T has sought the marginal usage of its business customers. The WATS overflow market for OCC services should be shrinking, as AT&T's two-part tariffs take their place in the market. The residence market is also difficult for an entrant. Many customers place few calls, but, if they open accounts with carriers, the carrier will incur some fixed monthly cost per account. This includes the billing and collection costs and the cost of dealing with customer inquiries.

There are no data available to me on actual calling patterns by time of day, length of haul, or class of customer. However, using the published access tariff rates and reported minutes of use by state, I constructed a pseudo point-to-point demand matrix. This translates into a revenue and access cost matrix.

The results of the analysis show that an OCC cannot profitably serve demand in the night-weekend rate period. The retained revenue is approximately eight-tenths of a cent per minute, which is not enough to pay for expected billing and collection costs. (I assumed that the carrier would have to offer a discount from AT&T's rates of 10 percent and received discounted access.)

Evening service could be profitable. The retained revenues average about 4.5 cents per minute, which should cover the billing costs. However, AT&T offers a 15% discount plan in this rate period, so to attract larger residence users, an entrant might have to offer a substantial discount. Unfortunately, residence users are likely to use both the evening and night-weekend periods much more than the business day. If I assume that they use each period equally and make no daytime calls, then the retained revenue would average 2.65 cents per minute. Billing and collection cost about 1 cent per minute, according to AT&T filings, so the net contribution to the OCC's fixed costs is about 1.65 cents per minute. A customer would have to use more than an hour a month to yield $1 to the carrier. If there were any fixed account maintenance cost it would have to be recovered from this, and what is left over is the return to the carrier's marketing investments. AT&T filings put its cost of selling an optional service to an existing customer at between $50 and $150 per account, depending on the service. Since AT&T knows its own customers' usage, and the OCCs do not, OCC costs would be higher. The OCCs should also be less likely to attract only the desirable hour-plus users. Even if a $50 marketing outlay were enough to attract only the right kind of customer, the chances of recovering it and earning a return seem small. Customers are not gained once for all, and there is always some random churning of accounts as people move.

I conclude, therefore, that the residence market is not contestable. Entrants face high fixed and unrecoverable costs to gain market share. If an entrant later wished to withdraw from the market, he could not sell his account list and recover the money. The buyer could not earn a return, if he paid the cost of their original acquisition for the accounts.

The small business market may be similar. The cost of persuading a single line customer to presubscribe may be too much to recover from the expected revenues. Larger business users remain to be considered. It is often said that the largest few customers account for a grossly disproportionate share of telecommunications expenditures. These customers are worth competing for, and the OCCs do have some share of their business. AT&T has argued that this is sufficient to show that competition is strong enough to make regulation unnecessary. At the time, more than two years ago, it met an OCC rejoinder that, while the OCCs did indeed serve the largest customers, they only served 7 percent of their demand. Whatever the current figures may be, large users have been able to get their needs met privately, if need be, for many years, and equal access is almost completely irrelevant to them. The service most relevant to these customers may be point to point high capacity links, for their use in internal networks. This service does not require a vendor to provide a ubiquitous network, nor much carrier investment. Smaller multiline customers, who make up the WATS market, are also worthwhile for carriers to pursue. This was also true without equal access.

In conclusion, the applicability of contestability theory to the intercity telephone business seems to be limited. Most customers are not worth competing for, and those that are may make up 20-30 percent of the total revenue. It is not yet clear whether the business obtainable from very large customers will support carriers large enough to make forays into adjacent markets, and so keep the incumbents there reasonably efficient in pricing. If private lines are the key to large customers, switched services are necessary for the rest. A successful entrant serving large users might thus be unable to affect the performance of other markets, without substantial extra investment.

Notes

1. This chapter represents the views of its author, who is solely responsible for its contents. Nothing contained herein should be construed as the views of my employer, Bell Communications Research, Inc., or of any of its owners or clients.

2. The FCC has begun a proceeding to decide on its future regulation of telephone companies, including AT&T. Total deregulation is not being actively considered. Direct price regulation may be chosen instead of rate-of-return regulation. I do not speculate on the outcome of this proceeding in this chapter, nor on its possible consequences.

3. In some cases the carrier number will be 950-XXXX and the same across the country. This service may continue even where equal access conversion have been made, for it enables carriers without operators of their own to offer service to customers away from their principal phone. This serves the same need as AT&T's calling card and third-number billing services.

4. To calculate AT&T's marginal cost, use the equation below:

Tariff Rate = Revenue Requirement / Industry Minutes

or $\qquad$ $t = RR/(A+O)$

where A=AT&T's minutes and O=Other Carrier minutes. AT&T's bill equals (Tariff Rate) * (AT&T's minutes) or A*t. Differentiating A*t with respect to A yields:

$$d(At)/dA = t + A\, dt/dA$$
$$= t + A\,[-RR/(A+O)^2]$$
$$= t - A(t\,/\,(A+O)$$
$$= t\,[(O/(A+O)]$$

That is, AT&T's marginal cost of expansion is the tariffed access charges times its rivals' market share, or about one-fifth of the tariffed rate.

5. Electricity utilities have constructed fiber along their aerial high voltage grids, and these may not run between major cities. Modern power plants are often quite far from cities for environmental reasons.

6. For a thorough discussion see Brown and Sibley (1986).

7. There has been an average 30+ percent switched service rate reduction since 1984. This is not a reduction in AT&T's share of the revenue from a call. It is the flow through of access rate reductions by the local exchange carriers.

8. The case must not be overstated. The logic of the analysis suggests the outcome, but it will doubtless take some time for the market to respond fully. AT&T's two part tariffs for midsize business customers are not yet fully deployed. I have also ignored the possible improvement in service reliability overall if several carriers are used and the gains very large customers can realize by playing carriers off against one another.

Reference

Brown, Stephen J., and David S. Sibley. 1986. *The Theory of Public Utility Pricing*. New York: Cambridge University Press.

9

COMPETITION AND COOPERATION IN DEREGULATED BULK POWER MARKETS
Scott R. Herriott

A special feature in *Electrical World* (1988) has made it clear that the deregulation of electric power generation, previously considered by many to be merely an academic issue, is very much on the minds of utility executives. Most commentators address technical aspects of the issue, such as the interpretation of "avoided cost" under the Public Utility Regulatory Policies Act of 1978 (PURPA), qualifications for cogenerating facilities under PURPA, transmission access for cogenerators and independent power producers, and the structure of competitive bidding systems for bulk power supply. Only a few have pointed explicitly to the organizational issues in deregulation. Joskow and Schmalensee (1983), for example, expressed grave doubts that the initiation of competition in bulk power markets could accommodate, without loss of economic efficiency, the organized cooperation that is necessary for least-cost planning and operation. These doubts are echoed by Martinson and Loria (1987) and by Casazza (1988).

Why should competition and cooperation be incompatible? The intuitive answer is that competition may cause firms to withhold the information that must be shared for cooperative planning or, if they disclose such information, that it will engender anticompetitive collusion or other violations of antitrust law. In this chapter, we seek to understand these problems more precisely. We will describe the types of cooperation that occur in contemporary power pools and examine what information must be shared, among whom, and what incentives this creates, if any, for anticompetitive behavior. This approach is important. The "whom" under deregulation can mean something very different than it does under the present system of power pooling among vertically integrated utilities. Proposals for deregulation and competition in bulk power supply typically recognize that the unregulated segment of the industry should be legally separated from the regulated portions. Thus, deregulation may permit the disaggregation of the industry into generation, transmission, and distribution firms. With this in mind, we will identify the information that must be shared within or among these three segments of the industry and investigate the incentives created thereby.

In the first section of this chapter, we will review the forms of bulk power competition anticipated or proposed by observers of the electric power industry. Having understood the purposes of competition, we will examine the types of economic interdependence that engender cooperation among electric utilities. Then it will be possible to consider the formal organization of cooperative interdependence and to assess its compatibility with the requirements of competition. The concluding section of the chapter summarizes the results of this analysis.

Deregulation and Competition in the Electric Utility Industry

The Federal Energy Regulatory Commission (FERC) exercises authority over all rates and terms of wholesale power transactions. As an experiment in releasing market forces among existing utilities, it authorized the Western Systems Power Pool (WSPP) to begin a two-year term of operation that started in May 1987 (Kemp 1987). The WSPP experiment gives the participating utilities greater freedom in information exchange and in the pricing of several types of generation sales and transmission services.

While these bulk power market experiments give us a vision of how certain competitive forces might operate in bulk power markets, the principal span in the bridge to a deregulated generation segment of the industry was erected in PURPA. PURPA created a class of non-utility producers, cogeneration facilities meeting certain technical standards for qualification, that would be allowed to generate power at wholesale without the obligation to serve the public's retail needs. Moreover, under PURPA, the public utility having the obligation to serve is required to purchase the cogenerator's excess energy at the utility's avoided cost. The meaning of "avoided cost" is the subject of much debate, particularly for utilities having excess capacity, but the prices allowed for cogenerated energy have stimulated a response far greater than the originators of PURPA anticipated. PURPA-qualifying facilities are typically very small, but in principle they can be of any size. The Midland Cogeneration Project in Michigan will ultimately consist of 12 gas turbines having a total capacity of 1343 megawatts (*Public Utilities Fortnightly* 1987a).

Non-utility generators that do not qualify for PURPA cogeneration status may still produce power at wholesale under FERC, but not under state, regulation. Many utilities are signing long-term contracts with these independent power producers (IPPs) in lieu of constructing and operating capacity themselves (*Public Utilities Fortnightly* 1987b). The practice is not even new. Consumers Power Company has had relationships with IPPs for 60 years (*Public Utilities Fortnightly* 1987c).

Some utility companies are moving out of the generation business entirely. Tucson Electric Power Company divested a generation subsidiary, Alamito Company, that has been taken private and operates solely as a wholesale firm (Yokell and Violette 1988). The Public Service Company of New Mexico has likewise proposed to reorganize as a generating company freed from state regulation and a distribution company that will continue to be regulated by the state.

The logic of PURPA was to allow market forces to create cogenerators whose low-cost energy could displace the higher cost of utility-generated energy during intermediate and peak-load periods. With the admission of capital charges in the avoided cost paid to qualifying facilities, PURPA is using market forces to displace the additions to generating capacity that the utilities would otherwise have to build for themselves. In June 1987, FERC Chairman Martha Hesse gave a speech expressing interest in opening up the market for new generating capacity by using competitive bidding systems, and, in March 1988, she outlined a "Phase II" of the deregulation plan, focusing on flexible pricing in wholesale generation and transmission. Significantly, Hesse emphasizes the importance of a bidding scheme that allows "all players to compete fairly in the same arena" (Haman-Guild and Pfeffer 1987). Subsequent discussion has centered on the merits of allowing IPPs, as well as PURPA-qualifying facilities and even the utilities themselves, to enter the competitive bidding.

Technically, eligibility to bid for the provision of new generation capacity requires that the bidder ultimately obtain access to the transmission facilities that link the potential generator with the distribution market to be served. Utility executives consider open transmission access to be the thorniest problem associated with bulk power competition. The Federal Power Act gives the FERC only very limited statutory authority to mandate the wheeling of power over transmission lines (Burns 1987), but several state regulatory commissions have empowered cogenerators and IPPs with open access as part of the states' competitive bidding schemes (Meade 1987; Radford 1987; Howard and Westfall 1988).

The transmission issue in competitive bidding schemes pertains only to access by IPPs or PURPA-qualifying cogeneration facilities to the purchasing utility, possibly across the transmission lines of another utility. This is termed wholesale wheeling. A more vexing issue is retail wheeling, where a non-utility generator sells power to a retail customer, such as an industrial plant, over a utility's transmission network. These transactions make the wheeling utility, in effect, a common carrier of electric energy. Open access is vigorously opposed by utility executives who fear the degradation of system reliability and the loss of their best retail loads, but in Texas, where competitive bidding for new capacity is also in use, the Public Utilities Commission has authorized retail wheeling—renewable-resource PURPA-qualifying facilities under 10 MW can sell power to end users under contract even without commission approval (Meade 1987). Casazza (1988) speculates that the present movement toward competitive bidding for new power generation will eventually require some form of open access to the transmission grid and that third-party sales and retail wheeling will inevitably follow. Lookadoo (1987) argues that the same political forces that resulted in the FERC Order 436 opening access to transmission in the natural gas industry could put pressure on electric utilities to accommodate third-party transactions.

The deregulation of electric power generation is likely to take place slowly, and it will be inconsistent across the United States, as different state utility commissions experiment with alternative formulations. In the intermediate term, a hybrid system will probably arise in which independent power producers and traditional integrated utilities continue to construct and operate generating plants. If an independent generating segment evolves, and if utilities follow Tucson's example by spinning off generation assets, then a disaggregated structure may be the long-term result. If this is so, the progress of deregulation in electric power generation points toward a scenario envisioned by Joskow and Schmalensee (1983). The generation segment might be disaggregated from transmission and distribution entities and left to operate subject only to FERC regulation in the bulk power market. Distribution companies are likely to remain regulated by the states as public utilities having an obligation to serve their customers' needs for electricity. The transmission entity, as a natural monopoly, will remain regulated or exist as a public corporation and may or may not be integrated with the distribution segment.

In such an organization of the industry, it would be obvious what types of competition and cooperation involve transactions and information exchanges within and among the generation, transmission, and distribution segments. This is the scenario of deregulation in which we will investigate these issues. The vision of competition is rather straightforward. Generating firms are rivals for the service of end-users' and distribution firms' long-term capacity needs and, in all likelihood, compete in a spot market for immediate energy sales. The required cooperation is less clear.

Cooperative Interdependence in Bulk Power Markets

Cooperation among electric utilities can reduce the participants' operating and capital costs in many ways. Here we review the types of cooperation exhibited in power pools (FERC 1981) in order to assess the economic characteristics of the interdependence that engenders this cooperation. In the subsequent section we will consider the forms of contract and ownership that are needed to organize the participants in bulk power markets to realize these advantages.

Cooperation in power pools takes shape in economy energy transactions, unit commitment, coordinated maintenance, spinning and capacity reserve transactions, emergency energy exchanges, agreements on voltage regulation and the control of reactive power flows, joint ventures in generating plants and transmission lines, and joint capacity planning and diversity exchanges. We will examine the economic interdependence underlying each form of cooperation, paying particular attention to the location of the "cooperation" along the industry's value chain—generation, transmission, and distribution.

Economy Energy Transactions

An economy energy exchange is a spot-market transaction between generating firms that have disparate short-run marginal energy costs. The higher-cost firm decreases its output and takes power over a transmission line from the lower-cost firm that increases its output correspondingly (with an allowance for transmission losses). When line losses are small, the economic interdependence among the participants is that of a simple exchange economy. In a commodity market, trade is beneficial to the participants because of the diversity in their preferences and endowments. In the economy energy market, it is due to the diversity of marginal energy costs. All participants have an incentive to trade with each other until the diversity is exhausted (marginal costs are equalized). This is the condition of short-run cost minimization. The outcome of this *competitive* discretionary trading admits a *cooperative* interpretation as a Pareto-efficient Nash equilibrium (Herriott 1985a).

Economy energy transactions are complicated, however, by the fact that electric energy cannot be directed to flow along a contractual path between the seller and buyer. It flows, to some degree, over all pathways by which the buyer and seller are interconnected. This transmission over indirect routes is termed *loop flow* and complicates economy energy transactions because it alters line losses (positively or negatively) on systems other than those of the buyer and seller. Simple market contracting does not compensate other utilities for this externality. Market inefficiency results. To correct this, the utilities must jointly be party to an agreement by which members are compensated for induced loop flows, or they may rely on courts of law for adequate compensation (Burns 1987).

Unit Commitment

Cold generating units may require several hours of preheating before they can be called into service, so a generating unit must be committed in anticipation of its actual use. When one generating firm commits a unit for another, it is providing a service in the present moment. When the commitment is bundled with a promise to generate and transmit economy energy in the near term, a *future commodity* is being exchanged. Future commodity markets differ from present commodity markets only in terms of the contractual hazards to which the participants are exposed. A future commodity can be promised but not delivered. In the natural gas industry, for example, there have been cases where producers abrogated their 30-day futures contracts in order to sell the gas at a higher price on the spot (present) market. The buyers in these cases see little value to recourse in the courts under contract law, but they do remember which firms break their contracts. When the number of players in a market is not extremely large, reputational effects can develop and induce participants to fulfill their contractual obligations.

Coordinated Maintenance

Generating firms periodically need to shut down a unit for scheduled maintenance. Though the duration of maintenance may be small relative to the period of active usage, the firm must continue to generate power to meet its obligations to its customers. In the absence of coordinated maintenance, each generating firm in a region would have to maintain some excess capacity to meet these obligations, even if maintenance is scheduled in off-peak periods. When the generating firms in a region can schedule their maintainance at different times of the year, this diversity makes advantageous the emergence of a futures market in generating capacity. The economic characteristics of this market do not differ substantially from the futures market in unit commitment, though the time into the future for contracted delivery is likely to be greater in this case and the hazards of contractual nonperformance somewhat higher. Reputation for reliability and trustworthiness sustain this market.

Emergency Energy Exchanges

Due to the unpredictability of generation failures, and the obligation of generating firms to serve their distribution and retail customers with a high degree of reliability, generating firms must carry capacity in excess of their predicted needs. For some firms, this may mean having extra capacity equal to the size of their largest generating unit. A more conservative firm may prepare to cover outages in its two largest units. When generation outages are weakly correlated among the generating firms in a region, the firms can reduce their total requirement of reserve capacity while maintaining the same reliability of service, if they know they can call on increments of capacity from other firms should they experience an outage in excess of their owned reserve capacity. These transactions in emergency energy or *back-up power* are not spot (present) market or futures market transactions. They are exchanges of a *contingent commodity*, a promise to deliver the commodity contingent upon the occurrence of some specific event (the outage). Markets for contingent commodities can exist just as spot and futures markets can, though they have additional hazards.

Contingent-commodity markets allocate risk. Insurance markets are a familiar example. Essentially the participants in emergency energy exchanging constitute a mutual insurance pool. These contingent commodity transactions are subject to the contractual hazards of futures markets—nonperformance at the contracted time—which reputation mollifies. In addition, insurance markets are subject to problems of adverse selection and moral hazard. Adverse selection is encountered by insurance firms whose policies, with rates based on population averages, are accepted only by the high-risk portion of the population. The process by which people select policies adversely affects the profitability of the insurance firm unless the firm can either directly observe the inherent risk of the prospective policyholder (and charge suitable rates) or cause the general population to self-select among a class of policies (by offering different levels of deductible and co-insurance rates). Moral hazard occurs when the insured, having obtained insurance, takes greater risks than he would have previously. Utilities that tend to "lean on the pool" (FERC 1981) by not investing sufficiently in the maintenance of generating units, exhibit this problematic behavior.

Spinning and Capacity Reserve Transactions

When generating firms in a pool reduce their total capacity requirements under emergency energy agreements, they often allocate the *deductible* by requiring all participants to maintain a capacity reserve of some percentage in excess of their demand. Firms that do not have this capacity may obtain it contractually from firms that have excess. *Spinning reserve* is the capacity available on units that are already running synchronized and are producing power or ready to do so at a moment's notice. It is used to meet unexpected changes in demand and to reduce the immediate impact of generation outages. *Capacity reserve* is a firm's excess over the expected peak demand of a year and is used as a back-up in the event of longer-term generator outages. For these transactions, the buyer often agrees to pay the capital and energy charge on a specific generating unit for a specific period of time (a few months to a few years). The capacity under contract is then counted toward the buyer's requirement. This, like the cases of unit commitment and scheduled maintenance, is a transaction in a future commodity.

Voltage Regulation

Electric power may appear to be a commodity, but is is actually differentiable in many ways. The reliability or interruptibility with which it is received by a user, the voltage level at which it is taken, its frequency and time of use are used to differentiate power. There is also a dimension of quality evident in the voltage profile of a particular generator. High-frequency components in the voltage and brief spikes in the voltage level can cause trouble in communications networks and harm to sensitive computing equipment. Irregularities in the voltage profile of a generator are dampened at greater distances from their source, but they still constitute a negative externality that one generator can produce in the interconnected network. Consequently, standards for voltage regulation are implemented by automatic excitation control systems in generators, but these standards must be imposed on the generating firms. A generator serving nonsensitive loads has no internal incentive to control voltage irregularities that may spill over and affect other loads. The interdependence among generators induced by this negative externality does not exhibit a market structure.

Reactive Power Flows

Reactive power is the *imaginary* component of the complex power generated in an electrical network. It does no physical work, but it contributes as much to transmission line losses as does the real power component. Reactive power is generated and absorbed respectively by capacitative and inductive loads in the distribution end of the industry. A distribution firm serving a large induction load, such as a set of industrial motors, will be drawing reactive power from the system. This reactive power must be supplied from somewhere. If it is not created by a capacitor bank located near the load, it will be necessary for the generating firms in the network to create the reactive power by overexciting their generators. This introduces reactive power flows throughout the network and increases line losses for everyone.

Like the loop flow and voltage regulation problems, reactive power flows exemplify a negative externality in the power grid. In this case, however, the externality is created by distribution firms ineffectively managing their load characteristics, not by generating firms. The negative externality induces a nonmarket economic interdependence among the distribution firms in the system.

Joint Ventures in Generation and Transmission

If the efficient scale of baseload coal and nuclear plants is near 1000 MW, a single utility is likely to experience substantial excess capacity when it brings a new plant on line. The magnitude of those plants is just too large relative to the rate of growth in a firm's demand. These plants are physically indivisible, and indivisibilities are known to create inefficiencies in economic systems. Generating firms have observed, however, that these large plants, though physically indivisible, can be legally partitioned and apportioned among a number of participants. With high-voltage transmission technology, the output of a baseload plant can be sent even a thousand miles. By joint venturing on new baseload plants and by apportioning their output, generating firms can avoid what would otherwise be excess capacity due to new plant additions. Under most joint-venture contracts, the owners contribute capital for the construction and operation of the plant and receive in return the right to a proportional amount of the plant's capacity and energy. If we neglect any advantages of risk-sharing under uncertainty about construction costs, we see that the participants share a commodity whose whole is equal to the sum of its parts. The purchase and sale of capacity in generating plants exhibits a market-like structure.

Joint Capacity Planning and Diversity Exchange

Among distribution firms that have load profiles of different shapes or peak loads that occur at different times of the year, substantial cost savings can be realized by planning jointly for the procurement (by contract or ownership) of capacity sufficient to meet their combined needs. The reason is intuitively simple. When peak loads occur at different times, the peak of the sum of the loads will be less than the sum of the individual distribution firms' peaks. In mathematical terms, the peak-load function is said to be subadditive in the load profiles of the distribution firms. If the cooperating distribution firms can take their wholesale power at a common point and transmit it among themselves, they can reduce the amount of capacity for which they have to contract.

The economic question is whether the actual cost of an optimally designed system is subadditive in the distribution firm's load profiles. The answer depends on assumptions about the optimization problem the distributors solve and on the forms of contract for capacity that are likely to emerge in a deregulated bulk power market.

One formulation of the capacity planning problem that gives insight into the structure of economic interdependence among distributors is the multiple-technology model of Crew and Kleindorfer (1976; 1986). In this version, a diverse set of generating technologies is available, each described by a pair (b,B) of numbers. The technology's cost per unit of energy produced is b (e.g., $/kw-yr), and the annualized cost of capacity is B (e.g., $/kw per year). Efficient technologies in the set lie on a piece-wise linear frontier, convex to the origin in the (b,B) space. Given the load-duration curve derived from a distributor's temporal load profile, it is a simple graphic exercise to identify the optimal amounts of capacity of each type of generating technology (e.g., Sherali et al. 1984). And it is not hard to show that the optimal cost function is subadditive on the space of temporal load profiles (Herriott 1985b).

The Crew-Kleindorfer multiple-technology model may yield insight into the capacity planning problem that distribution firms would face in a deregulated environment. The industry's experience at present with inter-utility sales of capacity suggests that the cost to the buyer will probably be decomposed into a capacity and an energy charge in long-term bulk power contracts. It is not easy to predict how the risk of capacity and energy costs will be shared between buyer and seller. The seller might bear all the risk by stating specific values of b and B in advance of the construction of generating capacity to support the contractual obligations. Or the buyer might bear the risk by agreeing to pay as a rental fee the annualized value of whatever it costs to build the plant (proportional to the amount of capacity contracted for) and to pay all operating costs under provisions for fuel-cost escalation, etc. Or some intermediate allocation of risk may obtain. Nevertheless, it makes sense to think of the distribution firm choosing a portfolio of bulk power contracts to meet its capacity needs at least cost, and these contracts will be described (explicitly or in expected value under uncertainty) by specific capacity and energy rates. Whether the long-term capacity is obtained by contract or by ownership, as long as the cost of transmission within the region does not exhaust the savings from avoided capacity, the cost of an optimal portfolio will be subadditive.

As a consequence of this subadditivity of procurement costs and the diversity of regional distribution loads, the distribution firms and large end-users in a region can reduce their total long-run costs by procuring their capacity requirements cooperatively. Unlike the case of joint ventures in baseload plants, here the whole is better than the sum of the parts.

In many parts of the United States, there is sufficient diversity in load profiles to warrant joint capacity planning among distribution firms. One of the more well-known examples of diversity exchange is the use of the Pacific Intertie (three 500 kv lines) to connect the Pacific Northwest winter-peaking loads with the Southern California summer-peaking loads. This economic inducement to cooperation is evident, however, over much smaller distance scales. Of the 38 distribution cooperatives in Georgia, about half are winter-peaking and half are summer-peaking. Even in central Montana, eight of the distribution coops are winter-peaking, two are summer-peaking, and three peak in the fall.

The point of this analysis is to show that a regional bulk power market, while not a natural monopoly, is a natural monopsony. Decentralized, independent decision-making by the distribution firms and large end-users is unlikely to bring forth the optimal mix of generating technologies. Collective optimization of procurement is necessary. Unlike the collective effort of generators to reduce short-run operating costs through economy energy transactions, this type of cooperation is engendered by a form of economic interdependence that does not admit interpretation as a market-like structure.

Cooperative Organization in Bulk Power Markets

Consider now the implications, for the organization of the industry, of the different forces of economic interdependence identified above.

Generating Firms

The generating firms must cooperate in economy energy exchange, unit commitment, maintenance coordination, spinning and capacity reserve transactions, emergency energy exchanges, voltage regulation, and joint ventures in baseload plants. With the exception of the loop-flow and voltage-regulation problems, each of these types of *cooperation* can be achieved under *competitive* behavior in a market-like context where decentralized decision-making can yield a Pareto-efficient outcome. Granted, the transactions in these markets may be complex, involving future and contingent assets. The hazards of contracting will certainly be present, but there are also strong forces that can mitigate against the necessity of hierarchically organizing this economic interdependence.

Consider the contractual hazards that might cause these market-like structures to congeal into administratively organized, hierarchical systems. Williamson (1979) has identified three principal characteristics of transactions that tend to cause the internalization of market transactions. The first is "small-numbers exchange relations" in which the parties to an exchange have few alternative buyers or sellers. As a result, abrogated contracts would be difficult to restore without economic loss, and bargaining power can be applied to the disadvantage of one party, if circumstances turn unfavorable. The second factor is the frequency of transaction. Williamson argues that unless the costs of organization can be spread over many instances of transaction, complex governance structures will be foregone in favor of simpler forms. The third factor is uncertainty. As uncertainty becomes greater, participants tend to internalize a transaction to gain greater control over the treatment of contingencies.

Small Numbers. The most serious source of contractual hazard is the condition of small numbers of market participants. As long as the number of participants in bulk power markets is reasonably large, there will be multiple sources of supply and demand for any type of bulk power transaction. As a rule of thumb, transmission losses over high-voltage lines are a few percent per hundred miles. Thus, where the transmission grid is available to carry power over hundreds of miles, there ought to be numerous participants in the market, and the generation segment is likely to be competitive in all its products.

Frequency. Interestingly, the frequency of transaction, which Williamson (1979) posited to contribute to the internalization of transactions within a unitary (hierarchical) form of organization, probably contributes to the use of simple contracts in a market context. Under repetitive and frequent transaction, trust and reputation can be built among the participants, reducing the perceived hazards of reliance on contract in lieu of ownership. Notice, however, that the formation of trust and reputation requires a smaller number of transactors in the market. There is evidently a trade-off between the need for large numbers of participants to strengthen the competitive character of the market and the need to maintain the potency of reputational effects. Arms-length contracting among generating firms will therefore achieve the benefits of *cooperation* where there is an intermediate number of generating firms (perhaps one or two dozen) in a regional bulk power market.

Uncertainty. Uncertainty is the third of Williamson's factors contributing to the internalization of transactions. If uncertainty is substantial, then the parties to an exchange must write extensive, costly contracts that anticipate all contingencies to which the relationship would be subject, or they must establish a governance structure in which unanticipated problems can be addressed and disputes resolved. Failing this, uncertainty in the behavior of exchange participants can be reduced by merger, managing the uncertainties administratively under common ownership.

While the reduction of uncertainties through horizontal integration may be a strong motivator of organizational—rather than market-based—transaction (Pfeffer and Salancik 1978), this effect is weak when there is a large number of participants in a market. Uncertainty alone need not force an administrative system for governing transactions. Consider the principal sources of uncertainty in the bulk power markets and how they can be dealt with under contract or ownership.

Capital and Fuel Cost Risks. Neither the generating firms nor the distribution firms in the market for long-term power contracts can predict the ultimate construction and fuel costs of a contemplated generating plant. The fuel costs are out of the control of each party, so this risk might be divided between the two. Generating firms, however, will have an incentive to participate in economic dispatch only if they specify to their customers in advance a particular energy charge, bearing at least some of the risk of changes in their operating costs. Capital costs, affected by both the ambient cost of money and the generating firm's expertise in construction, are to some degree controllable by the generator. So capital cost risks are likely to be borne, at least in part, by the generators. These uncertainties do not drive generating and distribution firms into common ownership.

Forecasting Risk. Distribution firms will err in their forecasts of future load profiles and capacity needs. Anticipating this, they may carry an excess of capacity contracts sufficient to serve their loads at prudent levels of reliability, and they will offer their retail customers interruptible service rates to spread the risk even further. If capacity is available for purchase, and contracts can be reassigned or resold to other buyers on the spot or intermediate-term market, then distribution firms will not need to stockpile as much excess in capacity contracts, and these uncertainties can be managed by market exchange rather than by ownership. The existence of multiple sources of supply and demand allows the short-term markets to solve the problem.

Availability Risks. Generating units are subject to forced outages. The interruptibility conditions in long-term bulk power contracts help spread this risk. Generating firms can internalize the risk by owning many generating units from which their contractual obligations can be met. Or they can participate in the exchange of emergency-energy contracts with other suppliers.

Nonperformance Risks. The principal difficulty with bulk power markets, in the view of Casazza (1988), is the risk that generators will be unable or unwilling to keep the promises made under futures or contingent-commodity contracts. What if a generating plant experiences an outage and the owner is unwilling to cover its capacity on the spot market? What if a plant takes longer to build than expected, yet contracts were written for the sale of energy after a particular date? What if a generating firm goes bankrupt? In Casazza's words, "financial penalties for failure to provide the capacity will not keep the lights on."

These risks can be allocated and governed in the same way that any supplier risk is handled. The buyer can choose to deal only with solid, reputable firms. The buyer can stockpile an excessive inventory. Or the buyer can purchase an option on alternative capacity by qualifying other vendors. The same apply to the bulk power market.

The purchasers can contract with larger generating firms that own and control an amount of capacity of sufficient magnitude that the unavailability or delay of a single plant represents a small risk relative to its total contractual obligations. By contracting for nonspecific capacity from large, reliable suppliers, rather than for the capacity of a specific plant, a distributor's contract is guaranteed by the generating firm's overall capacity, reputation, and capabilities. Alternatively, the purchaser could contract with multiple sources of supply and bear some risk of supplier failure by carrying an inventory of power capacity contracts somewhat in excess of that needed to cover load-forecasting risk. Third, the purchaser could bear risk by holding options for emergency capacity in its portfolio, just as generating firms might do to spread the risk of forced outages. Lastly, the buyers might just be prepared to go to the spot market for capacity in the event of a supplier failure.

If there is a sufficiently large number of generating firms in the market, the lights will stay on even if financial penalties have to be applied to compensate firms that are forced to seek higher-cost sources due to supplier nonperformance.

Of these alternatives, the most likely solution will be that wholesale purchasers deal with large, reliable suppliers. A large size internalizes the risks of plant unavailability or construction delays that would otherwise have to be allocated in a mutual insurance market among smaller generators. This implies that the deregulated bulk power market is likely to exhibit a minimum efficient scale of generating firm *above* the size of a single baseload plant. The efficient scale of a generating firm with baseload expertise could be as much as several thousand megawatts of capacity under ownership. This derivation of the efficient scale of generation incorporates both technological efficiency and contractual efficiency. Consistent with Williamson's formulations of the problem of defining the efficient boundaries of a firm, the efficient-scale organization minimizes the sum of production and transaction costs. If the minimum efficient scale is this high for baseload generators, then a regional bulk power market may have to cover a load of 20,000 MW in order to accommodate 10-25 generating firms. This is the order of magnitude of contemporary power pools.

Nonmarket Interaction Among Generators. The exceptional cases of interdependence among generators are loop flows and the regulation of voltage characteristics. Loop flows can be determined throughout a generation control area in the computerized solution of the load-flow problem that is necessary for optimal dispatching of generation subject to transmission constraints. Thus, a transmission entity may be needed to control generation and transmission levels and to prohibit energy sales that threaten system security.

Likewise, direct observation and control will be necessary to ensure that all generators maintain voltage standards. These functions will have to be enforced by an entity capable of penalizing substandard firms or enjoining them to upgrade their output. This might be the responsibility of the FERC in qualifying generating plants for inclusion in the network.

Distribution Firms

Distribution firms and large end-users must cooperate to reduce reactive power flows and to optimize the regional portfolio of generating units. As a condition of participation in a distribution pool, participants can be required to maintain standards or be subject to economic penalties. Where the cost reductions from joint planning are sufficiently large, participation in the pool will be of sufficient value that participants will comply with the requirement for membership. In practice, federations of rural distribution cooperatives require their members to maintain reactive power standards (often a power factor of .9 or higher) or be charged a higher rate for the energy they receive from the federation. Where the gains from cooperation are weak, the negative externality in reactive power flows may not be controllable except by an external body such as the state regulatory commission that oversees the distribution segment.

Competition and Cooperation

The roles of competition and cooperation in a deregulated bulk power market should now be clear. Generating firms compete for long-term contracts to serve the loads of distribution firms and large end-users. As long as generators bear some risk in the operating expenses of their plants, they will have an incentive to organize an energy broker or to implement central dispatching by the control center to effect economy energy exchanges and unit commitment. Even the exchange of maintenance and emergency energy among existing plants should not compromise their competition for new loads.

Their expertise is in building and operating generating plants with standards and reliability that maintain their reputation. This reputation serves them in their bidding for new capacity contracts let by distribution firms and in obtaining transactions, as buyer or seller, in the short-term bulk power market among generators.

Non-market cooperation takes place principally among the distribution firms. Their expertise is in their detailed knowledge of the needs of their end-users. By selling interruptible power, each distribution firm can develop a load-shedding sequence to be implemented if its end-users' demand exceeds the capacity for which it has contracted in the long-term and spot bulk power markets. Likewise, from its detailed knowledge of the consumers, it is uniquely suited to forecast load growth and future load profiles. The distribution pool aggregates members' demand forecasts and supplements them with regional information, such as states' economic development initiatives, to forecast regional loads as inputs to the regional capacity planning problem.

The problem of organizing a distributor pool is not trivial. Powerful coalitions may dominate decision-making to the disadvantage of minorities. But this problem is engendered by diversity and politics, not by any competitive economics. As important as the control of natural monopolies may be, it is beyond the scope of this chapter on competition and cooperation in bulk power markets.

The Transmission Segment

The discussion so far has not addressed the important role of the transmission segment of the industry. The transmission entity is a bridge between generation and distribution, interacting with both.

The transmission firm is more likely to be a service organization than a merchant buyer-reseller of electric power, for in the latter case it would be a monopolist to the distribution firms. It will be responsible for minute-by-minute load-flow analyses, both to ensure that all transmission lines are operated within their limits and to account for transactions among generating firms and between the generators and distributors. Having this load-flow information, the transmission entity is the natural candidate for the system control function, maintaining a power balance between generation and distribution. It could therefore operate a central dispatching system or economy energy broker as an agent of the generating firms. It would have to know the marginal cost curves of all participants' generating plants and would need to monitor the demand levels at the points of service to distribution firms and to other control areas and the generation levels at all plants in the control area.

With this cost and demand information, it could account for all transactions and bill generators and distributors accordingly. If it had records of all contracts, including spot sales and short-term exchanges for maintenance, emergency capacity, and the like, then it would be in a position to monitor the compliance of all parties with their agreements and to identify participants' obligations arising from loop flow.

To maintain the power balance, it must be able to shed load and/or control the output levels in generating plants. The latter is easy if a central dispatching system has been established, but in regions where the transmission entity performs a looser *pooling* function, load shedding may be its principal recourse.

The New England Power Pool performs such functions for its generating members. It has 46 participants, 22 with generating capacity and 24 without (FERC 1981), and it centrally dispatches all generation regardless of ownership. From records of plant output and service area usage recorded at five-minute intervals, it calculates monthly which generating firms were "buyers" and which were the "sellers" at any point in time, and it bills members for these imputed economy energy transactions using information about their marginal production costs.

The transmission entity may also need to act as an agent of the distribution firms. As we have seen, they are likely to plan their capacity requirements cooperatively and call forth from generating firms the plants needed in the future. But generation planning must be optimized jointly with transmission planning, so the transmission entity would have to work closely with the distribution pool(s) to determine the appropriate investments to be made in transmission capacity.

Summary and Conclusions

To determine whether the requirements for both competition and cooperation can be met in a deregulated bulk power market, we first defined the most likely scenario for deregulation and then analyzed the types of cooperative interdependence present in electric utility operations. The deregulation scenario consists of generating firms under FERC, but not state regulation, disaggregated from transmission and distribution. The transmission entity is likely to be a regulated utility or public corporation serving as a common carrier of bulk power, operating the regional control center, and recording all transactions between generators and distributors for financial resolution. The distribution firms are public utilities regulated by their states and charged with the obligation to serve their end-users' needs consistent with reasonable and prudent standards of service reliability. Generators and distributors transact principally for long-term bulk power contracts. A spot market will exist to rationalize the short-run operation of capacity among generating firms, meet unexpected needs, and dispose of unexpected surplus capacity. Long-term contracts are likely to incorporate demand and energy charges and may include terms pertaining to the interruptibility of the power.

When the generation segment of the industry is disaggregated from the distribution end, then almost all of the cooperative activities required among generating firms admit of a competitive interpretation as decentralized market exchange. Consequently, they should raise no antitrust concerns as long as the regional bulk power markets have a sufficient number of generating firms. One or two dozen generating firms, each capable of serving most of the region, appears to be the best number of competitors in a control area. This range of participants is large enough to give buyers flexibility in their choice of suppliers and reduce the bargaining power of individual participants, yet it is small enough to give potency to the participants' market reputations and thereby enhance the efficiency of the futures and contingent-commodity markets.

With some qualifications, the exchange of information essential for the efficient operation of a power system in the short and intermediate term appears to be consistent with the requirements of long-run competition. To compete for long-terms contracts to sell the output of the plants they construct and operate, the generating firms will want to give their potential customers information that demonstrates a history of timely construction and efficient and reliable operation. The forms of short- and intermediate-term "cooperation," having market structures, do not appear to require information that would compromise the competition for long-term contracts.

Economy energy transactions require participants to share marginal cost information; rather than being a trade secret, plant operating data could be revealed to convince prospective buyers that the technology performs to expectations. Maintenance energy transactions require sharing maintenance schedules, but this is unlikely to be strategically sensitive or lead to collusive behavior. Emergency-energy transactions are perhaps the most sensitive, as they affect a generator's ability to meet obligations and maintain a reputation for reliability. The market for back-up power, to operate most effectively, requires the publication of information from which participants' risks can be gauged. A firm's maintenance expenditures and forced outage history are together the best predictors of future outages. The latter is known to the system control center, but the detailed analysis of individual outages and the maintenance records of plants could be subject to misrepresentation. In the absence of member-specific information, a common risk is often assumed, even though that does not control the problem of moral hazard or permit the more reliable firms to pay lower premiums. Still, the experience of the New England Power Pool is telling: "While there have been disagreements with respect to appropriate reliability levels and the methods used to allocate capacity responsibilities to individual members, there is no evidence that competitive factors created or exacerbated these disputes" (FERC 1981, 68).

The problematic cases of interdependence among generators are the externalities of voltage regulation and of loop flow in economy energy transactions. The former may need to be controlled administratively by the FERC, but technical standards have not been obstacles to cooperation when there is reasonable agreement within the engineering profession. The need to account for loop flow, however, gives force to the argument that system control and load-flow calculation should be performed by a transmission entity disaggregated from generation and not directly controlled by generators. With these qualifications, it appears that none of the competitive market exchange relationships jeopardizes competitive bidding for the new long-term power contracts let by the distributors or their pool, so the *cooperation* among generators is not anticompetitive.

The distribution companies in the regional bulk power market incur a cooperative economic interdependence that does not admit a market interpretation. Facing in common a subadditive cost function for the optimal portfolio of bulk power contracts, their diversity of load profiles creates an incentive for cooperative planning. Organized cooperation among distribution firms, however, is not anticompetitive. There is no reason for the distribution firms to compete for bulk power contracts. They exist in a natural monopsony, despite the competitiveness of the bulk power market.

The essential expertise of generating firms is their reliability in constructing and operating generating plants. The expertise of distribution firms is in knowing their load characteristics, planning for a least-cost portfolio of capacity contracts, and in implementing load management in a socially efficient manner.

The key to a workable system of cooperation amid competitive bidding for new capacity is the ability of the transmission entity to serve, in some respects, as an agent of the generating firms, on the one hand, and of the distribution firms, on the other, while being disaggregated from both. It is a physical and informational intermediary, providing wheeling services and other accounting and billing services to both ends of the industry's value chain. It becomes the essence of the "electric utility," coordinating the operation of generating plants to maintain a power balance in real time and working with the distribution firms to plan adequate generation and transmission capacity for the distant future.

The economic requirements of cooperation in the bulk power market do not conflict with the requirements for competition. When there is a sufficiently large number of generating firms in the bulk power market, contractual arrangements should be able to allocate efficiently the risk induced by uncertainties about the capital and fuel costs of new generating units, deviations of load from forecast values, the availability of existing units, and the reliability of bulk power suppliers. It therefore appears that, with the exception of loop flow, the problems with deregulation do not lie in the economics of electric power production. Instead, they are found in the problems of using contracts and informal collaboration in lieu of authority to establish efficient relationships among technologically distinct elements of the electric power industry.

References

Burns, Robert E. 1987. "Legal Impediments to Power Transfers." In *Nontechnical Impediments to Power Transfers*, edited by Kevin Kelley. Columbus, OH: National Regulatory Research Institute.

Casazza, John A. 1988. "Free Market Electricity: Potential Impacts on Utility Pooling and Coordination." *Public Utilities Fortnightly* 121 (no. 4, February 18): 16-23.

Cohen, Linda. 1982. "A Spot Market For Electricity: Preliminary Analysis of the Florida Energy Broker." RAND Corporation Note N-1817-DOE.

Crew, Michael A., and Paul R. Kleindorfer. 1976. "Peak Load Pricing with a Diverse Technology." *Bell Journal of Economics* 7 (1): 207-231.

Crew, Michael A., and Paul R. Kleindorfer. 1986. *The Economics of Public Utility Regulation*. London: Macmillan Press.

Electrical World. 1988. "News Analysis." (January): 11-20.

Federal Energy Regulatory Commission. Power Pooling in the United States. U. S. Government Printing Office Report FERC-0049.

Haman-Guild, Renee, and Jerry L. Pfeffer. 1987. "Competitive Bidding for New Electric Power Supplies: Deregulation or Reregulation." *Public Utilities Fortnightly* 120 (no. 6, September 17): 9-20.

Herriott, Scott R. 1985a. "The Organizational Economics of Power Brokers and Centrally Dispatched Power Pools." *Land Economics* 61 (no. 3, August): 308-313.

Herriott, Scott R. 1985b. "Subsidy-free Allocation of Long-run Costs in Electric Utility Power Pools." Working Paper 84/85-4-13, Graduate School of Business, University of Texas at Austin, January.

Howard, Jeffrey H., and Richard A. Westfall. 1988. "The FERC Opens Pandora's Box." *Public Utilities Fortnightly* 121 (no. 5, March 3): 22-25.

Joskow, Paul R., and Richard Schmalensee. 1983. *Markets for Power.* Cambridge: MIT Press.

Kemp, William J. 1987. "The Western Systems Power Pool: A Bulk Power Free Market Experiment." *Public Utilities Fortnightly* 119 (no. 9, April 30): 23-27.

Lookadoo, Phillip G. 1987. "What Happened in the Gas Industry Can Happen in the Electric Industry." *Public Utilities Fortnightly* 119 (no. 11, May 28): 23-27.

Martinson, Linda, and Thomas W. Loria. 1987. "The Transitional Bulk Power Market." *Public Utilities Fortnightly* 120 (no. 11, November 26): 19-24.

Meade, William R. 1987. "Competitive Bidding and the Regulatory Balancing Act." *Public Utilities Fortnightly* 120 (no. 6, September 17): 22-30.

Pfeffer, Jeffrey, and Gerald Salancik. 1978. *The External Control of Organizations.* New York: Harper and Row.

Public Utilities Fortnightly. 1987a. "The Midland Cogeneration Project." 119 (no. 9, April 16): 42-45.

Public Utilities Fortnightly. 1987b. "Competitive Bidding and Independent Power Producers." 120 (no. 11, November 26): 43-45.

Public Utilities Fortnightly. 1987c. "Remarkable Remarks." 120 (no. 1, July 9): 6.

Radford, Bruce W. 1987. "Transmission Access for Cogenerators: Why Make It a Federal Question?" *Public Utilities Fortnightly* 120 (no. 6, September 17): 4-6.

Sherali, H. D., A. L. Soyster, F. H. Murphy, and S. Sen. 1984. "Intertemporal Allocation of Capital Costs in Electric Utility Capacity Expansion Planning Under Uncertainty." *Management Science* 30 (no. 1, January): 1-19.

Williamson, Oliver E. 1979. "Transaction-cost Economics: The Governance of Contractual Relations." *Journal of Law and Economics* 22 (October): 233-262.

Yokell, Michael D., and Daniel M. Violette. 1988. "Market Structure and Opportunities in the Electric Utility Industry Today." *Public Utilities Fortnightly* 121 (no. 1, January 7): 9-15.

10

DIVERSIFICATION, DEREGULATION, AND COMPETITION: COST OF CAPITAL IMPLICATIONS FOR ELECTRIC UTILITIES

Leonard S. Hyman
Heidimarie West

Diversification, deregulation, and competition are likely to affect the cost of capital of electric utilities by altering the risk levels of the existing utility business and by leading the utility into lines of business that may be riskier than electric service. They may require talents not yet residing in the utility as well as financial policies now alien to the organization. To the extent that the utility does not adapt its financial, managerial, governmental, and operational policies to the new environment, the utility may create greater risks than necessary for its owners and creditors (Crew 1980, 83). The guiding principle of utility finance has been to offset the lower business risk of the regulated monopoly by means of greater financial risk–leverage. What would happen to the utility's securities if the utility corporation's business risk rose as a result of competition, deregulation, and entry into diversified ventures, but the corporation kept financial ratios appropriate only to the regulated monopoly (ELCON 1987, 6)?

Diversification, Deregulation, and Competition Are Related

Competition may involve the unbundling of a service into regulated and unregulated segments. The utility—on its own or through affiliates—may want to provide unregulated services, too, or even branch out into other related areas, thus diversifying from its regulated core (Pollack 1987a, 1987b, 1987c). Competition means that alternatives are available. Regulators often objected to diversification on the grounds that the utility's attention would be diverted from a vital service that would not be furnished by others. If others can furnish the service, then the regulator may have less reason either to stop diversification or to regulate all aspects of the utility's business (ELCON 1987, 3). It is even possible that a utility's diversified—but related—venture could find new ways of serving customers outside the regulated framework, and thereby diminish the need for regulation.

Definitions

Diversification, in this chapter, means entry by the utility into sectors outside the currently regulated utility core business, excluding temporary investments and purchase of other regulated utilities. Diversification may be in three categories: portfolio investments, activities closely related to the utility core, and businesses unrelated to the core utility.

Natural monopolies have always faced some competition in that users could turn to alternative products or services, but the natural monopoly supposedly had the cost advantage of economies of scale that made it the lowest cost provider (Energy Information Administration 1986). For certain customers, the local utility may no longer be the low-priced supplier. Therefore, we define competition in the electric utility industry as the existence or potential existence of entities that are economical alternative suppliers of electricity to either the local utility or directly to consumers. Competition now exists in a number of ways:

- The utility may have to choose between generating its own electricity or buying from others,
- Various utilities or generators are already vying to sell in the wholesale power market, and
- The utility's customers may choose between self-generation, or purchase from the local utility or even purchase from an outside supplier.

If and when the transmission network is opened up to competitors, the choices will widen (Joskow 1987).

Deregulation is the rallying cry for those who believe that the present system of cost-plus-cum-rate-of-return regulation breeds inefficiencies (Hyman and Habicht 1986). Deregulation studies emphasize that generation, no longer a natural monopoly, should be freed from many existing regulatory constraints, and, perhaps, the generating function should be split off from distribution and transmission as well (Energy Information Administration 1986; Joskow and Schmalensee 1983). Total deregulation and forced divestiture of assets could come slowly. Some generation, however, might be exempted from rate-of-return regulation in the near future. Regulators, in addition, might remove the protection of rate-of-return regulation from certain large customers who have choices, and also exempt the utility from the obligation to serve those customers. And we may see, encouraged by the British models, a modification of regulation that emphasizes price rather than rate of return. A practical model of deregulation could involve partial or complete removal of rate-of-return pricing coupled with the cessation of obligation on the part of the utility to serve customers who wish to shop for service away from the local utility.

Competition and Deregulation

The opening of a formerly closed market to new entrants increases uncertainty for investors owning the current players in the market, and thereby raises cost of capital for those firms. If, however, the new entrants act only as suppliers of incremental power to existing utilities and do the job more efficiently, perhaps the new arrangements might reduce cost of capital for the utility which is no longer obligated to make large and risky investments in generation. To the extent that the new entrant's ability is superior to that of the existing utility, perhaps the overall cost of capital of electricity suppliers might be reduced. But if the new entrant has no such superior ability, then the overall cost of capital will remain unchanged. A local distribution company that signs a rigid take-or-pay contract from an independent generating company has almost the same risk as if it had built the plant, except if the utility's contract only goes into effect when and if the plant meets required operating schedules. The generating company that finances with a take-or-pay contract as security has shifted risk to the ultimate consumer as effectively as if a unitary utility still existed. The Federal Energy Regulatory Commission (1987) has ordered a study of competitive bidding for new generation.

Although utilities discuss competition as if it could be limited between suppliers to the utility, we doubt this is the case. Alternative generators may want access to the utility's disaffected customers, and some of the customers might not only self-generate but also attempt to sell excess power to others. That scenario could create additional risks, including loss of business by high cost utilities, political difficulties in passing on additional overhead to remaining customers, and difficulties in maintaining reliability within the network, unless the competitive system were designed properly.

Investors today have lost faith in the so-called regulatory compact, probably because they see regulators as failing to keep their part of the bargain.
The uneconomical fully allocated costs of new facilities, though, would have
made it impossible to keep the bargain even if regulators had tried to do so.
We are not yet certain that investors realize the possibilities or implications
of unfettered competition, although they do ask, more and more, about
whether utilities have competitive cost structures. The message is getting
across that competition will produce winners and losers.

A significant number of electric utility companies are vulnerable to competition. At least seven major electric utilities exhibit the following unhealthy
combination of characteristics: residential rates 10 percent higher and industrial rates 20 percent higher than the national averages, industrial business
accounts for over 30 percent of sales, rate increases are needed, and rates
are high for the region. At least nine major utilities have rates above their
neighbors, have industrial rates at least 20 percent above the industry average, and also have two of the following characteristics: residential rate 10
percent above the national norm, industrial sales account for over 30 percent
of total, or price increases expected. Still another five companies have
industrial rates 20 percent above average and industrial customers account
for over 30 percent of sales. In other words, using 1986 data, it appears that
at least 20 percent of major investor-owned electric utilities have characteristics that make them vulnerable to competition, especially for the industrial
load (Hyman 1987a).

Diversification

Diversification is not a new phenomenon. The old electric holding companies
had non-utility businesses. In the postwar period, natural gas utilities entered
a wide range of fields, though oil and gas exploration and production pre-
dominated. The non-Bell telephone companies also diversified, generally
into electronics or telecommunications-related businesses. The results of
such diversification were mixed. Andrew Carnegie once said, "Put all your
eggs in one basket and watch the basket" (Graham, Dodd, and Cottle 1962).
That is advice which managers seem loath to follow. In the 1960s, a few
electric utilities began to venture out of the core business, emphasizing fuel,
transportation, and real estate, but most did not. Expansion of the electric
utility itself required too much capital and management attention to allow
for diversions. No more than five or six companies developed significant
diversified operations through the 1970s. As construction efforts wound
down and cash flow increased in the 1980s, managements revisited diversifi-

cation. By the end of 1986, the scoreboard for 101 electric companies in the Merrill Lynch universe showed that half the industry was diversifying and could be categorized as follows:

- *High Level of Diversification* - Nine companies had non-utility investments that accounted for 20 percent or more of net assets or equaled 20 percent of common equity when only equity in subsidiaries was shown.
- *Medium Level of Diversification* - Thirteen utilities had non-utility investments that accounted for at least 10 percent (but under 20 percent) of net assets or common equity (equity accounting), or at least 7 percent of net assets or equity with a contribution to net income or net to common of 13 percent or more.
- *Low Level of Diversification* - Eleven utilities had non-utility investments involving at least 5 percent of net assets, equity, or of some measure of income.
- *Planned to Diversify* - Twenty-four utilities had investments that accounted for less than 5 percent of size or income, or had proposed to or had set up a holding company for diversification, or had announced diversification plans.

The most commonly cited reasons for diversification have been (Hyman 1987b):

- Cash flow in excess of the needs of the utility.
- Ability to reduce risk by having more than one line of business.
- Desire to remove the corporation's fate from the hands of regulators.
- Making temporary use of cash until needed in the utility.
- Adding growth to the corporation that would not have been possible due to poor prospects for the utility.
- Aiding the core utility by providing it or its customers with products or services that are better furnished in an unregulated manner.
- Making use of corporate assets and expertise in an optimal way.

Lessons Learned from Other Utilities

The electric utilities are following gas and telephone companies in diversifying and meeting up with competition, but many electric utility managements seem determined to repeat history.

Gas companies, especially pipelines, began to diversify in earnest during the 1960s. Portfolio diversification played a minimal role. Most emphasized activities that consumed natural gas, transported or distributed fuels, or explored for and developed hydrocarbons. The gas utilities tried to enlarge

Table 10-1. Number of Poor Years for Gas Industry Groupings

Merrill Lynch Groupings for Gas Industry	Companies in Sample	Number of Poor Years
Natural gas-distribution	16	0
Nautral gas-diversified	12	15
Natural gas-pipeline	11	8

Source: Merrill Lynch, Monthly Research Review (July 1987) and Standard & Poors , Stock Guide (August 1987).

their activities beyond both ends of the pipe, to encourage supply and demand. On the supply side, they were successful, although nonstandard efforts (such as LNG or synthetic fuels) proved to be costly diversions. On the demand side, however, gas utility managements demonstrated less acumen. The record for unrelated ventures has been mixed. Some managements may have been prompted by fear that the principal business of the corporation was in an inexorable slide, so that they had to find other businesses or cease to grow. As an indicator of overall results, for 39 gas companies in Merrill Lynch's universe, table 10-1 shows the number of times in 1983-1986 that companies had poor years (defined as a loss or a drop of 75 percent or more in earnings per share.

The poor years came about mainly from diversification. The utility business was reasonably steady.

Gas utility executives understood competition. They were always in competition with electric and oil heat, and their industrial and utility customers knew how to switch fuels. But, for much of the postwar period, demand grew steadily. There was plenty of business for everyone. Then, when supply tightened, industry executives may have worried about losing customers to other fuels. Did they dream that when shortage turned to glut, they would lose their monopoly on providing gas itself, that customers would make deals with producers, distributors could pit pipeline against pipeline, gas utilities would become transporters, owning production might saddle the pipeline with noncompetitive costs, "common carriage" and "bypass" would become common terminology, and that regulators would encourage academic notions about competition in order to reduce prices to customers instead of protecting the regulated industry? Competition came as a shock to most people, including investors.

Table 10-2 shows the results of diversification for the gas industry. The

Table 10-2. Gas Industry Investment

Unweighted Average of	Merrill Lynch Natural Gas Industry Groupings: Distribution	Diversified	Pipeline
Beta (5 year)	0.5	1.07	0.74
Five-year % return on equity (1982-1986)	12	10	13
Long-term debt % of capitalization (1986)	42	55	43
Five-year % annual earnings per share growth	-10	-34	-5
Five-year % annual dividend growth	5	4	5

Source: Merrill Lynch, Monthly Research Review (August 1987).

distribution companies diversified the least, often managing to collect transportation fees even when they lost direct billing to the customer, keeping their capitalization conservative. Using beta as an indicator, they were the least risky investments. The diversified companies made the most mistakes, were most leveraged, and had the highest betas.

Is it possible that gas companies diversified in order to reduce corporate risk and to improve competitive position, and thereby increased investor risk and cost of capital because they understood neither the markets they entered nor the supply and demand situation in their own markets?

In many ways the telephone situation is analogous. The telephone companies made few unrelated investments. Instead they concentrated on manufacturing equipment that they used (akin to gas utilities investing in hydrocarbons to fill their pipelines), with generally acceptable results. They also manufactured and sold telecommunications equipment directly to customers, underestimated competitive forces, had trouble understanding customer needs, and, often, took a beating. The companies also have offered long distance services directly to customers in a competitive market with a poor record of results to date. The telephone company, formerly integrated, seemed to want to keep all aspects of the telecommunications service within its grasp, but it lacked the skills to do so profitably.

Was an integrative strategy necessary to maintain the company's competitive position? Although many of the major telephone firms bury information about subsidiary profitability, we believe that non-utility operations have produced losses or lower and more volatile profits than the telephone utility. We expect improvement as those operations mature, but it is not yet clear that they all serve a strategic purpose. It is even less clear whether the telephone companies had to lose as much as they did to enter those businesses. Unfortunately, the reorganization of the industry does not allow the development of a table similar to table 10-2.

Competition came to the telephone industry as a result of:

- Technological changes that made it possible for others to enter parts of the business.
- Pricing that charged well above costs for certain services in order to subsidize others, thereby encouraging competitive entry against the overpriced services.
- Regulatory and legal moves that broke up integration or allowed competitive entry.

Those in the telephone industry, especially John de Butts of AT&T, understood the implications of competition, explained its social consequences, tried to slow down the onset of competition, and lost (Hyman, Toole, and Avellis 1987). One might even argue that competition came the way it did, with minimal input from telephone companies, state regulators and the mass of consumers, because those in the industry thought that they could stop it by arguing about service reliability and social equity. The Department of Justice, outside vendors, and large customers who were disadvantaged by the existing system had other ideas, and they won. The lessons that should be learned are:

- Entry into competitive markets is difficult, especially so for utilities that focus on too broad a definition of the end user of their service.
- Competition may come about despite good reasons to believe that some consumers may be hurt.
- Both competition and diversification can make investment riskier.

Telephone and gas utilities also found out that regulators object to the terms by which an affiliate of the utility serves the utility. But that is a lesson that electric utilities should have learned from their own experiences, although recent discussions of cogeneration and wholesale generating subsidiaries make us wonder if the lesson really did sink in.

Financial Analysis

Both diversification and competition will affect cost of capital either by actually affecting the financial results and risks of the utilities, in which case investors will adjust their demands to the new situation, or by causing investors to believe that diversification and competition will affect risk and profitability and, thus, adjust their demands before an event that may or may not happen. The market value of a utility might suffer too during the transition period from a primarily regulated, income-oriented investment vehicle to a more competitive or diversified company. This would arise as the company loses its traditional investors and does not yet convince still another group of investors that it will be successful in the new environment (Burkhardt 1986).

In July and August 1987 we surveyed a sample of institutional analysts, portfolio managers, and retail brokers and managers in order to discern attitudes toward diversification. The number of replies (37) was small, but the respondents encompassed many of the most knowledgeable and influential utility investors, with almost equal interest in the electric and telephone sectors. The results were:

- Portfolio investment or diversification into related sectors makes the investment more attractive, but diversification into unrelated businesses makes the investment less attractive.
- Diversification into unrelated sectors increases both risk of investment and cost of capital, but it is not clear that the same could be said for portfolio or related diversification.
- Two-thirds of those responding felt that diversification started to count in the evaluation of the investment only when it accounted for 10 percent or more of assets or earnings.
- Two-thirds of the respondents believed that utilities should modify financial policies (i.e., dividend payout or capitalization) when they diversified.

These general conclusions could not provide a basis for clear tests of attitudes toward individual securities. Those surveyed found it difficult to cite more than a handful of companies that had diversified significantly; cited a number of others that were talking more than doing; almost ignored some of the most prominent real diversifiers; differed as to how to classify the diversification (portfolio, related, unrelated); and paid little attention to telephone companies (possibly because telephone diversification was so close to the core business so as not to be considered diversification). Table 10-3 shows that the financial policies of utilities—whether diversified or not—appear similar. The most diversified companies have managed to earn a higher return on equity, and those companies either diversified or perceived to be so sell for a higher market/book ratio.

Are utilities diversifying simply because they have cash available to do so? Table 10-4 averages out projections of internal funds as a percentage of utility capital expenditure for 1987-1989 by diversification category. The actual diversifiers do project more available cash, and their higher standing in the market might also be because of superior cash flow, as opposed to expected superior deployment of the cash. Those utilities most cited by our respondents as diversifying, interestingly, did not have internal funds levels

Table 10-3. Averages for Diversified versus Non-Diversified Electric Utilities (August 15, 1987)

	No. of Cos.	Mkt./ Book (%)	Debt Ratio (%)	Beta	5-Year Aver. ROE (%)	Payout (%)	Pretax Int.Cov (x)
Industry							
All	93	137	47.9	0.64	13.8	67.0	3.4
Excluding nuclear	62	149	47.0	0.61	14.1	68.0	3.6
High level diversification							
All	10	156	46.9	0.60	15.2	64.0	3.6
Excl. nucl.	8	162	46.8	0.58	15.3	63.0	3.7
Medium level of divers.							
All	13	151	47.5	0.61	14.6	69.0	3.7
Excl. nucl.	10	161	47.0	0.59	14.1	69.0	3.8
Low level of divers.							
All	9	121	46.1	0.66	13.1	71.0	3.7
Excl. nucl.	6	126	44.4	0.59	14.0	67.0	4.3
Minimal or planned divers.							
All	23	140	45.4	0.62	13.9	65.0	3.6
Excl. nucl.	19	148	45.3	0.61	14.5	69.0	3.9
Most cited diversifiers							
All	8	161	46.8	0.62	14.5	68.0	3.7
Excl. nucl.	6	169	46.6	0.59	14.3	68.0	3.8

Notes: Excluding nuclear indicates that utilities do not have nuclear plant under construction or do not have completed plant that has not yet received rate order.
High level diversification - 12/86 diversification equals 20 percent or more of net assets, or common equity.
Medium level - diversification equals 10 percent or more of net assets or common equity.
Low level - Investment under 10 percent but at least 5 percent of assets or net income.
Minimal or planned - under 5% of assets and income.

as high as the other groups.

It is equally difficult to draw conclusions about competition, because of confusion as to its definition and impact. Table 10-5 shows data for the companies that we previously defined as vulnerable, divided into those with and those without large industrial load (industrial load being most vulnerable to competitive forces).

Companies that are vulnerable to competition seem to have financial

Table 10-4. Internally Generated Funds of Electric Utilities 1987-1989

	Number of Companies	Average Internal Funds % of Utility Capital Expenditures
Industry		
All	101	92
Excluding nuclear	71	89
High level divers.		
All	10	152
Excl. nucl.	8	161
Medium level divers.		
All	13	113
Excl. nucl.	10	113
Low level divers.		
All	9	112
Excl. nucl.	6	106
Minimal or planned		
All	23	125
Excl. nucl.	19	133
Most cited diversifiers		
All	8	84
Excl. nucl.	6	82

Source: Merrill Lynch estimates.

policies that are at least as risky as those of the industry as a whole. Many advisors believe that vulnerable utilities should engage in even riskier financial policies, over the short term, in an attempt to reduce rate increases. However, it is more likely that the stock market will react negatively when the utilities put in more leverage in order to—supposedly—reduce cost of capital and, thereby, reduce costs to customers. The low market/book ratios of the vulnerable companies may indicate that investors are already adjusting to risk, whether they see that risk as derived from present or expected financing policies, from high cost nuclear projects, or from the realization that the market for electricity will not support the price required to provide a full regulatory return on investment.

Perhaps the best way to tackle the questions of diversification, competition, and cost of capital is to examine the data for a wide variety of industries as shown in table 10-6. The sample is biased in the sense that Merrill Lynch's universe excludes many smaller or financially troubled companies; information on financial companies is incomplete and not completely comparable

Table 10-5. Electric Utilities Vulnerable to Competition (August 15, 1987)

	No. of Cos.	Mkt./ Book (%)	Debt Ratio (%)	Beta	5-Year Aver. ROE (%)	Payout (%)	Pretax Int.Cov (x)
Industry							
All	93	137	47.9	0.64	13.8	67.0	3.4
Excluding nuclear	62	149	47.0	0.61	14.1	68.0	3.6
With high							
industrial load	7	86	50.3	0.70	14.7	68.0	2.3
Without high							
industrial load	11	107	48.1	0.68	13.8	67.0	2.8
All vulnerable							
Excl. nuclear	5	88	48.7	0.64	13.9	67.0	3.0

Note: Vulnerable is defined as having residential rates 10 percent higher and industrial rates 20 percent higher than national average, rate increases needed, rates higher than those of neighbors. *High industrial load* is defined as over 30 percent of system sales.

with the balance of the sample; and the data collection procedure tends to distort loss situations so they have to be omitted from some calculations. In a sense, the sample is dominated by large, successful, mature firms. The lesson of table 10-6, though, is as follows:

- With the exception of the natural gas diversified and pipeline groups, the utilities have significantly lower betas, presumably indicating a lower assessment of risk by the market.
- All the utility groups have far higher debt and dividend payout ratios than industrial groups.
- Industrial returns earned on equity are generally higher for industrials than for utilities.
- Utilities sell at market/book ratios significantly below that of industrials.

The average bond rating is close to single A, for utilities, financial firms and industrials (table 10-7), thus indicating that the various industries have balanced their business and financial risks in order to get an average rating (Hyman et al. 1987). If utilities add to leverage in order to raise funds to go into riskier businesses, or continue present leverage policies that are suited for the old low risk utility business while they are diversifying, will that increase cost of equity or debt capital? If the utility business becomes riskier due to competition (i.e., more like other industries), will continuance of the traditional leverage affect cost of equity capital? The answer to both ques-

Table 10-6. Averages For Merrill Lynch Industry Groups, Sorted by Beta in Descending Order (August 15, 1987)

	Beta	Debt Ratio (%)	5-Year Payout Ratio (%)	Return on Equity (%)	5-Year Market/ Book Ratio (%)
Quartile[a]					
I	1.31	30.0	30.2	14.9	331
II	1.12	29.0	39.5	13.4	373
III	1.06	33.5	24.7	14.6	324
IV	0.92	26.4	39.3	15.0	283
Large Industries[b]	1.08	30.0	40.0	16.0	362
Financial Industries[c]	1.15	51.0	37.0	15.0	188
Natural Gas					
Diversified	1.10	51.9	70.0E	10.0E	169
Pipeline	0.87	45.2	70.0E	13.0E	190
Distribution	0.66	43.4	69.2	12.0	148
Electric	0.64	47.9	67.4	13.8	137
Telephone	0.63E	40.0E	62.8E	13.2E	199

[a] 40 industry groups, excluding financial, real estate, and utilities; each group with market value of $5.0 billion, consisting of more than 4 companies in group.
[b] 53 Merrill Lynch industrial groups with market value of $8 billion or more, excluding financial and real estate corporations, but including utilities.
[c] Six financial industries, each with more than four participants and $5.0 billion of market value.
Source: Merrill Lynch, Monthly Research Review (August 1987).

tions should be "yes."

Sale and leaseback deals have become common, especially for troubled electric utilities. They put off the necessity of rate relief, and they diminish the need for disallowances and other punitive accounting and regulatory treatment that often follows from a rate order that does not recognize the need for a big rate increase. Those deals serve competitive, political, regulatory, and financial purposes in the intricate game of utility regulation and finance. They keep the utility in the game. They give the players time to reorganize, cut costs, and strike deals. They levelize costs, thereby diminishing the need for an immediate rate increase, but they also diminish the ability to lower rates later in the life of the asset. In other words, this financial

Table 10-7. Bond Ratings by Industry Group

Merrill Lynch Industry Groups	Mean[a]	
Industrials by Beta Quartile		
I	A-	
II	A	
III	BBB+	
IV	A-	
	Moody's	S&P
Natural Gas[b]	A3	A-
Electric[b]	A	A-
Telephone[b]	A2	AA
Financial[c]	A1	A

[a] For each industry, unweighted average of Moody's and S&P ratings. Group mean is unweighted average of industry means. Stated in S&P format.
[b] All ratings in Merrill Lynch, *Utility Trading Options* (August 4, 1987).
[c] All ratings in Merrill Lynch, *Financial Institutions Rating Guide* (August 1, 1987), excluding governmental and government-guaranteed agencies.

wizardry enables the company to price more competitively now, but then shifts the risk of competition to the future. A competitive industrial firm, faced with the problem of marketing an uncompetitive product, would write down assets, or simply market the product if the direct costs of production were less than the price, figuring that other costs are sunk. The average widely held industrial firm, though, is not saddled with a huge debt burden, all sorts of obligations to owners of fixed income securities, and thousands of shareholders who bought the stock specifically for a handsome dividend payout. (The trend to leveraged buyouts and use of debt to buy in equity in order to fend off raiders is not only creating a large amount of low-rated debt but, sooner or later, will bring up the question of what financial policies really are appropriate in competitive industries.)

The dividend payout ratio of utilities is far higher than that of industrial firms. That policy could be justified on the grounds that:

• Utility earnings are stable, being derived from a natural monopoly selling an essential service, so there should be few instances in which the company would have trouble meeting the dividend.

• Shareholders should have a choice whether to reinvest earnings by purchasing new shares or putting the money elsewhere.

• When money is not needed in the utility, regulators may penalize the utility for its retention, and might also make it difficult for the utility to invest in non-utility ventures.

- Shareholders buy utility shares as income vehicles and do not desire to have earnings reinvested in activities with which management is unfamiliar.

If, however, the utility industry is moving toward more competition and diversification, the earnings stream could become less predictable. Shareholders might choose to own utilities not just for dividends but also because they expect earnings to be reinvested in a way to increase profitability. Regulators will interfere less with financial policies. And the dividend payout should move down. Utilities entering competitive situations should plan a new dividend policy, and should start on that path soon.

Will profitability increase as utilities become more like other businesses? The successful industrial firms of table 10-6 earned more on equity during a period of good economic conditions, admittedly taking greater risk to do so. Differences in accounting procedures, as well as inconsistencies in the data collection and manipulation process, make us cautious, though, in concluding how much better industrials did. Perhaps diversification will moderately improve utility profitability, if the utility's management can do as well in the new field as those experienced in it. Eventually, if regulators remove themselves from the picture, utilities might become more profitable in their core businesses, but not until a shakeout of incompetents, hothouse competitors, and shrinking of oversupply takes place.

Finally, would becoming more like other businesses produce a better stock price? Undoubtedly managements of utilities grouse about their market/book ratios: too low when adjusted for risk, return earned, prospects, etc. This is not an issue to be dismissed lightly, but in the past one could draw a line that showed a rough correlation between return on equity and the market-to-book ratio, and utilities seemed to fall close to where the line predicted. In other words, they sold at a low market-to-book ratio because they earned a low return on equity. At the time of writing of this chapter (August 1987), utilities seem to sell at prices far below what would be indicated by their returns on equity. That may be an aberration brought about by the lack of interest in stable companies during a speculative stock market. Or it may indicate that the market believes that utilities are riskier than before and have poorer prospects. We believe that the recent ratios have more to do with the state of the market than with philosophical questions about the direction of utility profitability. (In the October 1987 market collapse, utility stocks did move back closer to former relationships.)

Conclusion

This is not the place to examine cost of capital theory. We have tried to keep this discussion on a mundane level—the utility view of the world—and we intend to end it that way. Basically, a business has some cost of capital determined by its inherent characteristics, and this determines a market value of sorts. As a result of financial, legal, and tax institutions, it may be possible to increase the market value of the business by changing financial policies (such as dividend payout or the use of leverage), at least up to an appropriate point. After that point, the policies increase risk too much and market value may fall. In most industries, which are more variable and riskier than utilities, the market-enhancing policies have included lower debt and payout ratios than for utilities. Now either utilities are attempting to enter other fields, or the utility field is becoming more like others due to to competition. That leads us to one of two possible conclusions:

- All other industries have chosen the wrong combination of financial policies to maximize market value.
- The utilities will have to adopt financial policies more like those of other industries as the utilities become more like other companies.

In our view, some utility managements and investors are stumbling into a new era of diversification and competition. They are confusing short-run, ad hoc solutions to immediate problems with long-run policy. And they are ignoring the questions of appropriate financial policies and cost of capital that could have as much impact on the market value of their companies as will structural changes within corporations and their industries.

References

Burkhardt, Daniel A. 1986. "The Individual Investor's Perspective on Utility Stocks." P.U.R. Utility Conference (February).

Crew, Michael A. (ed.) 1980. *Issues in Public Utility Pricing and Regulation.* Lexington MA: Lexington Books.

ELCON. 1987. "Electricity's Future." Special Report by the Electricity Consumers Resource Council, Washington (July).

Energy Information Administration. 1986. "Financial Analysis of Investor-Owned Electric Utilities." Washington, D.C.: Energy Information Administration (November): 63.

Federal Energy Regulatory Commission. 1987. "Hesse Outlines Competitive Bidding Options for Electric Generating Capacity." Washington, D.C.: Federal Energy Regulatory Commission (June).

Graham, Benjamin, David L. Dodd, and Sidney Cottle, with Charles Tatham. 1962.

Security Analysis: Principles and Technique. New York: McGraw-Hill.

Hyman, Leonard S. 1987. "Intra-Industry Combination: What Is It and Does It Make Sense?" Merrill Lynch Institutional Report (April).

Hyman, Leonard S. 1987. "Vulnerability to Competition." Merrill Lynch Institutional Report (August).

Hyman, Leonard S., et al. 1987. "Electric/Telecommunications Bi-Monthly Review." Merrill Lynch Institutional Report (September/October).

Hyman, Leonard S., and Ernst R. Habicht, Jr. 1986. "State Electric Utility Regulation: Financial Issues, Influences, and Trends." *Annual Review of Energy.*

Hyman, Leonard S., Richard C. Toole, and Rosemary M. Avellis. 1987. *The New Telecommunications Industry.* Arlington: Public Utilities Reports.

Joskow, Paul, and Richard Schmalensee. 1983. *Markets for Power: An Analysis of Electric Utility Deregulation.* Cambridge, MA: M.I.T. Press.

Joskow, Paul. 1987. "Competition and Deregulation in the Electric Utility Industry." M.I.T. Center for Energy Policy Research Policy Division Paper. Cambridge, MA: M.I.T. Press (May).

Pollack, Andrew. 1987. "New Era for Electric Utilities: Residential Rates Might Rise." *New York Times* (August 11): A1.

Pollack, Andrew. 1987. "Non-Utility Electricity Rising." *New York Times* (August 12): D1.

Pollack, Andrew. 1987. "Shopping Around for Electric Power." *New York Times* (August 13): D1.

11

THE FINANCIAL FALLOUT FROM CHERNOBYL: RISK PERCEPTIONS AND REGULATORY RESPONSE
Catherine C. Eckel
Theo Vermaelen

Introduction

In this chapter we explore the effect of the Chernobyl nuclear accident on the returns of nuclear electric utilities in the United States. We use the accepted market model to analyze the impact of the accident on stock prices in two periods: (1) the period immediately following the announcement of the accident on April 28, 1986; and (2) the period surrounding the release of the Soviet report detailing the circumstances of the accident on August 18, 1986. The study is in the spirit of the work on the financial effects of the Three Mile Island nuclear accident by Bowen, Castanias, and Daley (1983) and Pulley and Hewlet (1985), and it confirms and extends Fields and Janjigian (1987). Our technique is first to estimate the impact of the accident on each utility in our sample, to test for individual and aggregate effects for nuclear and nonnuclear firms, then to explain differences in effects across firms using what we know about the regulatory environment of nuclear utilities. We find that nuclear utility stock prices were negatively affected by the accident, and the magnitude of the effect is related to the nuclear "exposure" of the utility. The release of the report had a positive effect, partially offsetting the initial impact. We also discuss the expected effect on nuclear liability and safety regulation and the government response to the accident.

The Accident

In the early hours of Saturday, April 26, 1986, Reactor No. 4 at the Chernobyl Nuclear Power Plant in the Soviet Union exploded, and several tons of radioactive material were released into the atmosphere. The explosion sent up a three-mile-high radioactive plume, hailing the worst recorded nuclear accident in history. Radiation detectors in neighboring countries gave the first indication, during the weekend, that something had gone wrong within the Soviet Union. On Monday, the Soviet Union acknowledged the disaster, and the news reached the United States press late that afternoon. On Tuesday, all major news agencies carried stories of the accident, but not until Wednesday was it given headline status. As the seriousness of the accident became apparent, there was also a good deal of speculation that the regulation of nuclear utilities would be tightened.

Although it was recognized that the accident might have serious implications for the future profitability of United States utilities, other information lessened its perceived impact. An article in the *Wall Street Journal* discussed the differences in design between reactors in the two countries. The Soviet RBMK-1000 reactor was graphite-moderated and water-cooled. Only one commercial reactor in this country uses a graphite moderator—the Fort St. Vrain plant in Plattsville, Colorado, owned by Public Service Company of Colorado—and it has a helium coolant, believed to pose much less risk for fire than the water-cooled Soviet plant. A *New York Times* report also stressed design differences, noting that United States plants, "unlike the Soviet reactor in the accident, have steel and concrete containment structures designed to prevent the escape of radiation" (*New York Times*, April 30, p. A1). As the nature of the accident gradually became known, the Dow Jones Average for Utility Stocks fell from 186.6 on Monday morning to 179.6 at Wednesday's close—a total of 3.75 percent.[1]

Speculation about the cause of the explosion and the severity of the damage continued through the summer.[2] It wasn't until August 18 that a translation of a Soviet report was released, explaining in detail the events that caused the accident and the damage that resulted. The report revealed the significant contribution of the design characteristics to the severity of the accident, characteristics which differ from United States designed reactors. The predominant cause of the accident was described as operator error during a test, when many safety systems were disconnected or overridden.

This report, coupled with news coverage highlighting the significant differences in safety requirements of the two countries, seemed to calm United States investor fears. The good news sent the Utility Stock Average up by 1.57 percent over the period between August 15 and August 19 surrounding the release of the report.

Arguably, the Chernobyl accident altered expectations about both the likelihood and magnitude of a serious nuclear accident, by providing an unprecedented example. On the other hand, plant safety regulation and construction standards in the United States are very different from their Soviet counterparts. In addition, the aggregate liability of nuclear utilities in the United States for damages resulting from a serious accident is limited, by the Price-Anderson Act of 1957 and its subsequent amendments, to $660 million per accident. Both safety regulation and the liability limit would tend to lessen the effect of the accident on investor evaluations of nuclear utilities.

However, by chance, the reform of both nuclear plant licensing regulation and the Price-Anderson Act were subjects of Congressional inquiry at the time of the accident. Nuclear utilities in the United States were immediately affected by the mix of perceptions that resulted from the accident and from its interaction with existing and expected regulation.

Substantial differences in design and safety standards between Soviet and United States plants were highlighted by the report released in August. This information may have completely offset the negative impact of Chernobyl on the perceived probability of an accident. The accident itself, however, may have had a lasting impact on expected regulation.

In this chapter, we analyze the effect of the accident at the Chernobyl nuclear plant on the perceptions of United States utility investors and examine the regulatory response to concerns raised by the accident. Using data on the rates of return to electric utility firms with and without nuclear generating capacity, we obtain estimates of the changes in investor perceptions about the risk of a nuclear accident and about the cost associated with expected changes in regulation. According to the efficient markets hypothesis, all new information about the expected cash flows and risk characteristics of a firm is immediately incorporated into the stock price, affecting the return on the stock and its beta. Under the maintained hypothesis of efficient financial markets, we analyze the changes in returns resulting from the accident and from the release of the Soviet report. We then discuss the actual legislative response to the new information provided by Chernobyl.

Regulatory Environment

At least two categories of utility regulation are important for predicting the impact of the Chernobyl accident: the limit on liability for an accident, and safety and licensing regulation. In 1957 Congress passed the Price-Anderson Act which constructed a two-tier liability system for nuclear utilities. The first layer was private insurance provided by a group of insurance firms, equal at the time to $60 million, the maximum the insurers were willing to provide. If an accident exceeded $60 million in damages, the second tier would come into play. It limited the *aggregate* liability of nuclear utilities for a single accident to $560 million—the $60 million plus $500 million initially provided by the government.

The 1975 extending legislation provided that large nuclear accidents would be covered, not by government insurance, but by a pool of all owners of nuclear facilities. Premiums would be assessed retroactively in the event of a large accident and would equally divide the cost of an accident among all operating nuclear plants, up to the ceiling amount of $5 million per nuclear unit. The cost to each unit would be the same, regardless of the "riskiness" of the plant. Damages in excess of $60 million plus $5 million times the number of nuclear units then operating could only be handled by a special legislative provision of the federal government. In return for the liability ceiling, the industry agreed to a waiver of defenses. Thus legal proceedings designed to determine liability for an accident would be eliminated, and claims could be processed quickly. (See Wood (1982) or Dubin and Rothwell (1987) for studies of the incentive effects of Price-Anderson.)

Subsequent amendments to the act have raised the limit to $660 million—$160 in private insurance plus the pool of at most $500 million, $5 million per operating plant (the 100th plant was licensed in 1986). The most recent amended limits to the Act expired in August 1987. Although commercial plants that were already licensed or that held a construction permit before the expiration date are grandfathered under the old limits, government plants and new commercial plant construction are no longer covered. Congress has been unsuccessful so far in its attempts to renew or revise the limits.

In addition to liability limits, the Nuclear Regulatory Commission regulates the safety of nuclear plants and controls their operation through licensing and construction requirements. The regulation of nuclear utilities is complex and involves every stage of the design, construction, and operation of the plants. Reform of the licensing stage of regulation was under consideration at the time of the accident. Planning for the evacuation of the area surrounding nuclear utilities in the event of an accident was of particular concern. Both liability and licensing regulation are discussed in more detail below.

Chernobyl and Share Prices

Financial theory tells us that the value of a firm is the discounted present value of the expected cash flows or profit stream. The discount rate depends on the beta, the correlation of those cash flows with the market portfolio (or the overall level of business activity). High cash flows and a low correlation with the market affect the value of the firm positively. (See, for example, Sherman (1974), chapter 7.)

The financial impact of the Chernobyl accident can be analyzed in terms of its effect on these components. An increased probability of a serious accident, tighter regulation, or more strict licensing requirements should negatively affect expected cash flows. If investor expectations are so affected by the accident, the firm's share price should experience a negative capitalization proportional to the additional expected cost. Firms will see negative abnormal (market adjusted) returns during this period, and the effect will differ across firms, depending on the nuclear "exposure" of the firm.

Because of uncertainty about future regulation, the accident may also increase the expected variability of returns. Higher variability may affect cash flows through, say, an increase in the cost of insurance, but, as accidents do not tend to be systematically correlated with other business risk, it should not affect the stock betas. We assume betas are constant in the analysis that follows, and that capitalizations resulting from the accident are due solely to the impact on expected cash flows.[3] This can be decomposed into the change in expected cost of an accident and the change in regulatory cost. Each is discussed in turn.

Cost of an Accident

Consider the single period expected cost of an accident at a nuclear utility. Prior to the Chernobyl accident, investors assigned probabilities to accidents of different sizes, and these expectations were incorporated into the stock price—the collective perception of shareholders about the value of the firm. For simplicity, suppose that there are only two possible types of accidents, small and large. The expected cost of an accident consists of the probability of a small accident times its cost plus the probability of a large accident times its cost. The Chernobyl accident is likely to have affected both the subjective probability of a large accident and its cost, leaving perceptions about small accidents unaffected.

The cost of a large accident includes both the firm's loss of plant—the direct destruction of shareholder wealth from loss of the reactor itself—and liability-related costs. Both would depend on the number and size of plants owned by a firm, as well as the risk characteristics of the plant, such as location, design, etc., and could differ considerably across utilities.

The plant-loss portion of the change in expected cash flows depends on the revised probability of an accident and the value of nuclear generating assets. Chernobyl may have affected both the extent of destruction investors expect a major accident to cause, and the likelihood of its occurrence.

If liability is limited, as under Price-Anderson, to an amount L times the number of operating plants N, the change in the expected cash flows due to the liability costs alone would be the revised probability times L*N and is proportional to the number of plants owned. Since the liability is shared equally, the probability is of an accident anywhere among the members of the insurance pool and should be equal across utilities. If investors expect a new liability limit to come into effect as a result of the accident, the change will be greater, but it is still proportional to the number of operating plants.

If investors do not believe the liability limit will stay in effect, the impact on cash flows may depend on the amount of nuclear assets, as well as on location and design of the plants. Finally, if investors do not know the extent of nuclear plant ownership, but are aware only of substantial owners of nuclear facilities, the impact on expected cash flows may be constant across all firms for whom investors are aware of significant nuclear involvement.

Regulatory Risk

The remaining effect on expected cash flows arises from the impact of the accident on expectations about licensing and safety regulation. While the Chernobyl accident may not have told investors much about the probability of an accident, it may have revealed new information about the cost and difficulty of evacuation of large populations. While the subsequent report may have eased fears about the likelihood of an accident, it probably did little to offset expectations about increasingly strict regulation of evacuation plans, something which has been and continues to be a major regulatory issue, particularly for unlicensed plants.

Changes in expectations about safety regulation in response to the accident should affect all nuclear utilities, and the effect should depend on the size of the nuclear assets, the inherent riskiness of the plants, and the expected cost to the firm of regulation to improve safety.

Because licensing regulation was under consideration at the time of the accident, investors may have expected an immediate tightening of licensing requirements or tighter enforcement of existing statutes. Utilities with as yet unlicensed facilities are likely to have been affected the most by this increase. This expected cost will depend on the value of the unlicensed nuclear assets of the firm.

The August report would not have offset the effect of the Chernobyl accident on the licensing aspect of regulatory expectations, largely because of the importance of evacuation plans for these new plants.

In sum, we look for relationships between the size of the capitalization and the number and size of operating plants and the size of new plants. Because investors may not be aware of particular characteristics of plants or of the relative magnitude of nuclear involvement, but only of whether or not the firm has any operating or new nuclear facilities, we also test for the effect of classifications of firms alone.

Stock Return Data and Estimation

Data

We estimate the impact of the Chernobyl accident on a sample of firms consisting of all electric utilities listed on the CRSP tapes whose generating operations are located in the United States. There are 96 firms in all, 55 with nuclear plants which were operating at the time of the accident or scheduled to begin operating in 1986. Of the remaining 41, four had plants at varying stages of construction, expected to become operational after 1986. Thirty-seven had no nuclear involvement. Nearly all operating commercial nuclear units are covered in our sample; one firm (Centerior) was eliminated because of a major reorganization that took place on April 29, 1986.

Two periods are analyzed: (1) April 28, 29, and 30, the accident announcement period; and (2) August 15, 18, and 19, the period surrounding the release of the Soviet report. We choose a three-day period in April because, although the accident was completely unanticipated, the news of what had occurred arrived slowly. The accident was more or less rumored on Monday, the 28th; significant information was available on Tuesday; and by Wednesday the nature of the accident was fairly clear. We also choose a three-day period for the report announcement. News of the report may have leaked on Friday the 15th; on Monday the report was released; and on Tuesday a full account of the report was carried by the *New York Times*.

We collected daily data using the CRSP tapes on stock returns of the 96 firms from 110 days prior to the accident to 150 days after, including the report announcement period, for a total of 261 observations per firm. Data on nuclear ownership were collected from several government publications and industry periodicals.[4]

Estimation

The most common method for analyzing the effects of unanticipated events is the analysis of residuals from security returns regression models such as the "market model" or CAPM. (See Schwert (1981) for a discussion of this methodology.) We estimate the excess returns associated with the Chernobyl accident and with the release of the Soviet report on the accident using an alternative method, Zellner's Seemingly Unrelated Regression (SUR), which is a simultaneous estimation technique. The use of SUR in event studies was pioneered by Schipper and Thompson (1983).[5] SUR offers several advantages over the traditional "event study" technique, arising from the fact that it incorporates cross-firm information in the estimation. In the traditional technique it is assumed that excess returns are independent across time and across firms. For events that occur at the same time for all firms, particularly if the firms are in the same industry, this assumption is clearly violated. Strong contemporaneous correlation across firms biases the hypothesis tests usually performed in the analysis.

If all equations in the system contain the same explanatory variables, the SUR coefficient estimates and standard errors will be identical to ordinary least squares (OLS) estimates. The main advantage of the technique is then in hypotheses testing. Simultaneous estimation facilitates tests of cross-equation relationships and uses the appropriate full system variance-covariance matrix in testing for significance.[6]

We estimate a system of 96 equations, one for each firm, of the following form:

$$R_{it} = \alpha_i + \beta_i R_{mt} + \sum_{a=1}^{3} \delta_{ia} D_a + \sum_{r=1}^{3} \mu_{ir} D_r + e_{it}, \quad i=1,\ldots,96$$

where:

R_{it} = the observed return on the common stock of firm i at time t

α_i, β_i = market model parameters

R_{mt} = the return on the value weighted market portfolio of all NYSE stocks

D_a = dummy variables equal to 1 on each of the days of the accident announcement period (April 28, 29, 30)

D_r = dummy variables equal to 1 on each of the days of the Soviet report announcement period (August 15, 18, 19)

δ_{ia}, μ_{ir} = coefficients representing the effects of the announcements.

e_{it} = residual, assumed normal, iid for a given firm across time (serially
    independent, and independent of the rhs variables)

These 96 equations are "stacked" and estimated jointly. Notice that the estimated coefficients for the effects of the accident and the report can differ across firms.

Results

Estimates of the Effect of the Chernobyl Accident

The initial estimates of the parameters are shown in table 11-1a for utilities with operating nuclear units and table 11-1b for utilities without operating nuclear units. The company name and number are shown in the first column, followed by the beta. Estimates of the betas are statistically significant at at least the .1 level for all except one utility. The average betas are .628 for nuclear utilities and .543 for nonnuclear and are within the range of previous studies.[7] The next three columns contain the estimated announcement effects for April 28, 29, and 30, followed by the sum over the three days, the aggregate effect of the accident announcement. The last four columns contain estimates for August 15, 18, and 19, followed by a sum of the three daily effects.

Of the 55 nuclear utilities, 27 (or 49 percent) report statistically significant negative effects for at least one day of the accident period—6 firms on April 28, 18 on April 29, and 10 on April 30. Nineteen show a statistically significant sum. Of the 41 utilities classified as nonnuclear, 5 (or 15 percent) report significant negative effects—1 firm on April 28, 2 on April 29, and 3 on April 30—and one a significant positive effect (firm 42). Four show a statistically significant sum. The average three-day return across firms for the accident period is -0.0350 for nuclear utilities; -.0095 for nonnuclear.

In the report announcement period, 18 (or 33 percent) of the nuclear utilities report significant positive effects on at least one day. Eleven show a positive aggregate effect. Nine (or 22 percent) of the nonnuclear utilities had significant returns on one or more days, and one of these was negative (firm 45). Three show a significant positive sum. The average three-day return across firms for the report announcement period is 0.0209 for nuclear utilities and 0.0037 for nonnuclear. From this there appears to be a much stronger impact of the accident and the subsequent report on nuclear utilities. These and additional hypothesis tests are summarized in table 11-2.

The traditional event study tests the statistical significance of sums (or means) of effects across firms. This is equivalent to testing the sums of

Table 11-1a. Parameter Estimates, Nuclear Utilities

Company	Firm	Beta	Apr.28	Apr.29	Arp.30	Sum(Ap)	Aug.15	Aug.18	Aug.19	Sum(Au)
AZP Group	1	0.5708‡	-0.0418‡	-0.0139	-0.0157	-0.0714‡	-0.0023	0.0068	0.0090	0.0136
Am.Elec.Power	3	1.0720‡	-0.0078	-0.0084	-0.0082	-0.0244	-0.0035	-0.0061	0.0107	0.0012
Atlantic City El.	4	0.5734‡	-0.0098	-0.0237*	-0.0371	-0.0705‡	-0.0112	-0.0022	0.0084	-0.0050
Baltimore G&E	5	1.0709‡	0.0007	-0.0032	0.0021	-0.0004‡	0.0098	0.0213*	0.0250*	0.0561†
Boston Edison	7	0.2833‡	-0.0113	-0.0177*	-0.0179*	-0.0469†	0.0328†	0.0058	0.0022	0.0408*
Carolina P&L	8	0.6425‡	-0.0064	-0.0059	-0.0114	-0.0237	-0.0092	0.0043	0.0225*	0.0177
Cen.Hud.G&E	10	0.4536‡	-0.0093	-0.0263*	-0.0230	-0.0586*	-0.0118	0.0021	0.0105	0.0008
Cen.ME Power	12	0.5961‡	0.0113	- 0.0165	0.0029	-0.0023	-0.0165	0.0047	0.0206	0.0089
Cen.VT PSC	13	0.1791*	-0.0120	-0.0099	0.0021	-0.0198	-0.0018	-0.0016	0.0228*	0.0194
Com.Edison	16	0.6628‡	-0.0099	-0.0514‡	0.0079	-0.0534‡	0.0087	-0.0015	-0.0026	0.0046
Com.En.Sys.	17	0.4818‡	-0.0094	-0.0069	0.0009	-0.0153	0.0087	0.0092	0.0055	0.0233
Con.Edison	18	0.8483‡	-0.0059	-0.0125	-0.0022	-0.0206	-0.0032	-0.0045	0.0139*	0.0061
Cons.Power	19	0.6469†	-0.0332	-0.0260	0.0402	-0.0190	-0.0045	0.0068	-0.0010	0.0013
Delm.P&L	21	0.4003‡	-0.0059	-0.0131	-0.0056	-0.0247	0.0152	-0.0014	0.0238*	0.0375*
Dom.Res.	23	0.6598‡	-0.0060	-0.0136	-0.0079	-0.0276*	0.0096	-0.0021	0.0205*	0.0280*
Duke Power	24	0.7906‡	-0.0088	0.0009	-0.0100	-0.0179	0.0123	0.0057	0.0163*	0.0342*
Duquesne Li.	25	0.3065*	0.0000	-0.0053	-0.0118	-0.0171	-0.0090	0.0544*	0.0187	0.0640*
Eastern Util.	26	0.4941‡	-0.0362†	-0.0312*	-0.0590‡	-0.1265‡	0.0106	0.0076	-0.0044	0.0137
FPL Group	28	0.8268‡	-0.0065	-0.0038	-0.0040	-0.0143	0.0107	-0.0084	0.0016	0.0039
Florida Prog.	30	0.5428‡	-0.0128	-0.0096	-0.0150	-0.0373*	0.0055	-0.0021	0.0112	0.0145
GPU (TMI)	31	0.6663‡	-0.0028	0.0054	-0.0269*	-0.0243	0.0024	-0.0020	0.0221*	0.0226
Green Mt.Po.	32	0.2032*	-0.0077	-0.0053	0.0020	-0.0110	0.0062	0.0193	-0.0056	0.0199
Gulf States	33	0.6780‡	-0.0303	0.0192	0.0045	-0.0066	0.0319	0.0011	0.0038	0.0369
IE Industries	36	0.6906‡	-0.0025	-0.0254*	-0.0092	-0.0372*	0.0021	0.0172	0.0103	0.0295
Illinois Power	38	0.5835‡	-0.0344†	-0.0235*	0.0103	-0.0476*	0.0066	-0.0016	0.0454‡	0.0504†
Iowa IL G&E	40	0.4374‡	-0.0117	-0.0319†	0.0005	-0.0431*	-0.0053	0.0038	0.0166	0.0151
KS City P&L	43	0.5507‡	-0.0023	0.0092	0.0003	0.0073	0.0229	-0.0181	0.0299*	0.0348
Kansas G&E	44	0.3893†	-0.0030	0.0018	0.0126	0.0113	0.0098	-0.0153	0.0183	0.0128
LI Light	46	0.8016‡	-0.0138	-0.0337	-0.0486*	-0.0962*	-0.0042	-0.0244	-0.0108	-0.0393
ME Pub.Svc.	49	0.3260†	-0.0201	-0.0073	-0.0551‡	-0.0825†	-0.0023	-0.0099	0.0239	0.0118
Mid.So.Util.	50	0.8742‡	-0.0120	-0.0291*	-0.0225*	-0.0636	-0.0031	0.0437†	0.0191	0.0597*
NE Elec.Sys.	55	0.7384‡	-0.0027	-0.0252*	-0.0008	-0.0287	0.0048	0.0209	0.0049	0.0306
NY St. E&G	56	0.5496‡	-0.0182	-0.0276*	-0.0195	-0.0653†	0.0044	-0.0053	0.0108	0.0099
Nia.Mohawk	58	1.0161‡	-0.0285*	-0.0058	-0.0133	-0.0477	0.0029	-0.0052	0.0246	0.0223
NE Util.	59	0.7896‡	-0.0031	-0.0237*	0.0014	-0.0255	0.0064	0.0218	0.0150	0.0433*
No.State Po.	61	0.9597‡	-0.0092	-0.0169	0.0154	-0.0107	0.0268*	0.0175	0.0113	0.0555†
Ohio Edison	62	0.6230‡	-0.0091	-0.0080	-0.0091	-0.0262	0.0033	0.0101	0.0066	0.0200
Pacific G&E	65	0.8443‡	0.0084	-0.0092	-0.0244*	-0.0252	-0.0031	0.0031	0.0260*	0.0260
PA P&L	67	0.5186‡	0.0052	-0.0078	-0.0070	-0.0096	0.0065	0.0011	0.0062	0.0137
Phila.Elect.	68	0.7158‡	-0.0170	-0.0084	-0.0020	-0.0274	-0.0035	0.0029	0.0165	0.0160
Portland GE	69	0.6872‡	-0.0032	-0.0273*	-0.0124	-0.0428*	-0.0033	0.0234*	0.0111	0.0312
Pub.Ser.–CO	71	0.6051‡	-0.0318*	-0.0063	-0.0009	-0.0389	0.0050	0.0058	0.0082	0.0189
Pub.Ser.–NH	73	0.7459‡	-0.0141	-0.0050	-0.0592*	-0.0783*	-0.0023	0.0128	-0.0122	-0.0017
Pub.Ser.–NM	74	0.5594‡	-0.0456	0.0047‡	0.0175	-0.0234	0.0085	-0.0051	0.0186	0.0220
Pub.Ser.Ent.	75	0.8337‡	-0.0166	-0.0031	-0.0094	-0.0292	0.0050	-0.0048	0.0068	0.0070
Rochtr. G&E	77	0.4923‡	-0.0157	-0.0382†	-0.0257*	-0.0795‡	-0.0064	0.0175	0.0236*	0.0348
S.Diego G&E	78	0.5864‡	-0.0065	-0.0184*	-0.0057	-0.0306	0.0096	-0.0143	-0.0059	-0.0106
SCANA	80	0.4591‡	-0.0216*	-0.0047	-0.0161	-0.0424	-0.0088	0.0040	0.0149	0.0100
So.Cal.Ed.	82	1.0315‡	0.0007	0.0010	-0.0105	-0.0088	-0.0002	0.0118	0.0157	0.0273
Southern Co.	83	1.0135‡	-0.0135	0.0047	0.0025	-0.0062	-0.0032	0.0031	0.0120	0.0120
Union Elec.	90	0.6408‡	-0.0083	-0.0056	-0.0103	-0.0242	-0.0033	-0.0024	0.0124	0.0067
United Illum.	91	0.4339‡	0.0158	-0.0763‡	-0.0479†	-0.1084†	0.0088	0.0244	0.0071	0.0403
WI Elec.Po.	94	0.4985‡	-0.0027	-0.0089	0.0006	-0.0109	-0.0028	0.0021	0.0185*	0.0178
WI P&L	95	0.5002‡	-0.0022	-0.0169*	-0.0101	-0.0292	-0.0001	0.0274†	0.0264†	0.0538‡
WI Pub.Ser.	96	0.3963‡	-0.0101	-0.0105	0.0010	-0.0196	-0.0024	0.0024	0.0039	0.0040
Sum		34.5417‡	-0.6113*	-0.7620†	-0.5503*	-1.9236‡	0.1707	0.2876	0.6911*	1.1494*
Mean		0.6280‡	-0.0111*	-0.0139†	-0.0100*	-0.0350‡	0.0031	0.0052	0.0126*	0.0209*

Key: Statistically significant at *=0.1, †=0.01, ‡=0.001 level.

Table 11-1b. Parameter Estimates, Nonnuclear Utilities

Company	Firm	Beta	Apr.28	Apr.29	Arp.30	Sum(Ap)	Aug.15	Aug.18	Aug.19	Sum(Au)
Allegheny Po.	2	0.5851‡	-0.0027	-0.0019	0.0131	0.0085	-0.0053	0.0029	0.0100	0.0076
Black Hills	6	0.3781‡	0.0251	0.0029	0.0221	0.0501	-0.0019	-0.0013	0.0050	0.0017
Central & SW	9	0.8897‡	-0.0109	-0.0118	0.0000	-0.0227	0.0039	0.0015	0.0086	0.0141
Cen. IL PS	11	0.5922‡	-0.0187	-0.0170	0.0044	-0.0313	-0.0156	-0.0234*	0.0044	-0.0346
Cilcorp	14	0.4601‡	0.0010	-0.0163	0.0032	-0.0120	-0.0029	-0.0243*	-0.0127	-0.0399*
Cincin. G&E	15	0.8438‡	-0.0032	-0.0030	0.0098	0.0036	-0.0120	-0.0065	0.0143	-0.0043
DPL, Inc.	20	0.6248‡	-0.0241*	0.0103	-0.0004	-0.0142	0.0208	-0.0021	0.0095	-0.0134
Detroit Ed.	22	0.6314‡	-0.0161	-0.0085	-0.0172	-0.0419*	0.0190	-0.0085	0.0081	0.0186
Empire Elec.	27	0.3552‡	-0.0112	-0.0024	0.0099	-0.0036	0.0084	-0.0018	0.0031	0.0097
Fitchburg G&E	29	0.1044	-0.0021	-0.0008	-0.0278	-0.0308	0.0047	-0.0088	0.0053	0.0012
Hawaiian Elec.	34	0.5173‡	-0.0067	-0.0086	-0.0040	-0.0193	-0.0027	-0.0019	0.0075	0.0028
Houston Ind.	35	0.7788‡	-0.0105	-0.0128	-0.0020	-0.0253	-0.0028	0.0019	0.0230*	0.0221
Idaho P&L	37	0.6967‡	-0.0026	0.0061	0.0125	0.0160	-0.0198	0.0113	0.0011	-0.0074
Interstate Po.	39	0.2906‡	-0.0069	-0.0134	0.0044	-0.0159	0.0062	-0.0100	0.0121	0.0083
Iowa Res.	41	0.6426‡	-0.0090	-0.0071	0.0108	-0.0053	-0.0079	-0.0118	0.0147	-0.0050
IPALCO Ent.	42	0.6702‡	0.0001	-0.0112	0.0232*	0.0120	-0.0006	0.0069	-0.0014	0.0049
Kentucky Util.	45	0.3756‡	-0.0094	-0.0117	-0.0188*	-0.0399*	-0.0001	0.0031	-0.0291†	-0.0261
Louisville G&E	47	0.5114‡	-0.0096	-0.0106	0.0049	-0.0153	-0.0026	0.0041	0.0120	0.0135
MDU Res. Grp.	48	0.6149‡	-0.0084	0.0022	0.0168	0.0105	-0.0026	-0.0063	0.0053	-0.0036
Midwest Energy	51	0.7092‡	0.0118	-0.0031	0.0063	0.0151	-0.0032	0.0028	0.0055	0.0051
Minnesota Po.	52	0.4811‡	-0.0004	0.0107	0.0151	0.0255	-0.0183	-0.0179	-0.0044	-0.0406
Montana Power	53	0.4707‡	-0.0022	-0.0141	-0.0065	-0.0228	-0.0053	-0.0017	0.0002	-0.0068
Nevada Power	54	0.4812‡	-0.0127	0.0032	-0.0192	-0.0287	-0.0181	-0.0073	-0.0002	-0.0256
Newport Elec.	57	0.2114*	0.0108	0.0009	0.0029	0.0147	0.0040	-0.0184*	0.0109	-0.0035
N.IN Pub.Svc.	60	0.6696‡	-0.0133	-0.0277	0.0239	-0.0172	-0.0256	-0.0014	0.0370*	0.0099
Oklahoma G&E	63	0.7998‡	-0.0030	-0.0060	0.0099	0.0009	-0.0032	0.0081	0.0145	0.0193
O&R Util.	64	0.3454‡	-0.0018	-0.0015	-0.0182*	-0.0215	-0.0052	0.0255*	0.0196*	0.0399*
Pacificorp	66	0.5938‡	-0.0059	-0.0097	0.0031	-0.0125	0.0045	-0.0015	0.0145	0.0175
Potomac Elec.	70	0.6075‡	0.0030	-0.0135	0.0070	-0.0035	0.0105	0.0112	0.0112	0.0328
Pub.Ser.of IN	72	0.7538‡	-0.0039	-0.0055	0.0014	-0.0080	-0.0041	-0.0126	0.0097	-0.0070
Puget Snd. P&L	76	0.6252‡	-0.0149	-0.0193	-0.0080	-0.0421*	-0.0032	0.0031	0.0110	0.0109
Savannah E&P	79	0.6257‡	0.0097	0.0085	0.0100	0.0282	0.0204	0.0308*	-0.0003	0.0509*
Sierra Pac.Res.	81	0.5419‡	-0.0136	-0.0071	-0.0022	-0.0229	-0.0075	0.0126	0.0098	0.0148
So.Indiana G&E	84	0.3443‡	-0.0025	-0.0167	-0.0026	-0.0218	-0.0025	0.0038	0.0055	0.0067
SW Pub. Ser.	85	0.6617‡	-0.0026	0.0014	0.0033	0.0021	-0.0062	-0.0018	0.0179*	0.0100
TECO Energy	86	0.5693‡	-0.0027	-0.0108	0.0096	-0.0038	-0.0028	0.0053	0.0003	0.0028
TNP Ent.	87	0.3085†	-0.0079	-0.0402†	0.0174	-0.0308	-0.0125	-0.0122	-0.0057	-0.0304
Texas Util.	88	0.7090‡	-0.0019	-0.0157	-0.0020	-0.0197	0.0014	0.0094	0.0087	0.0196
Tuscon G&E	89	0.5784‡	-0.0027	-0.0096	0.0074	-0.0050	-0.0068	0.0019	0.0159	0.0110
Utah P&L	92	0.3527‡	-0.0185	-0.0056	0.0199	-0.0043	0.0198	0.0061	0.0007	0.0266
WA Wtr.Power	93	0.2677†	0.0027	-0.0238*	-0.0132	-0.0343*	0.0151	-0.0055	0.0082	0.0178
Sum		22.2709†	-0.1985	-0.3206	0.1300	-0.3891	-0.1044	-0.0347	0.2911	0.1521
Mean		0.5432†	-0.0048	-0.0078	0.0032	-0.0095	-0.0025	-0.0008	0.0071	0.0037

Key: Statistically significant at *=0.1, †=0.01, ‡=0.001 level.

coefficients δ_{ia} and μ_{ir} on the dummy variables D_a and D_r across firms, since the coefficient on each event dummy is the abnormal return for that trading day. Part 2 of table 11-2 contains the results of cross-equation tests of these parameters. F-tests are reported for each day of both test periods, and for the aggregate effect in each period, for both nuclear and nonnuclear firms.

For the accident period, we can reject the null hypothesis that the sum of effects across nuclear firms is zero for each day (April 28, 29, and 30) at (at

Table 11-2. Hypothesis Tests

1. Individual firm tests	Number of firms rejecting Ho: Effect=0		
	All (n=96)	Nuclear(n=55)	Non-Nuclear (n=41)
a. accident effects			
April 28=0	7	6	1
April 29=0	20	18	2
April 30=0	13	10	3
Total*	31	27	5
Sum(April 28-30)=0	23	19	4
b. report effects			
August 15=0	2	2	0
August 18=0	10	5	5
August 19=0	19	14	5
Total*	27	18	9
Sum(Aug. 15-19)=0	14	11	3

2. Traditional tests: tests of $\sum_i \delta_{ia}, \sum_i \mu_{ir} = 0$		F-statistic	Pr. > F
a. Accident effects			
April 28:	Nuclear firms	4.940	.026
	Nonnuclear firms	0.856	.355
April 29:	Nuclear firms	7.625	.006
	Nonnuclear firms	2.219	.136
April 30:	Nuclear firms	3.912	.048
	Nonnuclear firms	0.359	.549
Aggregate effect (April):			
	Nuclear firms	15.917	.0001
	Nonnuclear firms	1.071	.301
b. report effects			
August 15:	Nuclear firms	.3853	.535
	Nonnuclear firms	.2367	.627
August 18:	Nuclear firms	1.093	.296
	Nonnuclear firms	.026	.871
August 19:	Nuclear firms	6.310	.012
	Nonnuclear firms	1.841	.175
Aggregate effect (Aug.):			
	Nuclear firms	5.777	.016
	Nonnuclear firms	.166	.684
3. Tests of equality across firms			
a. $\delta_{ia}=\delta_a{}^*, \mu_{ir}=\mu_r{}^*$ for all i, a, r		1.720	.0001
b. $\sum \delta_{ia}=\delta^*$, for all nuclear firms, and $\sum \delta_{ia}=\delta^\circ$, for all nonnuclear firms		1.659	.0001
c. $\sum \mu_{ir}=\mu^*$, for all nuclear firms, and $\sum \mu_{ir}=\mu^\circ$, for all nonnuclear firms		1.650	.0001

* Some firms had significant effects on more than one day, so the total is not equal to the sum over the three days as reported here.

least) the .1 level of significance, and for the aggregate effect at .0001. Clearly the negative capitalization was significant for these firms taken together. However, nonnuclear utilities do not show a significant sum for any day or for the entire period.

There is weaker evidence of an effect in the period in which the Soviet report was announced. For nuclear firms, we can reject the null hypothesis of zero effect for only one day (August 19, the day following the release of the report), and for the three-day period at only the .016 significance level. For nonnuclear firms, again, there is no evidence of an effect for the firms taken together, for any single day or in total.

Part 3 of table 11-2 contains tests of the hypothesis that the effects are the same across firms. We can easily reject this hypothesis, even when firms are separated into nuclear and nonnuclear.

Why Are the Effects Different?

To explore the sources of the inequality of the effects across firms, we perform regression analysis, using for each firm the aggregate effect of the accident and of the report as the dependent variables. The model we use is based on the discussion in section 11.3:

$$Accident\ (or\ Report) = a_1 + a_2*Liability + a_3*NukMW + a_4*NukDum + a_5*NewMW + a_6*NewDum + e$$

The variables are defined as follows:[8]

Accident: sum of the abnormal returns for April 28, 29, and 30, the period following the accident at Chernobyl.

Report: sum of the abnormal returns for August 15, 18, and 19, the period surrounding the release of the Soviet report.

Liability: (number of nuclear plants owned * $165 million)/equity (Firm equity was calculated as shares of common equity outstanding as of April 1, 1986, multiplied by the closing share price on April 1.) This is expected to carry a negative sign, capturing the increase in the expected likelihood of a large nuclear accident with limited liability.

NukMW: (megawatts of nuclear capacity)/equity. This is also expected to carry a negative sign, capturing the expected additional cost of destruction of assets due to an accident and of more stringent expected safety regulation.

NukDum: a dummy variable equal to 1 if the utility owns nuclear assets. Could capture an imperfect assessment by investors of either of the above, due to imperfect information.

NewMW: (megawatts of nuclear capacity under construction)/equity. Expected to carry a negative sign, reflecting additional expected licensing costs.

NewDum: a dummy variable equal to 1 if the utility has nuclear capacity under construction. An alternative specification to capture licensing costs.

e: residual, assumed normal, mean 0, constant variance.

OLS regression results are shown in table 11-3.[9] In the equations with Accident as the dependent variable, the intercept is negative and statistically significant at .05 or better. In equation (11.1), which includes all the variables discussed above, all variables have the expected sign; however, only NukDum and NewMW are statistically significant (both at better than .01). The number of plants owned (which determines Liability) and the size of nuclear assets (NukMW) are insignificant. NewDum is significant only at .17. Unfortunately, Liability, NukMW, and NukDum are so highly collinear, with correlation coefficients of between .72 and .94, that the effects cannot be separated. Similarly, NewMW and NewDum have a correlation coefficient of .73. Equation (11.2) is specified with only the two dummy variables, and

Table 11-3. Regression Results

Dependent Variable = Market Adjusted Return for April 28-30 (t-statistics in parentheses)				
	Independent Variable:			
Dependent	*Accident*		*Report*	
Variable	*Eq. (11.1)*	*Eq. (11.2)*	*Eq. (11.3)*	*Eq. (11.4)*
Intercept	-.008	-.007	-.003	.003
	(-2.131)	(-2.040)	(1.101)	(1.130)
Liability	-.021		-.030	
	(-.383)		(-.609)	
NukMW	-.008		.010	
	(.525)		(.734)	
NukDum	-.021	-.019	.014	.017
	(-2.922)	(-3.798)	(2.328)	(4.048)
NewMW	-0.54		-.010	
	(-2.719)		(-.597)	
NewDum	-.012	-.028	.006	.003
	(-1.370)	(-4.830)	(.869)	(.630)
R^2 (Adjusted)	.356	.325	.129	.150
F-Statistic	11.48	23.85	3.82	9.36
(significance)	(.0000)	(.0000)	(.0035)	(.0002)

both again carry the expected sign. The effect of new capacity is larger in magnitude and somewhat more significant than operating capacity, and both are significant at .001. For utilities with capacity under construction as well as operating nuclear assets, the effects are compounded. The fit for this equation is nearly as good as for (11.1); this provides some evidence that investor knowledge of the precise ownership of utilities is imperfect.

Equations (11.3) and (11.4) contain estimates for the same specifications using the impact of the release of the Soviet report as the dependent variable. In (11.3), only NukDum is statistically significant, with the expected positive sign. In magnitude, it appears to offset about two-thirds of the initial impact of the accident. There is no similar offsetting positive effect for new capacity. The same pattern is evident in equation (11.4), except that the effect of the accident appears to be fully offset by the information contained in the report for firms with operating nuclear capacity.

These results support our hypotheses that the magnitude of the effect of the accident depends on nuclear exposure. There is evidence that nuclear ownership and nuclear capacity under construction, per se, are more important than the precise size or liability involved. The effect of the accident does not appear to be related to liability, at least not in any detectible way. Investors seem to distinguish only whether a utility has nuclear capacity, and whether it has capacity under construction. However, it does appear that Chernobyl had a significant, lasting effect on expectations about the future cash flows for as yet unlicensed nuclear facilities. This is probably related to the additional information and increased concern about evacuation plans in the event of an accident, and their likely impact on the ultimate cost of obtaining operation licenses for these plants.

Regulatory Response

Two major pieces of nuclear legislation were being considered in Congress at the time of the Chernobyl accident: the renewal of the Price-Anderson Act and a reform of nuclear licensing procedures. Delays following the accident ultimately prevented any legislation on either subject from being passed in that session.

Before the accident, it was reasonable to assume that both houses of Congress would enact legislation reauthorizing the Price-Anderson Act during the 99th session, though with an increase in the liability cap. The House committees supported Price-Anderson legislation carrying a liability cap of between $2.4 and $8.2 billion, compared with the current level of $660 million, per accident. Just before the accident, industry lobbyists had actively sought the lower limit. On April 30, the House committee delayed its expected vote to lower the limit. A member of the committee said in explanation of the delay, "This industry . . . is living in a different world than a week ago" (*Engineering News Record*, May 8, 1986, p. 12). It was speculated that, because of the disaster, industry supporters in Congress would vote against the lower limit for fear of what their constituents would think. The House finally approved legislation with a liability cap of $6.5 billion, but not until August.

The Senate had similar pending legislation, but was very divided as to the liability limit. The Energy subcommittee submitted a low $2.2 billion cap, while the Environment and Public Works Committee supported a $10 billion cap. The trade press published speculative reports that Chernobyl may have foreclosed the Price-Anderson debate for the year, and they were correct. The Senate and House failed to reach a consensus on the liability limit or on licensing reform by the end of the session.

Pending licensing reform legislation also met with delays as Rep. Markey of Massachusetts, an opponent of nuclear energy, used the accident to call for more public testimony on the issue, delaying a markup session (Subcommittee on Energy Conservation and Power of the House Committee on Energy and Commerce). Prior to the accident, the Subcommittee was on the verge of consolidation of three competing bills to go forward with a consensus proposal for full licensing reform. The proposed legislation was aimed at one-step licensing, in which the construction and operating permits would be granted at the same time, and at design standardization concepts. "Washington sources" were quoted to say that the Chernobyl accident had given Markey a great deal of ammunition, and that this essentially foreclosed any nuclear legislation for the 99th Congress.

It seems clear that the accident increased uncertainty about both types of regulation. However, delay was predictable almost immediately and can be seen as the only reasonable compromise strategy at the time. The tentative compromise reached with the industry over the liability limit was unsustainable in the face of the accident. Talk of higher liability led industry lobbyists to delay, preferring to operate under the grandfathered provisions of the old Act to a new, excessively strict ceiling. Fears of stricter licensing regulation, particularly involving evacuation plans in the event of an accident, also led the industry to delay. The industry preferred to wait until Chernobyl was less vivid in legislators' memories. This, in turn, made it easier for legislators to delay their decision.

The Price-Anderson amendments expired in August 1987, without fanfare. As of this writing, Congress has still not passed extending legislation for

Price-Anderson, though there are bills before both houses. The Senate bill calls for a $6.8 billion liability cap, and the House bill calls for a $7.02 billion cap, both of which are considerably higher than the level the industry had hoped for. No action has been taken on licensing reform.

Conclusions

The Chernobyl accident resulted in a negative (market adjusted) return for electric utilities with nuclear capacity. This return averaged 3.5 percent over 3 days following the accident. The magnitude appears to be greater for utilities with larger nuclear exposure, both in term of operating capacity and plants under construction. Utilities with as yet unlicensed capacity under construction also experienced a larger negative return, equal on average to 2.8 percent more than other nuclear utilities. The release of the Soviet report resulted in an offsetting positive effect for utilities with operating nuclear capacity, but not for those with capacity under construction. These results are consistent with the notion that the accident altered investor perceptions about regulatory cost. Subsequent legislative inaction has borne out expectations of tighter, more costly regulation. Licensing reform has been abandoned, and Price-Anderson limits, if reenacted, promise to be higher than was expected prior to the accident. Both aspects of regulation should have a greater impact on new, unlicensed nuclear capacity.

Notes

Virginia Polytechnic Institute and INSEAD, respectively. The authors thank Cathleen Long, Paul de Wouters, and David Allen for research assistance, and B. Craig, A. Fields, V. Janjigian, J. Johnson, R. Lamy, D. Orr, L. Pulley, R. Sherman, and W. Wood for their help and comments. We also thank Joseph Schuh and Krishna Hegde, the discussants for this paper on the conference program, for their helpful criticism. We are especially grateful to Michael Crew for his encouragement, and for his guidance in shaping the final draft.

1. The Utility Average includes stocks of 15 firms and weights nuclear firms rather heavily. Nine of the 15 operated nuclear plants at the time of the accident, and two additional firms had plants under construction.

2. Edwards (1987) provides a careful description of the long-term physical and social effects of the disaster in the Soviet Union.

3. We discuss the effects of the accident on volatility and correlation with the market in more detail in another paper (Eckel and Vermaelen, 1988).

4. These include: Energy Information Administration (1987), *Moody's Public Utility Manual* (1987), and *Nuclear News* (1986) world list of nuclear power plants.

5. Smirlock and Kaufold (1987), a recent study of the effect of the Mexican default on United States banks, also illustrates the use of this technique in event studies. Although SUR has some clear advantages over the more traditional method, its adoption has been slow.

6. There is some evidence that the usual F test used to test cross-equation restrictions is

somewhat biased in SUR, particularly for small samples, though the bias is much less serious than the assumption of independence. Schipper and Thompson (1985) and Binder (1985) suggest statistics whose exact distributions are known for hypothesis testing in these systems. We plan future tests of this nature.

7. See, for example, Berk (1981, 155), who reports betas of .63-.84 for large utilities; Naill et al. (1986) report average betas of .53 for all utilities.

8. We use measures of exposure relative to equity, measured as the stock price times shares outstanding on April 1. Because our dependent variable is a return, this is a more appropriate specification than raw exposure measures alone.

9. The equations were also estimated with two additional variables: the debt/equity ratio, measured as [1 - (common equity/total capitalization)]; and a variable measuring the restrictiveness of the regulatory environment. Neither had a statistically significant coefficient in any specification; their inclusion did not affect the signs, magnitudes, or significance of the other coefficients. The results are not reported here, but are available from the authors on request.

References

Berk, Joel, ed. 1981. *Public Utility Finance and Accounting: A Reader.* Cambridge, MA: Harvard Business School.

Binder, John J. 1985. "On the Use of the Multivariate Regression Model in Event Studies." *Journal of Accounting Research* 23(1):370-383.

Bowen, Robert M., Richard P. Castanias, and Lane A. Daley. 1983. "Intra-Industry Effects of the Accident at Three Mile Island." *Journal of Financial and Quantitative Analysis* 18(1):87-110.

Department of Energy, Energy Information Administration. 1987. *Inventory of Power Plants in the United States 1986.* DOE/EIA-0095(86), August.

Department of Energy, Energy Information Administration. 1987. *Commercial Nuclear Power 1987: Prospects for the U. S. and the World,* July.

Dubin, Jeffrey A., and Geoffrey S. Rothwell. 1987. "Preparing for the Improbable: Safety Incentives and the Price-Anderson Act." California Institute of Technology, Social Science Working Paper 642 (May).

Eckel, Catherine C., and Theo Vermaelen. 1988. "The Capital Market Fallout from Chernobyl." VPI Working Paper, Xerox.

Edwards, Michael. 1987. "Chernobyl: One Year After." *National Geographic* 171(5):632-653.

Fields, M. Andrew, and Vahan Janjigian. 1987. "The Effects of Chernobyl on Electric Utility Stock Prices." Department of Business Administration, University of Delaware (April) Xerox.

Moody's Public Utility Manual. 1987.

Naill, Roger F., H. Donald Burbant, and Sheryl Sturges. 1986. "Least-Cost Planning for Combination Gas & Electric Utilities." *Public Utilities Fortnightly* 118 (no. 3, August 7): 36.

Nuclear News. 1986. "World List of Nuclear Plants." (August): 91-94.

Pulley, Lawrence B., and James G. Hewlet. 1985. "Financial Market Reactions to the Accident at Three Mile Island." Working Paper No. 85-023, School of Business Administration, College of William and Mary (October).

Schipper, Katherine, and Rex Thompson. 1983. "The Impact of Merger-Related Regulations on the Shareholders of Acquiring Firms." *Journal of Accounting Research* 21(1):184-221.

Schipper, Katherine, and Rex Thompson. 1985. "The Impact of Merger-Related Regulations Using Exact Distributions of Test Statistics." *Journal of Accounting Research* 23(1):408-415.

Schwert, G. William. 1981. "Using Financial Data to Measure the Effects of Regulation." *Journal of Law and Economics* 24(1):121-158.

Sherman, Roger. 1974. *Economics of Industry*. Boston: Little, Brown.

Smirlock, M., and Howard Kaufold. 1987. "Bank Foreign Lending, Mandatory Disclosure Rules, and the Reaction of Bank Stock Prices to the Mexican Debt Crisis." *Journal of Business* 60(3):347-364.

Wood, William C. 1982. *Insuring Nuclear Power: Liability, Safety, and Economic Efficiency*. Contemporary Studies in Economic and Financial Analysis, series edited by Edward I. Altman and Ingo Walter, volume 38. Greenwich, CT: JAI Press.

INDEX